JN083069

Urban Development and Social Change in Megacities in East Asia

Seoul, Tokyo and Shanghai in the Past and Present

Urban Development and Social Change in Megacities in East Asia

Seoul,Tokyo and Shanghai in the Past and Present

Edited by
Dukjin Chang
Daishiro Nomiya
Haidong Zhang

Chuo University Press

Research series 3
The Institute of Social Sciences
Chuo University

Editor
Dukjin Chang
Daishiro Nomiya
Haidong Zhang

Urban Development and Social Change in Megacities in East Asia
Seoul,Tokyo,and Shanghai in the Past and Present

ISBN 978-4-8057-1342-6

Published by Chuo University Press
742-1 Higashinakano, Hachioji-city
Tokyo, 192-0393 Japan

Contents

Introduction

Shanghai, Seoul and Tokyo in Sequential Social Change

Dukjin Chang
Daishiro Nomiya
Haidong Zhang

Since the World War II, Japan, South Korea, and China have experienced a series of very interesting combinations of social change. Some of them suggest that the three countries might follow predetermined sequential paths. It was Japan that first achieved economic growth. The real growth rates of Japanese economy came close to 10 percent in the latter half of the 1950s and then remained double digit for the entire 1960s. Next came South Korea. For most of the 1970s and 1980s South Korea's GDP growth fluctuated around 10%. China's growth rate began to rise in the 1980s and hit its peak in the 1990s. Japan's economic recession started in 1991 with the collapse of asset bubble and then, as is well known, led the country into the 'lost two decades.' Since the Asian financial crisis of 1997/8, South Korea has been going deeper and deeper into the low-growth tunnel. The signals of economic slow-down in China began to be witnessed since the 2008 global financial crisis. At least on the surface the three countries look similar: they have followed the same cycle of economic booms and bursts by 10-year intervals. This also means that the three countries have experienced the same cycles of industrialization and deindustrialization in a sequential manner. Of course we do not blindly interpret this sequence as the uni-linear evolutionary social change, which was once influential in the early stage of the post- World War II social sciences. However, at least in a few different aspects, it is hard to deny that the three countries have followed very similar paths of sequential social change.

It is not just the ups and downs of the economy that the three countries have experienced sequentially. Take urbanization for an example. If we look at the percent of the population living in city areas, Japan already reached 80% in the 1980s. It was 2000 when South Korea reached the same figure. China is expected to reach the same level of urbanization in around 2050. What about aging? The percent of population aged 65 and over in Japan is now above 25 percent, after already hitting 12.1 percent back in 1990. South Korea is now well known for its fastest speed of aging in the world. Even with this kind of speed, the country only reached 12.7 percent in 2014, equivalent to 1990 Japan. In other words, there is a 25-year gap in terms of the state of aging between the two countries. However, South Korea will catch up with Japan sooner or later because the speed of aging is faster in the country. There is no downplaying the speed of aging in China, where the elderly population reached 10.6 percent in 2014 which is not much different from South Korea. For a long time everyone knew that aging would become a big social issue in China, where they maintained one-child policy for over 30 years to suppress rapid population growth. With this one-child policy it is clear the country is destined to witness faster aging. Although South Korea had maintained a very strong population control policy until 1995, with two-children policy very strongly recommended but not mandated, this contributed to maintain the level of population reproduction. China is already experiencing a new phenomenon often termed 4-2-1 families. A 4-2-1 family is a family composed of a couple(2), each of them having two parents(4), and one child(1) to support. It becomes very difficult for the couple, who are the only breadwinners, to support four parents and one child.

What about industrialization and deindustrialization? In Japan and South Korea the industrial sector now only accounts for one fourth of all employment (25.8% in Japan and 24.4 percent in South Korea as of 2013). Now the service sector is responsible for about 70% of all employments in both countries. China's industrial sector explains 30.1 percent of all employment as of 2013. It may not appear to be a big difference given the comparable figures are about 25 percent in Japan and Korea. However, we should not forget that this figure in China is not on the decline but on the rise. The industrial sector in China was only 18.2 percent in 1980 and constantly bulged to 30.1 percent in 2013. What is now happening in Chinese employment is what happened in Japan and Korea until 1980s, i.e., the simultaneous growth of industrial and service sectors.

As we have discussed so far, at least in a few aspects, the three countries appear to have followed the same paths of social change in a sequential manner. Why? Behind these common experiences in different points in time lie macro trends such as industrialization, deindustrialization, aging, and, above all, globalization. In this sense we might compare the three countries to passengers in different compartments of a same train. However, these common macro trends might be experienced very differently by the people of the three countries. Let us suppose that we are sitting in different compartments of a same train and the distance between any two compartments is long enough. The scenery outside the window constantly keeps changing. While the passengers in the last compartment are seeing beautiful lakes, those in the first compartment might well be running in the deep mountains. The same scenery seen by the passengers in the first compartment some time ago is now being seen by those in the last compartment. The lakes might have been beautiful with the sunlight glistening on the water when the passengers in the first compartment saw it, while it might be dismal when those in the last compartment see it with a sudden arrival of dark clouds.

We can think of two different conceptions of time: physical and historical time. The three countries are in different stages of historical time while at the same time living in the same physical time. China is the only country where the middle class is increasing while polarization is deepening in the rest of the world. In a country like China, rising up to the middle class means riding the wave of industrialization and urbanization. In contrast, shrinking middle class in countries like Japan and Korea may mean deindustrialization and globalization. According to a Gallup survey conducted in 1989, 75 percent of Koreans reported that they belonged to the middle class. Twenty four years later in 2013, a survey conducted by the Korean Sociological Association showed that the same response dramatically dropped to 20.2 percent(Jaeyeol Yee 2014). Japan, once boasting a society of 'one hundred million all in the middle class' (Chiavacci 2008), has now become a 'gap society', where which hospital one is born in may determine the rest of his or her life (Sato 2000). Of course this 'return to inequality' is not confined to Japan and Korea but a global phenomenon (Alderson and Nielsen 2002). This is so because deepening inequality is on the one hand prompted by the changes in industrial change and on the other affected by financial flows and cross-border migration on a global scale.

These three East Asian countries are riding in the same train in the sense that they are experiencing the same macro trends in today's world. However, they are in different compartments of that train because they have different socio-economic, political and historical conditions. Depending on which compartment they are in, the same macro trend affects people in these countries in different ways.

Now what are these macro trends that affect our lives? We will expound in detail our answer to this question in the concluding chapter of this book. As a way to introduce readers to our field of study, we may draw a conceptual map as a first step to start our endeavor to answer this question. It is a map created out of the understanding and interpretations of the authors of this book. The authors of this book had had a series of meetings; in the last meeting, they were asked to list up the macro trends that they thought were important, together with their understanding of how these macro trends were connected with each other. Utilizing the answers from the authors, we have come up with three networks of relationships across macro trends, which are shown in Figures 1 through 3.

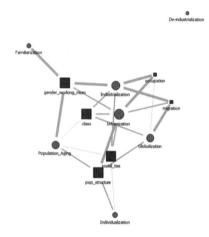

<Figure 1-1: Network of Causalities between Macro Trends and Social Phenomena in Shanghai>

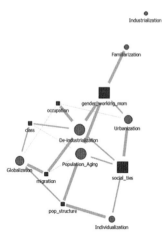

<Figure 1-2: Network of Causalities between Macro Trends and Social Phenomena in Seoul>

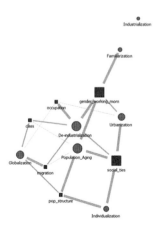

<Figure 1-3: Network of Causalities between Macro Trends and Social Phenomena in Tokyo>

In these figures, circles denote macro trends and rectangles do major social phenomena that we deal with in this book. These trends and social phenomena are intertwined in a complicated way, influencing and being influenced by one another. Thicker links between two nodes (whether circles or rectangles) denote that proportionally more authors agreed on the existence of causality between them. Bigger circles or rectangles mean proportionally more authors agreed that they are important macro trends or social phenomena. 'Central' factors that are related with many other trends or phenomena are located at the center of the network. 'Peripheral' factors that are related with only a marginal number of trends or phenomena are located toward the periphery of the network.

Before we try to interpret each of these figures, let us compare Figure 1 to Figures 2 and 3. One thing that is obvious is Figures 2 and 3, Seoul and Tokyo respectively, look quite similar, while Figure 1, Shanghai, is significantly different. Very simply, it means that the interconnections among macro trends and social phenomena in Seoul and Tokyo are similar, while they are quite different in Shanghai. If we recall the conception of 'historical time', Tokyo is riding in the first compartment, Seoul in the middle, and Shanghai in the last in the train of macro trends. The figures suggest that the first and the middle compartments have now entered a section where they share similar scenery while the last compartment is still seeing a different scenery.

If we look more closely into the figures, we can see that the most important factor that distinguishes between Shanghai and the other two cities is industrialization/deindustrialization. In Figure 1 (Shanghai), the most central trends are 'industrialization' and 'urbanization.' 'Deindustrialization' is still a small trend that is located in the upper right corner. Although it is often said that the vast regions of China where there is a huge gap between cities and rural areas with a fast growth rate are experiencing a simultaneous process of industrialization and deindustrialization, Figure 1 shows that the former is still a much more central trend than the latter. On the other hand, 'deindustrialization' and 'aging' are the most central in Seoul and Tokyo (Figures 2 and 3), while 'industrialization,' which once defined these two cities, is now an isolated factor in the upper right corner. If the social changes in Shanghai are led by 'industrialization' and 'urbanization,' those in Seoul and Tokyo are led by 'deindustrialization' and 'aging.'

If we focus on the importance of each macro trend, 'urbanization' takes up a second most important trend in Shanghai, while it is aging in Seoul and Tokyo. While urbanization in Shanghai is a central factor which has relationships with many other factors such as stratification, social ties, occupational structure, migration, gender, and population structure, it has become a much less important factor with relationships with only a limited number of trends and phenomena such as gender, social ties, and occupational structure in Seoul and Tokyo.

In all three cities 'individualization' is related with both population structure and social ties. However, the strengths of those relationships are more or less different as we can see from the different width of the links. It may be taken for granted that individualization is related with population structure. As the birth rate goes down, younger generations become smaller in size as compared with older generation. This is reflected in the size and composition of family; an average family size becomes smaller, with a smaller number of children. If we add fragmented social ties to this down-sized generation, then individualization becomes a taken-for-granted phenomenon.

There is no doubt that observation of macro-trends and their interconnections are helpful in our understanding of the extent of similarities and differences across three countries. Employing observations of macro trends only, however, may leave us rather insensitive to changes and transformations taking place in our everyday life. In this regard, it may be useful to view changes as individual experiences. Here we take up "eating" as an exemplary observational field. Our question is how eating as social practice has changed over time in three countries. Using personal accounts from college students, we try to shed light on yet another aspect of social change in three countries.

Our focus here is the phenomenon called "eating alone." Traditionally eating as a social act has been associated with the idea of together-ness, as it often involves "the others" with whom one interacts in the form of seating together and having conversation with eye contact. Recently this traditional "eating together" appears to be receding; rising instead is "eating alone." Eating alone is still a social act, as it carries various social meanings born out of the act itself.

Eating alone is something that cannot be socially recommended in China. One Chinese student who is currently studying abroad in a college in Seoul replies to a question whether he has ever eaten alone in his college years in China as follows.

"You never have a chance to eat alone in China. If I run out of money on Sundays, I can simply go to the street where there are many restaurants. I come across senior students all the time, and they invite me to their social gatherings taking place in nearby restaurants. I can easily join them, meet with people, eat and drink."

Eating practice of a college student in Korea in 1980s was much like that in present China. In fact, the authors of this book would have lunch with their friends almost every day. Students who finished their classes early waited for their friends whose classes ran late to eat together. Today, eating practice among college students shows a stark contrast to the dining scene in a Korean college in 1980s. College students more frequently than before choose to eat alone not only when it is inevitable but because they prefer eating alone. A Korean student in 2016 answered as below when asked why he ate alone.

> "Because we take different classes, we're gonna have to wait if we want to eat together. You can easily waste 30 minutes. I don't want to waste my time, and I don't want my friends to feel the pressure that they have to wait for me. Because everyone knows this, no one feels sorry if his or her friends do not wait."

How do we make sense of the change in eating practice in a college in Korea? One way to answer this question is to interpret it as a shift resulting from macro-level transformation. Social ties created by eating together in 1980s often worked as important social capital with which we exchanged help for a long time to come. In 1980s Korea was an industrializing country, where the economy was growing fast, the windows of opportunity for college students kept becoming wider and wider with time. Friends who used to wait for each other for lunch grew up to become significant players in various areas of society after graduation. They perform better and better with the help of social capital which they used to exchange among themselves. It could have been nothing more than friendship in the micro-level lives of individuals, but from the perspective of the macro trend there were enough incentives to invest in social ties.

In contrast, eating alone in today's Korea is closely related with uncertain future and competitive pressure. Taking time and effort to eat with others means on the one hand that this person is not a social outcast when viewed by other people but on the other he or she is creating and re-creating social ties with these meal-mates. To create and manage social ties is more necessary when there is a long future horizon of a 'career.' If the available number of jobs decreases and the longevity of stay in whatever jobs that exist becomes shorter, there is much less such necessity. Then there is little reason left to take time and effort to eat with others.

Even in the changing macro trends from industrialization and growth to deindustrialization and stagnation, people still have friends. However, they now have much less incentives to invest 30 minutes in such friendship. These windows of opportunity, becoming much narrower than that in the past, may reflect strong and constant competitive pressure. Numerous youngsters fiercely compete with each other to enter the narrow door that would lead eventually to decent employment. Young people who do not otherwise have a moment a day to escape competition want to breathe at least while they eat.

A college senior student in Japan, currently doing activities for job hunting, said he eats alone according to his own wish. He continues:

> "I want to take some rest at least when I eat. My friend might have been offered a regular employment position while I am still preparing for my job. Or, even if we are both preparing for jobs, we always end up talking about another friend who got a decent job. That way I end up thinking about getting a job throughout my lunch. I would rather eat alone and listen to music with my smartphone. This is an indispensable temporary relief for me."

Here again, rather stagnant Japanese economic performance in recent years and its consequential effect on the activity of a college student can be observed. When did Japanese college students began their practice of eating alone? Some Japanese authors of this book recall that it was late 1970s through early 1980s when practice of eating alone in a college restaurant began to prevail. In 1970s, Japan saw a sudden economic downturn after the oil shock in the early phase of 1970s.

The practice of eating in a college scene may be only a small part of what we experience in everyday life. It may be possible, as shown above, to find a plausible account that explains the differential practice of eating between China, Korea, and Japan and its change over time in respective countries. However, we still have countless social interactions in numerous social fields. Our sense of change itself may come from the sum of small changes that people experience in their everyday lives. Given the existence of many small changes in our life, then we may have to prepare for multiple ways that link between our everyday sense of change and macro-trends and transformations behind it.

This book is our first step to understand what we are currently experiencing in Korea, China, and Japan. Observing three countries and providing plausible explanations for the similarities and differences in respective transformations in a comparative perspective is, to say the least, a bold endeavor. It would be an insurmountable task to observe every single aspect of social change that takes place in all parts of these three countries. Also, as we have shown in this introduction, we prefer to go back and forth between the observations of macro-level trends and micro-level social interactions in our effort to interpret social change we are currently experiencing. Added to these limitations are relative paucity of literature and the data; There are studies that discuss social change in Korea, China, and Japan. However, we find few research work that studies maro-and micro-transformations in many aspects of social life in these three countries in an explicit comparative manner. Also, macro-level data are limited; they are not evenly limited, but rather skewed toward urban areas. For example, socioeconomic indicators for urban areas are rather resourceful in all three countries, but not for non-urban areas. Furthermore, there is a good amount of literature that discusses change in social interactions in urban areas. For these reasons, in this book, we set ourselves to focusing on the observations of three mega cities in respective countries, Seoul, Shanghai, and Tokyo. These cities have abundant resources for our use of macro and micro data, as well as a body of literature discussing their transformations. In the next 9 chapters, we will proceed our analysis, using the data on three mega cities in the main and employing country-level data when necessary as supplementing the main data.

This book has 11 chapters, including introduction and conclusion. Our approach to the agenda discussed above is to observe people' life from three different angles: economic, social sphere, and individual. After Chapter 2, where an overview of the cities of Seoul, Tokyo, and Shanghai is laid out, we start our investigation into the changes in the economic sphere found in our three mega cities. Chapter 3 discusses change in social mobility patterns. Chapter 4 looks at job structure and its change. Chapter 5 goes deep into the issues and problems working mothers in modern cities. From Chapter 6 through 8, we shift our attention to the changes in social sphere. Chapter 6 explores change in the household size and the trend behind it. Chapter 7 faces squarely social issues of today: death alone, eating alone, and me-generation. Chapter 8 focuses on community change and policies to cope with the problems associated with community life in big cities. Chapter 9 and 10 turn to the changes in the individual sphere that. Chapter 9 deals with the structure of trust, and Chapter 10 discusses people's attitudes toward changes associated with globalization. Summarizing all the findings in these analytical chapters, we try to provide answers to the questions we set in this introductory chapter.

In many times during this book project, we realize that we still have a long road ahead of us to grasp the true nature of change in big cities in three countries. We just hope this book marks a new start with which we continue our effort to understand the life in East Asian mega cities and societies.

ACKNOWLEDGEMENTS

Compiling a book out of writings of contributors from multiple countries was quite a task. Not only did we have countless meetings to discuss the contents of the book, we also exchanged numerous on- and off-line communications during the compilation work. More often than not in the meetings, language barriers set in, which kept us from moving forward in a satisfactory manner. Many times we thought that we would never complete this book project. Indeed, without help and encouragements from people around us, we are certain that we would never be able to write these acknowledgements. The publication of this book still feels like a miracle.

Our acknowledgement goes to the individuals, who helped facilitate the communication between the contributors. They helped translate several of the chapters into English so that the authors could focus on improving their arguments. Among many, the first to mention is Kim Jisun. She was immensely instrumental. She worked tirelessly to interpret Korean writings into English, so that contributors from other countries were able to understand the arguments made by the Korean contributors. Our thanks also go to Kim Hani and Kim Suna, who helped us in the final phase of the editing work. While we are unable to mention all their names here, we had other Chinese, Japanese, and Korean friends who have contributed to the production of this book.

REFERENCES

Alderson, Arthur S. and François Nielsen "Globalization and the Great U-Turn: Income Inequality Trends in 16 OECD Countries" American Journal of Sociology Vol. 107, No. 5 (March 2002), pp. 1244-1299 (56 pages).

Chiavacci, David (Summer 2008). "From Class Struggle to General Middle-Class Society to Divided Society: Societal Models of Inequality in Postwar Japan". *Social Science Japan Journal.* **11** (1): 5–27.

Sato, Toshiki. 2000. *Japan as Unequal Society: Good-bye to the Middle Class Society (fubyōdō shakai nihon: sayonara sō-chūryū).* Chuo Ko-ron New Books (Chūō kōron shinsha).

Yee, Jaeyeol. 2014. "The Coming of a Humble-Class Society Where the Middle Class Has Disappeared." (Jungsanchung i Sarajin Sominsahoe eui Dungjang), Part 3 in *Do You Belong to the Middle Class?* co-authored by Wontaek Kang et al. 21st Century Books.

2

Seoul, Tokyo and Shanghai: An Overview

Wonnho Jang
Tatsuto Asakawa
Xiaocong Lu

This chapter gives a basic overview of Seoul, Tokyo and Shanghai. It will first detail the past development trajectories taken by the three cities and then go on to analyze their relative strengths and weaknesses by comparing their economic, social and demographic characteristics.

1. THE DEVELOPMENT OF SEOUL, TOKYO AND SHANGHAI

We will first look at how the three cities have expanded with modernization. All three cities have greatly developed during the twentieth century period of modernization to become cities on a global scale.

(1) The Development of Modern Seoul

When Hanyang (present-day Seoul during the Joseon period) became the new metropolitan center of the Josen Kingdom in 1394, it encompassed everything within the fortress walls and the surrounding locality. These boundaries stayed fixed even when Japan set up government offices and designated a resident general to rule over the city. All of Seoul (known as Gyeongseong at this time), except for Yongsan—an area where many Japanese resided, had its boundaries fixed within the four main gates of Old Seoul up until the mid-1930s.

During the later stage of the Japanese colonial period beginning in 1936, Korea's first urban plan known as "The Land Plan of Gyeongseong City" was implemented. In January 1936, an expansion plan for Gyeongseong, including an adjacent town *(eup)*, 8 townships *(myeon)*, 71 villages *(ri)* and areas of 5 other villages, was finalized and starting in April was officially carried out. Through such expansions, Gyeongseong grew 3.5 times in size to a total sur-

1906   1936

1949   1963   1973

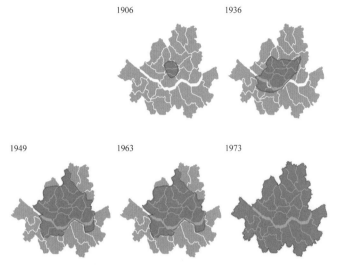

Figure 2-1: The Expansion of Seoul
Source: The Seoul Institute (2007)

face area of 135.36km[2]. The present-day Yeongdeungpo-gu or Yeongdeungpo district (excluding Daerim-dong or Daerim neighborhood) and the Dongjak-gu region (excluding Sindaebang-dong and Sadang-dong) were the first wards south of the Han River to become part of Gyeongseong.[1]

After South Korea was liberated on August 15, 1949, Gyeongseong underwent an elevation in status and was renamed Seoul Independent City. Throughout this process, Seoul expanded to include several townships *(myeon)* and villages *(ri)* in Goyang and Siheung counties previously a part of Gyeonggi Province. At the time, Seoul's total surface area was 269.73km[2] with a total-population of 1.418 million people.

The target population of Seoul outlined in the 1949 expansion plan was two million residents. However, when Seoul's population reached that target of two million in 1960, a new target of five million was set in 1963. The adjacent five counties, 84 townships and villages were incorporated soon after, increasing Seoul's total surface area 2.3 times to 613.04km[2].

In 1973, with the incorporation of Goyang county, Sindo township, Jin Gwannae village and Gupabal villageof Gyeonggi Province, Seoul's total surface area expanded to 627.06km[2]. In the late 1980s, the city of Seoul adjusted its administrative borders of the new city. As a result, Seoul's administrative region was composed of 25 autonomous districts and 423 administrative districts with a total surface area of 605.25km² which covered 0.6% of the country's total surface area.

(2) The Development of Modern Tokyo

In 1603 Tokyo, known as Edo at the time, began its development process in 1603 when Tokugawa Ieyasu was appointed shogun of the city. Edo had for some time been a central place tied to Japanese politics and culture. By the mid-18th century, the city grew into a metropolis with a total population of more than 1 million people, becoming the largest city in Japan in terms of population.

Edo was renamed Tokyo after the Meiji Restoration in 1868, the same year the Tokyo Metropolitan Government Building was built. In 1869, Tokyo be-

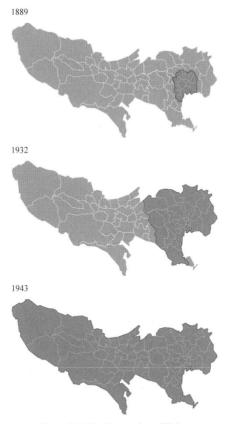

Figure 2-2: The Expansion of Tokyo
Source: Eicha, *"Para-para Map, Tokyo Metropolitan City"*

came the capital city of Japan with Emperor Meiji's relocation to the city. In 1889, after the installment of the municipal organization system, Tokyo was made up of a total of 15 districts

Tokyo borders were unchanged until 1932 when as a result of the city's Great Expansion Policy the number of districts increased to 35. In 1943, Tokyo prefecture and Tokyo city merged together to form the current Tokyo Metropolis. During this process, the city was divided into 35 special wards.

In 1947, under the new Local Autonomy Law, the number of wards in Tokyo decreased from 32 to 22 in March and then increased to 23 wards in July as Nerima ward was carved out of Itabashi ward. To this day, Tokyo has been comprised of 23 special wards, 26 cities, 5 towns and 8 villages.

(3) The Formation of Modern Shanghai

With the signing of the Treaty of Nanking between China and the United Kingdom in 1842 at the end of the Opium Wars, Shanghai became one of China's five trading ports. In 1854, after the establishment of an autonomous administration system during the Taiping Rebellion, Shanghai was broken up into concessions independent of the Chinese authorities and began its rapid devel-

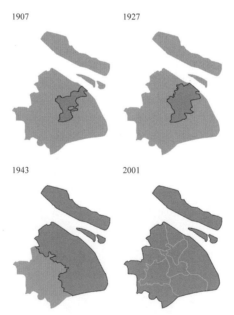

Figure 2-3: The Expansion of Shanghai
Source: Sina Shanghai (2015.9.9)

opment process.

Shanghai prefecture or Shanghai-hyun (present day Shanghai) established its first borders in 1907 and was made up of 24 districts at the tame. With the establishment of Shanghai Municipal Government in 1927 alone with the merging of Shanghai prefecture with its adjacent prefectures, the borders of Shanghai were reestablished to include 30 total districts.

The administrative region of Shanghai was expanded to 8 districts and 7 suburban districts in 1943 after the international settlement area and the French concession were returned to the Wang Jingwei regime. The composition of Shanghai's districts continued to change in response to the transformation of Shanghai's municipal system. At the time the Chinese Nationalist Party reclaimed Shanghai in 1945, the city was comprised of 17 districts and additional special districts.

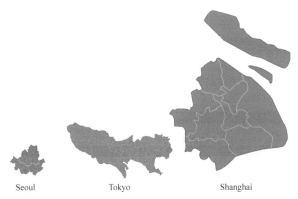

Seoul   Tokyo   Shanghai

Seoul
Total Surface Area 605.25km²
Population 1,0297,138
Population Density 17,013.03 person/km²

Tokyo
Total Surface Area 2,190.90km²
Population 13,378,578
Population Density 6,106.43 person/km²

Shanghai
Total Surface Area 6,340.50km²
Population 24,152,700
Population Density 3,809.27 person/km²

Figure 2-4: The Total Surface Area and Population of the Three Cities

In 1949, with the establishment of the communist regime in China, Shanghai became a municipality directly-controlled by and a center of Chinese industry. Although Shanghai's central position was at times threatened by the rapid development of other cities including Shenzhen of Guangdong province in a process that was spurred by China's reform and open door policy during the 1980s, the development of Pudong in the 1990s cemented Shanghai's position as China's economic, financial and trading core. Currently, Shanghai is made up of 16 districts and a prefecture ten times the size of Seoul with a total surface area of 6340km².

(4) Current Size and Population of Seoul, Tokyo and Shanghai

Figure 2-4 compares the sizes of Seoul, Tokyo and Shanghai. As shown, Shanghai is a metropolis ten times the size of Seoul. Tokyo is also considered a large city being 3.5 times the size of Seoul. In comparison to the other two cities, Seoul's population density is much higher. However, some parts of the other two cities like Tokyo's 23 wards and Shanghai's central area have similar population densities as Seoul.

Table 2-1: The Economic Competitiveness Rankings of Seoul, Tokyo and Shanghai

Index	Seoul	Tokyo	Shanghai
Global Power City Index (GICI), 2016	6th	3rd	12th
Global Financial Centres Index (GFCI), 2016	7th	6th	20th
The world's Most Influential Cities, 2014	16th	5th	16th
Prime International Residential Index (PIRI),	16th	59th	3rd
Global Cities Index (GCI), 2016	11th	4th	20th

Source: The Asia Business Daily (2014.3.16); Yonhap News Agency (2014.8.19);
AT Kearny (2016); Knight Frank (2016); The Mori Memorial Foundation (2016)

2. COMPARING THE ECONOMIC COMPETITIVENESS OF SEOUL, TOKYO AND SHANGHAI

Seoul, Tokyo and Shanghai are leading economic hubs in Asia. As capital cities of South Korea and Japan, Seoul and Tokyo, hold a great deal of political influence. All three cities are economically influential in Asia as shown in Table 2-1.

As can be seen in table 2-1, according to the Global Power City Index published by The Mori Memorial Foundation in 2016, Seoul, Tokyo and Shanghai rank 6th, 3rd and 12th place, respectively. Both Seoul and Tokyo have maintained high rankings in this index, with Tokyo inparticular ranking 4th place for eight consecutive years and jumping to 3rd place in 2016. This demonstrates Tokyo's capacity to attract influential global workers and industries to the city.

In the Global Financial Centers Index published by London's consulting group Z/YEN, Seoul scored 718 out of 1000 and ranked 7th place. This is three places higher than it scored in the 2013 rankings, illustrating its high pace of development, the highest out of all Asian cities. Tokyo has continued to maintain its ranking of 3rd place and Shanghai ranks 20th place, the second highest of Chinese cities and right behind Shenzhen at 18th place.

All three cities also rank high on American business magazine Forbes list of The World's Most Influential Cities. Notably, Seoul and Shanghai are ranked 16th characterrized "rising stars," i.e. cities with the potential to rank in the top ten in the near future (Yonhap News, 2014).

This pattern is also reflected in real estate prices as shown in the Prime International Residential Index (PIRI) published by Knight Frank, a real estate agency highly regarded among international real estate agents. The index ranks Shanghai 3rd place due to its 14% annual increase in real estate prices. This puts Shanghai at the top of the ranking of cities in China as well as all of Asia. Seoul ranks 16th place with its 6.3% increase in real estate prices while Tokyo places 59th with a 0.8% increase, a rate that is indicative of a temporary halt brought about by the 1993 collapse of the asset price bubble.

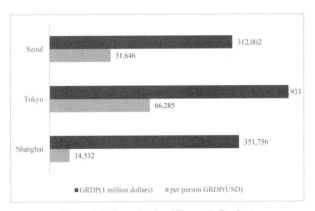

Figure 2-5: Gross Regional Domestic Product
※Seoul and Shanghai, 2014 statistics; Tokyo, 2013 statistics
Source: Seoul: Korean Statistical Information Service (2016)(Seoul); Statistics Division, Tokyo Metropolitan Government Bureau of General Affairs (2014)(Tokyo); Bureau of Shanghai (2015)(Shanghai)

Figure 2-6: Ratio of Secondary Industry Workers
※Seoul and Tokyo, 2010 statistics; Shanghai, 2014 statistics
Source: The Seoul Research Database, The Seoul Institute; Statistics Bureau of
Japan (2015)(Tokyo); Statistics Bureau of Shanghai (2015)(Shanghai)

The Global Cities Index, published in *Global Cities* (2016) and written by AT Kearney who examines the global indexes of 125 cities, has placed Seoul, Tokyo and Shanghai in 11th, 4th and 20th places, respectively. We can safely assume that these three cities exhibit high economic competitiveness in the major indexes.

We can now compare their economic indexes to draw out the distinct characteristics of the cities. First, a comparison of the gross regional domestic product (GRDP) levels of the three cities reveals Japan's total GRDP to be more than 2.5 times that of Seoul and Shanghai.

To be specific, Tokyo's GRDP per capita is twice that of Seoul and four times that of Shanghai. In this sense, Tokyo's economy towers over Seoul's and Shanghai's. On the other hand, Shanghai's GRDP per capita is less than half that of Seoul's, but due to its population being twice as large as Seoul's, its total GRDP is higher.

The ratio of secondary industry workers out of the total population shows Shanghai to have highest percent of secondary industry workers at 34.9% and Tokyo with a somewhat high percentage at 17.6%. These high ratios are due to the fact that the two cities are metropolitan hubs that include small to mid-size cities or counties. On the other hand, Seoul's percentage of 6% demonstrates that the city has become a consumer city rather than a production-based city. Shanghai's high ratio is evidence of the high number of factories in the city, which has led to environmental pollution in the city and the surrounding region.

3. COMPARING THE SOCIAL INDEXES OF SEOUL, TOKYO AND SHANGHAI

This section will compare the three cities using an array of social indexes that revel their socio-cultural characteristics

According to the statistics of the Safe Cities Index published by The Economist Intelligence Unit (EIU), a research and analysis division of the renowned London weekly *The Economist*, Tokyo ranked 1st out of 50 cities. The rankings of the two other cities were 24th for Seoul and 30th for Shanghai respectively. The EIU has analyzed that the safety of the cities is closely associated with the country's wealth and economic development except for Seoul. According to EIU's Worldwide Cost of Living report, Seoul ranked 8th while Tokyo and Shanghai ranked 11th in cost of living. Tokyo, a city that had ranked 1st place in cost of living for many years, has recentry been outranked by other cities as a result of the weakening value of the Japanese yen.

Table 2-2: Comparison Social Indexes of Seoul, Tokyo and Shanghai

Index	Seoul	Tokyo	Shanghai
Safe Cities Index, 2015	24th	1st	30th
Worldwide Cost of Living Index(WCOL), 2016	8th	11th	11th
QS Best Student Cities, 2016	10th	3rd	39th
Youthful Cities Index, 2016	21th	12th	37th
Quality of Living Index, 2016	73th	44th	101st

Source: DECODE(2016); Economist Intelligence Unit(2015); Mercer(2016);
The Economist (2016.3.10)

Meanwhile, the three cities have high ranking as ideal places for young people to settle in. The 2016 Youthful Cities Index, based on an international annual survey of young people around the world and published by Canada's consulting firm DECODE, placed all three cities in the top 40. Notably, Tokyo at 12th place was recognized as a highly attractive place for youth. Seoul was at 21st placed, also on the higher end, while Shanghai was placed 37th in the rankings, the lowest of the three cities. This pattern was also reflected in the ranking for best cities for academic pursuits. United Kingdom's annual publication QS Best Student Cities ranking rated Tokyo, Seoul and Shanghai at 3rd, 10th and 39th place, respectively.

The Quality of Living Index report released by the American consulting firm Mercer analyzes 450 cities worldwide and reports ranking for the top 230 rank-

22

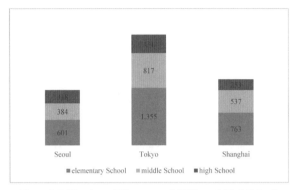

Figure 2-7: Number of Elementary, Middle and High Schools
※Seoul, 2016 statistics; Tokyo, 2014 statistics; Shanghai, 2015 statistics
Source: Center for Educational Statistics Information(Seoul); Tokyo Metropolis(Tokyo); Shanghai Municipal Education Commission(Shanghai)

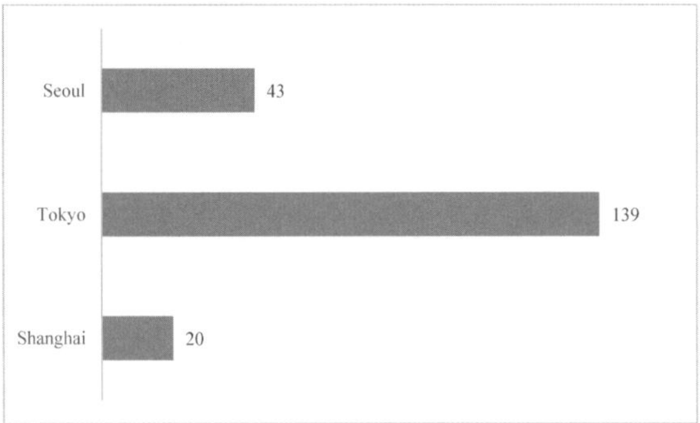

Figure 2-8: Number of 4 Year Colleges
※Seoul, 2016 statistics; Tokyo and Shanghai, 2014 statistics
Source: Center for Educational Statistics Information(Seoul); Tokyo Metropolis(Tokyo); Shanghai Municipal Education Commission(Shanghai)

ings. This report placed Seoul, Tokyo and Shanghai at 73rd, 44th and 101st place respectively. This index, utilizing results from an analysis of 39 diverse factors associated with quality of living for city dwellers, placed the three cities in the mid-range tier. [2] This was in contrast to the high rankings the three cities had in the economic indexes. A conclusion can be drawn that Seoul, Tokyo and Shanghai are economically influential cities globally but fall short in terms of providing high-quality living environments as measured by social and cultural indexes.

The next section will explore the characteristics of the three cities by comparing the various social indexes of the cities. First, we will look at the indexes related to education.

The figures for the total number of elementary, middle and high schools puts Tokyo in the top position. This suggests that Tokyo has a stronger foundation for primary and secondary education than the other two cities. On the other hand, while Shanghai has twice the population of Seoul, the number of schools in the two cities is nearly the same. In this respect, it could be said that Shanghai's foundation for primary and secondary education falls short compared with Seoul and Tokyo.

The educational indexes of the three cities diverge further for higher education. The number of four-year colleges in Tokyo is three times that of Shanghai. Shanghai's low number of four-year colleges is in part due to its low rate of college entrance and in part due to the large-scale college-policy pursued by the city.

Figure 2-9 shows the spatial distribution of college graduates in the three cities. The figures indicate the differences in the distribution of college graduates within the three cities. It can be seen that Seoul's college graduates are centrally located in the financially affluent ward of Gangnam while Tokyo's college-degree holders are spatially spread out among the 23 wards.

In the case of Shanghai, there is a high college graduates in the city center and Pudong. This provides indirect evidence of spatial segregation existing in the city. Taking into account the fact that college graduates' earnings are relatively higher than non-college graduates, we can conjecture that Seoul's wards north and south of the Han River are spatially segregated while Tokyo's 23 wards do not exhibit a high degree of spatial segregation. For Shanghai, there are signs of spatial segregation in the main city area of Shanghai and Pudong but not to the degree exhibited in Seoul.

When it comes to the number of libraries, Tokyo's library count is at 387, twice that of Seoul and 15 times that of Shanghai. As the high number of schools suggest, Tokyo exhibits the highest quality of educational facilities followed by Seoul and Shanghai.

On the other hand, Seoul has the most number of hospitals followed by Tokyo and Shanghai. However, this does not mean that Seoul provides the highest quality of medical services out of the three cities. A look at the number of hospital rooms reveals a total count of 80,400 rooms in Seoul, 120,700 in Tokyo and 110,700 in Shanghai. By these numbers, we can conjecture that Seoul provides medical services centrally through private clinics while Shanghai utilizes

24

Unit: %

Seoul

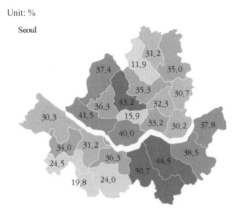

Tokyo

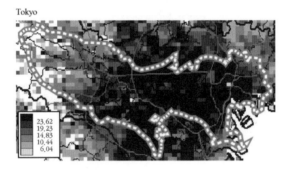

Shanghai

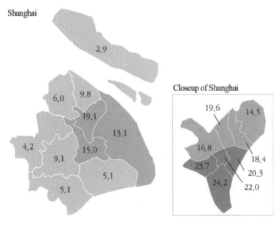

Figure 2-9: Spatial Distribution of College Graduates

Source: Seoul City(2015)(Seoul); Statistics Bureau of Japan(2010)(Tokyo);
Statistics Bureau of Shanghai(2015)(Shanghai)

Figure 2-10: Number of Libraries

※Seoul, 2015 statistics, Tokyo and Shanghai, 2014 statistics

Source: The Seoul Research Data Service (Seoul); National Diet Library (Tokyo); Statistics Bureau of Shanghai (2015)(Shanghai)

Figure 2-11: Number of Hospitals

※Seoul and Shanghai, 2015 statistics, Tokyo, 2013 statistics

Source: The Seoul Research Data Service(Seoul); Tokyo Metropolitan Government Bureau of Social Welfare and Public Health(2014)(Tokyo); Statistics Bureau of Shanghai(2015)(Shanghai)

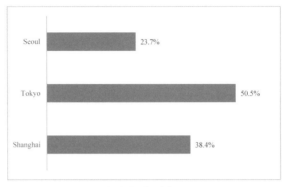

Figure 2-12: Ratio of Green Area
※Seoul, 2015 statistics; Tokyo, 2013 statistics; Shanghai, 2014 statistics
Source: The Seoul Research Data Service (Seoul); Geospatial Information Authority
of Japan (Tokyo); Statistics Bureau of Shanghai (2015)(Shanghai)

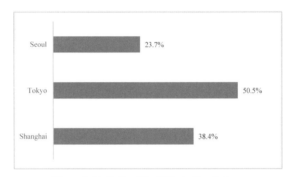

Figure 2-13: Ratio of the Elderly Population
※Seoul, 2015 statistics; Tokyo, 2010 statistics; Shanghai, 2014 statistics
Source: The Seoul Research Data Service (Seoul); Statistics Bureau of Japan (2010)
(Tokyo); Statistics Bureau of Shanghai (2015)(Shanghai)

large-sized general hospitals.

A comparison of the percentage of land designated as green areas shows
Seoul as having the lowest percentage out of the three cities. However, this is
mainly due to the fact that the two other cities include small to mid-scale cities
and counties that are in the process of being urbanized. It is important to take
note that Shanghai has a lower green area ratio than Tokyo even though the city
encompasses large rural agricultural areas including Songming county. This
might reveal Shanghai's relative shortcomings in environmental protection.

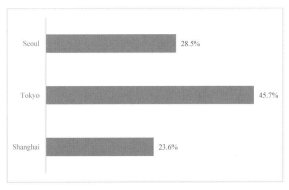

Figure 2-14: Single Person Household

※Seoul, 2015 statistics; Tokyo, 2010 statistics; Shanghai, 2014 statistics

Source: The Seoul Research Data Service (Seoul); Statistics Bureau of Japan (2010)

(Tokyo); Statistics Bureau of Shanghai (2015)(Shanghai)

4. DEMOGRAPHIC CHARACTERISTICS OF SEOUL, TOKYO AND SHANGHAI

In this section, the demographic characteristics of the three cities will be compared in detail.

The ratio of the elderly population to the total population in the three cities can reveal interesting details of the cities. The fact that Tokyo's elderly ratio is higher than Seoul's is not unexpected for Japan as it has faced an aging society problem for years, but it is surprising to find Shanghai's elderly ratio to be higher than Tokyo's. This ratio can be explained by Shanghai's numerous rural farming and fishing villages populated by the elderly.

With 45.7% of the city as single person households (SPHs), Tokyo surpasses the other two cities in the SPH ratio to total households. This ratio is unusually high in Tokyo with close to one out of two households reporting as SPH. This might indicate a higher individualistic quality among the young in Tokyo compared to its Seoul and Shanghai counterparts. In Tokyo, it is not unusual for the elderly population to reside separately from their children, hence another reason for the larger ratio of SPHs in the city.

Figure 2-15 illustrates the spatial distribution of SPHs in the three cities. The distribution reveals different patterns and characteristics of the three cities. In Seoul, most young SPHs are concentrated south of the Han river including in Gwanak ward and Gangnam ward while the elderly SPHs are concentrated north of the river. We can conjecture that the elderly SPHs of Seoul are from relatively low economic backgrounds considering that wards north of the river have a lower economic standing than the wards south of the river. On the other hand, SPHs among the young and the elderly in Tokyo are somewhat equally distributed within the city for the most part. In the case of Shanghai, the elderly SPHs are more concentrated in the city center while the young are more likely to reside in the periphery. We can conjecture that in Shanghai, the elderly SPHs have a higher economic standing than young SPHs.

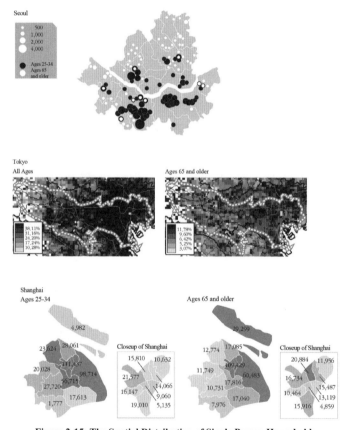

Figure 2-15: The Spatial Distribution of Single Person Households
Source: The Seoul Institute (2012)(Seoul); Statistics Bureau of Japan (2010)(Tokyo); Statistics Bureau of Shanghai (2015)(Shanghai)

The number of foreigners in Seoul is nearly three times that of Tokyo and

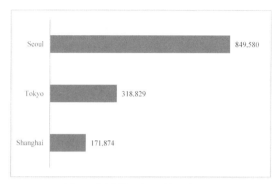

Figure 2-16: Number of Foreigners
※Seoul, 2015 statistics; Tokyo, 2010 statistics; Shanghai, 2014 statistics
Source: The Seoul Research Data Service(Seoul); Statistics Bureau of Japan(2010)
(Tokyo); Statistics Bureau of Shanghai(2015)(Shanghai)

five times that of Shanghai.. This is due to the recent surge of Korean-Chinese or *joseon-jok* in Daelim-dong and Jayang-dong in Seoul. Additionally, the higher number of foreigners in Seoul is evidence of South Korea's relatively more open policies to foreigners compared with Tokyo and Shanghai.

Figure 2-17 illustrates which areas have high concentrations of foreigners within the three cities. From this figure, we can see how Shanghai and Tokyo are different from Seoul. There is a high concentration of foreigners in the economically deprived areas of Seoul whereas the spatial distribution of foreigners in Tokyo is spread out throughout the 23 wards. In the case of Shanghai, the foreigner population is concentrated in the economically advantaged areas including the central city and Pudong. This implies that foreigners residing in Seoul are economically deprived relative to their counterparts in Shanghai. In Tokyo on the other hand, the foreigner is diverse in terms of their economic status.

NOTES

1   Because Yeongdeungpo was developed to support the Japanese military industry, it was added to Gyeongseong city.
2   According to the index, the best ranked city was Vienna, Austria, while the lowest ranked city was Baghdad, Iraq.

REFERENCES

AT Kearney. (2016). *Global Cities 2016.*
DECODE. (2016). Available at: http://www.youthfulcities.com

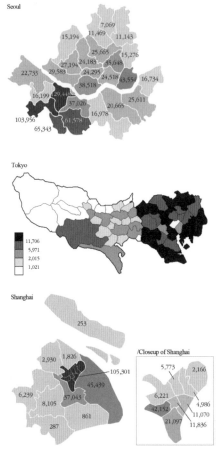

Figure 2-17: Spatial Distribution of Foreigners

Unit: Number of Foreigners

Economist Intelligence Unit. (2015). *Safe Cities Index 2015*.

Eicha. *Para-para Map, Tokyo Metropolitan City*, 2004 Available at: http://mujina.sakura.ne.jp/history/13/index2.Html

Geospatial Information Authority of Japan. *Statistical reports on the land area by prefectures and municipalities in Japan*. Available at: http://www.gsi.go.jp/KOKUJYOHO/MENCHO-title.htm

Knight Frank. (2016). *The Wealth Report 2016*.

Korean Educational Development Institute. *Korean Education Statistics Service*. Available at: http://kess.kedi.re.kr/index

Korean Statistical Information Service. (2016). *GRDP Per Person, GRNI and Personal Income*. Available at: http://kosis.kr/statHtml/statHtml.do?orgId=101&tblId=DT_ 1 C65

Mercer. (2016). Available at: https://www.imercer.com/content/mobility/quality-of-living-cityrankings.html

Ministry of Education, Culture, Sports, Science and Technology of Japan. *School Basic Survey*. Available at: http://www.mext.go.jp/b_menu/toukei/chousa01/kihon/1267995.htm

National Diet Library. Available at: http://www.ndl.go.jp/index.html

QS Top Universities. (2016). Available at: http://www.topuniversities.com/city-rankings/2016

Seoul City. (2015). *2015 Seoul Survey*. Available at: http://stat.seoul.go.kr/jsp3/stat.book. jsp?link=2&cot=007

_____. Seoul Statistics, Available at: http://stat.seoul.go.kr

Seoul Community Support Center. *Seoul Village Making Project Policy*. Available at: http://www. seoulmaeul.org/programs/user/eng/introduction.html

Shanghai Municipal Education Commission. Available at: http://www.shmec.gov.cn/web/xxgk

Shanghai Municipal People's Government. Available at: http://www.shanghai.gov.cn

Sina Shanghai. *Eight Pictures to Understand the Changes in Shanghai's Regionalization over a Century*. September 9, 2015. Available at: http://sh.sina.com.cn/ news/b/2015-09-09/detail-ifxh-qhuf8271562-p2.shtml

Statistics Bureau of Shanghai. (2015). *Shanghai Statistical Yearbook*. Available at: http://www.stats-sh.gov.cn/data/toTjnj.xhtml?y=2015

_____. (2016). *2015 Statistical Communique of Shanghai on the National Economic and Social Development*. Available at: http://www.stats-sh.gov.cn/sjfb/201602/287258.html

Statistics Bureau of Japan. (2010). 2010 National Census. Available at: http://www.stat.go.jp/data/ kokusei/2010/

_____. (2015). *2014 Economic Census for Business Frame*. Available at: http://www.stat.go.jp/data/ e-census/index.htm

Statistics Division, Tokyo Metropolitan Government Bureau of General Affairs. (2014). *2014 Tokyo Statistical Yearbook*. Available at: http://www.toukei.metro.tokyo.jp/tnenkan/tn-index.htm#h21

The Asia Business Daily. *Seoul Places 7th as a Global Financial City.1st Place Goes to New York*. March 16, 2014.

The Economist. *Worldwide Cost of Living Survey*. March 10. 2016.

The Mori Memorial Foundation. (2016). Available at: http://mori-m-foundation.or.jp/english/index. shtml

The Seoul Institute. (2007). *Seoul through a Map (2007)*. Available at: https://www.si.re.kr/map

_____. (2012). *Where Do Single Person Households Live in Seoul?*. Available at: https://www.si. re.kr/node/45487

_____. (2015). *Transition of Seoul's Administrative Regions and Development of Urban Spaces*. Available at: https://www.seoulsolution.kr/node3182

_____. *The Seoul Research Data Service, Understanding Seoul by Indexes*. Available at: http://data. si.re.kr/index

_____. *Looking at Seoul's Statistics*. Available at: http://data.si.re.kr/statistics-seoul

Tokyo Metropolis. (2014). Available at: http://www.metro.tokyo.jp

_____. *2014 Report on School Basic Survey*. Available at: http://www.toukei.metro.tokyo.jp/gakk-ou/2014/gk14qg10000.htm

Tokyo Metropolitan Government Bureau of Social Welfare and Public Health. (2014). "Medical Facilities in Tokyo Metropolitan Area: Report based on the 2014 Survey on the Medical Facilities in Tokyo Metropolitan Area". Available at: http://www.fukushihoken.metro.tokyo.jp/kiban/cho-sa_tokei/iryosisetsu/heisei26nen.html

Yonhap News Agency. *Seoul, the World's 16th Influential City by Forbes*. August 19, 2014.

3

Social Mobility in Three Cities**

Haidong Zhang
JiYoung Kim
Yoshimichi Sato
Yelin Yao

As outlined in Chapter 3, three cities—Seoul, Tokyo and Shanghai—share the characteristic of receiving a high influx of young population compared to other cities. Migration is an act that is highly energy-consuming for migrants as they adapt and form new networks in new places. Despite this fact, in 2015 alone we have seen large population moves into the cities including 459,000 to Seoul (Statistics Korea, 2016), 397,000 to Tokyo (Statistics Bureau of Japan, 2015) and 9.81 million to Shanghai (Statistics Bureau of Shanghai, 2016).

The reasons for migration include various population, cultural, social and educational resources as detailed in Chapter 2. In order to acquire these re-sources, however, people need to have economic resources that usually comes paired with employment. Therefore, we can conjecture that the three cities are enticing due to the job opportunities they offer.

It is important to understand that the three cities were not always at the core of economic or job opportunities. Most jobs at the cities were formed within the past century. Looking at Korea we can see a five-fold growth in the past centu-ry from 3,260 jobs in 1969 to 15,537 in 2016. What phenomenon can we ob-serve by combining the trends in migration and diversification of jobs in the three cities?

We would like to analyze this phenomenon by using the keyword and con-cept of "social mobility." Social mobility is defined by an individual or group moving from one social strata to another and usually measured by occupational change (Hong and Koo, 2008). Social mobility is possible in a society where economic resources, social opportunities and privileges are equally distributed or in places where the channel to advance to a higher social status is flexible. A society where social mobility is openly achievable can be understood as having a system that backs up personal achievements and efforts compared to societies that are more rigid. Social mobility can also be tied to a level of hope for a city.

Before observing the level of hope in the cities, we will first outline the historical background of migration and social mobility as well as how the three cities have addressed these issues in the past. Then, we can discuss recent social mobility opportunities and level of hope found in the cities.

1. CITIES FORMED BY MIGRATION

(1) Migration, a Fate of Modern Society

Alvin Toffler (1980) who has categorized the development of civilization based on energy sources used, pointed to the "second wave," or the beginning of industrialization, as when modern society started. The "first wave" before the industrialization was characterized by an agrarian society powered by human and animal labor as well as energy sources from nature including solar and wind power. Since agriculture was tied to a physical land, societies at this time were physically rooted.

People's lives drastically changed with the introduction of mass production fueled by fossil fuel. Development of technology that buttressed mass production continued to produce new machines. The large number of factories produced as a result led to creation of railroads to transport fuel. Most of the labor force created by the "first wave" agrarian revolution moved to the city to find work.

The move to the cities, therefore, was like fate for migration laborers. Toffler sees the modern society as different from the past societies due to the fact the society has forced people to migrate. Today's modern society is filled with workers who are able to move to different regions depending on circumstances.

(2) The Appearance of New Occupations

The modern society developed by migration of people has many distinct characteristics from agrarian societies. One of them is the diversification of occupations. Past agrarian societies that were based on settlement and limited in moving to other areas showed similar occupations over generations. However, intergenerational change for families that have moved to cities show different jobs for children of parents who used to be factory workers.

Mass education was offered to cultivate eligible individuals that can increase productivity at factories. Other developments made to encourage productivity of workers included advancements in medicine, public health and leisure-related industries. In the city, alongside factory workers, other industry workers increased including teachers and caretakers. The development of mass production also created a new line of work which involved managing, organizing or selling factory products. These people who were in charge of middle-level management are also known as white-collar workers. Although these people did not participate in the production process, their roles were deemed invaluable since their job efficiency was directly related to sales and production levels.

Another backdrop for the creation of new occupations was the "third wave," a phase represented by the spread of information and globalization. After the World War II, information network that had once been used for military and economic purposes became utilized for product management, distribution and sale. At this time of post-industrial society, occupations became even more diversified. Daniel Bell (2006) saw post-industrial society as a society where economic and occupational structures would be changed due to expansion of service-based economies and increase of professional technicians among others.

What is important to take note is that the new occupations are not accessible for anyone but only accessible to people who have received at least a high school education or have special skills (Hong, 2005). It is true that even laborers working for a factory are categorized as either skilled or unskilled laborers and measured by the quality of their work. With time and experience, unskilled laborers have potential to become skilled. However, the occupations created by a highly advanced industrial society are different from jobs that can be managed by experience alone. There is now an educational requirement attached to occupations before starting work.

The development of an industrial society and the coming of a post-industrial society have diversified jobs for the cities. In this process, jobs have been categorized as jobs that can be replaced and jobs that cannot be replaced. According to this categorization, occupations are ranked, workers are paid according to the wage system and social status has been emphasized. These changes have increased the interest and desire in people for social mobility.

2. DIVERSIFIED PERSPECTIVES FOR ANALYZING SOCIAL MOBILITY

Social mobility is a concept characterized by the move in social status from one strata to another (Hara and Seiyama, 1999). As mentioned previously, social mobility has gained attention along with the new social structures brought on by advanced industrial societies and the coming of a post-industrial society.

We need to analyze social mobility in the three cities according to when industrial society was fully established and post-industrial society was advanced.

The next section will look into how analytical perspectives for analyzing social mobility are diversified. Because social mobility measures changes in social status between generations and since social status is commonly measured by occupations, we need to check if there exists a survey using the same question across generations. Since social structure changes like industrial and post-industrial societies as advanced by Toffler and Bell are changes happening nationwide and even transnationally, not many surveys collect data using cities as units. Therefore, instead of focusing on consistency in units, we have prioritized securing data on Korea, Japan and China that includes the three cities of interest.

(1) Japan: End of Middle Class and Reduced Social Mobility

It was in the early1900s that industrialization in the West led to a general raise in economic levels. However, in Japan, it took another fifty years for absolute poverty to disappear, which was after World War II. Known as the Japanese economic miracle, during the high economic growth between post-World War II and end of the Cold War, job structure in Japan changed drastically. Primary industry workers declined drastically and wholesale and retail trades expanded. After the 1980s, occupations in professional, management, clerical and administrative, sales and service sectors increased as well.

Many people in Japan experienced changes in occupation as more jobs were created due to the change in the industrial structure. Discourse and collection of data on social mobility have existed before the industrial structure was well established starting from the 1950s. Japan first participated in an international joint research in 1951 titled "Program of Cross-National Research on Social Stratification and Social Mobility." From 1955, The National Survey of Social Stratification and Social Mobility or SSM Survey was carried out every decade in Japan (Hara and Seiyama, 2002).

SSM survey collects data for both the respondents and their families on their education levels, occupation and subjective SES levels. Based on data from SSM survey including the Japanese sample, Lipset and Bendix (1959) predicted a greater level of intergenerational social mobility than expected for industrial societies and that inequality will be reduced due to it. With further contention provided by Featherman, Jones and Hauser (1975) that industrialized societies will eventually experience similar social mobility patterns, a hopeful sentiment on good job prospects and social equality in the future became widespread in Japan.

This positive attitude on social openness and equal society is also found in the survey results. According to the annual National Poll on Life Quality Survey that was first carried out in 1958, people who have reported their life quality status to be "middle/high," "middle," and "middle/low" was past 80% in the mid-1960s and over 90% after 1970. Based on this data, Japan has coined the term "1 million middle class" referring to the national population of 1 million at the time. Paired by the high economic growth, the belief in Japan's openness and equality was further strengthened.

However, this belief was questioned with the crash of the bubble economy in the mid-1990s. Based on SSM survey data, Toshiki Sato (2000) contended that with change in industrial structure, many people in Japan have experienced more abundant lives but the gap between the rich and poor still remained. Also, with the barrier to getting a white-collar job becoming greater, he added there will be certain job positions and social strata that cannot be achieved by effort alone.

What are recent social mobility patterns like in Japan? Since SSM survey includes nationwide samples, data on Tokyo is included. However, since the survey collects data through a random sampling method, Tokyo sample is very limited to offer good data on social mobility. To add, the survey data for 2015 is yet to be released. Therefore, we will observe Japan's social mobility patterns by looking at national data from 1955 to 2005.

We must pay attention to two perspectives to determine whether a society has an open system for social mobility. Satoshi Miwa and Hiroshi Ishida (2008) observed actual social mobility termed "absolute mobility" and relative social mobility opportunities termed "relative mobility" to analyze social mobility patterns and effects caused by father's occupations.

In order to measure "absolute mobility," both "total mobility rate" and "dissimilar index" need to be observed. The total mobility rate includes both upward and downward mobility while "dissimilar index" represents the gap between social status at birth and social status achieved. Higher numbers for both mean high intergenerational mobility but since total mobility rate measures both upward and downward mobility, a higher rate does not reflect higher upward mobility. However, a high dissimilar index does mean higher upward mobility. A high total mobility rate and low dissimilar index can be interpreted as increased downward mobility.

Figure 3-1 shows total mobility rate and dissimilar index of people who have different jobs from their fathers by gender using SSM survey data from 1955 to

2005. We can see in figure 3-1 that total mobility rate including both upward and downward mobility has continually increased for men since 1955 to decline for the first time in 2005 to the same level measured in 1985. The dissimilar index that measures the difference between social status at birth and achieved social status increased up until 1975 but steadily decreased to 17.7, which is an index lower than that measured in 1955. These numbers mean that intergenerational mobility is slowly declining in Japan and barrier between social classes are getting higher.

Unit: %
Male

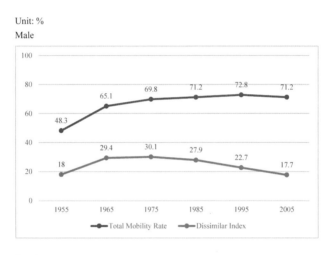

Female

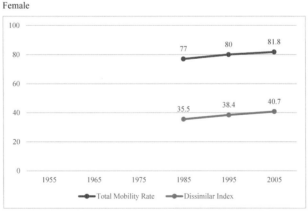

Figure 3-1: Social Mobility Rate and Dissimilar Index Trends
Source: arranged by the authors based on Satoshi Miwa and Hiroshi Ishida (2008).

Ever since women were included in the survey from 1985, total mobility rate increased continually. Dissimilar index also steadily increased from 35.5 to 40.7 evidencing an active upward mobility. The reason why women's social mobility is shown up as more active in Japan can be based on many reasons. One of the main reasons put forth by Taro Miyamoto (2011) was the restructuring of family during the high growth period in Japan where the state actively supported a family structure of a working husband and a stay-at-home wife. The tax system that used to charge higher tax to married women was changed in 2016 as Japan entered an era of low birth rate and aging society and as need for women's labor force became reevaluated. The active upward mobility pattern shown in survey results for women can be interpreted as the weakening of the past social structures that used to bind women.

We can now observe relative mobility results to observe for social mobility trends. Relative mobility measures the likelihood of an individual's job to be different from their father's to estimate possibility of social mobility. An index called "intergenerational stability" that measures similarities between intergenerational occupations is utilized. The higher the rate, there is higher likelihood of intergenerational occupations to match, which evidences lower social mobility.

Intergenerational stability rate by occupation is shown in figure 3-2. Based on eight occupational categories in SSM survey, which include professional, administrator, clerical worker, sales and service worker, skilled manual worker, semi-skilled manual worker, unskilled manual worker, agriculture, forestry, and fishery, we look at the trends of intergenerational stability rate.

Figure 3-2 shows male responses to intergenerational stability rate on eight occupation categories from 1955 to 2005. The "agriculture" category that used to be the main job category in 1950s had a high intergenerational stability rate around the 1960s but steadily decreased since then. Occupations in professional, management and sales sectors that have increased with the onset of industrialization show highest intergenerational stability rate. More specifically, occupation in management has increased in stability rate until 1995 but decreased in 2005 to a level recorded in 1965. Intergenerational stability rate declined for clerical and administrative work since 1985 but started increasing again in 2005. For occupations in sales, intergenerational stability rate has steadily rose starting from 1975. Excluding management positions, occupations in professional work, clerical work and sales have shown increased mobility rate relative to other occupation categories, showing more younger people are employed in these jobs. Lastly, it is important to note that for unskilled work

40

Unit: %
Male

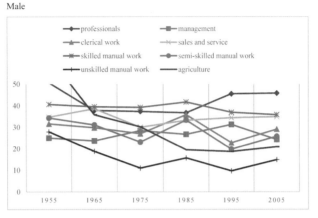

Female

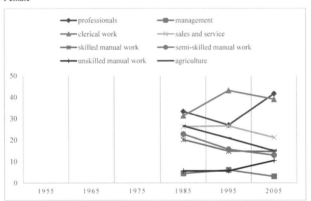

Figure 3-2: Intergenerational Stability Rate Patterns
Source: arranged by the authors based on Satoshi Miwa and Hiroshi Ishida (2008).

positions, intergenerational stability rate has fluctuated frequently but stayed lower than other occupations.

Intergenerational stability rate for women in figure 3-2 shows that except for increased stability rate for professional and low-skilled jobs, all other occupation categories including management, clerical, sales, agricultural, skilled and semi-skilled work have declined in rate. This shows that women are indeed influenced by father's occupations. Fluctuating patterns are shown for intergenerational stability rates for occupations like administrative, clerical, sales and management work that increased with the industrial structure change. This pattern might be interpreted as women being more likely to seek for newly created jobs in the 1980s but later being influenced by father's occupations in the 1990s.

Japan could be characterized as a society with active mobilization due to the fact downward and upward mobility rates are both active. However, declining dissimilar index shows that the path to upward mobility is getting narrower. To add, for jobs that are highly affected by father's occupations including low-skilled, agricultural and management work, social mobility remains fixed.

(2) Shanghai: City with Growing Middle Class

As mentioned previously, social mobility as a concept gained attention with the changing economic structures in society and diversification of jobs. Industrialization and modernization were introduced in China after Japan in a compressed fashion. Shanghai, our city of interest, is known to have experienced a large inflow of population during the industrialization and urbanization processes. Wang (2008) categorized population migration into active and passive responses to urbanization: active actors moved automatically from rural areas to cities to find jobs and passive actors were drifted into the cities involuntarily with the flow of urbanization.

Whether the migration was voluntary or involuntary, population increased in the cities during urbanization. And as industrialization was advanced, intergenerational social mobility became strengthened. Before examining social mobility in Shanghai, we can look at China's mobilization trends nationwide shown in figure 3-3.

As shown in figure 3-3, when looking at China as a whole, total mobility rate has steadily increased: total mobility rate was 35.3% between the years 1949 to 1977, 39.3% between the years 1978 and 1991 and 60.1% between the years 1992 and 2006.

The late effects of modernization and urbanization is well displayed by the greater mobility rate shown during the periods between years 1978 and 1991 and between years 1992 and 2006 compared to periods between years 1949 and 1977 and between years 1978 and 1991. China as a whole can be characterized as a society with social openness and relatively active mobilization.

However, when looking at total mobility rate post-2005 in Shanghai, we see a resemblance to Japan's trends shown in mid-2000s.

Although China lagged behind Japan and Korea in modernization and urbanization, Shanghai took on the role of delivering fast-paced development and

Unit: %
China

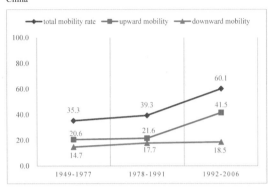

Japan

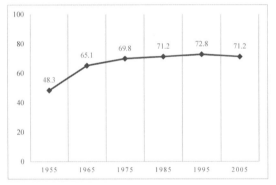

Figure 3-3: China's Total Mobility Rate
※Japanese data only shows total mobility rate for reference.
Source: arranged by the authors based on "2006 Chinese Social Survey"
and Satoshi Miwa and Hiroshi Ishida(2008).

attracting labor force from different countries as a central city. Shanghai's mobilization as shown by its total mobility rate has increased rapidly in the past six
years from 61.7% in 2005, to 66.3% in 2008 and to 76.4% in 2011. However,
from 2011, Shanghai is experiencing a different trend showing decline in both
upward and downward mobility. Li Qiang (2016) contends that reduced mobilization is likely to be based on four factors. First, since most new jobs created
during post-industrial stages including jobs in real estates, finance and technology require higher education, many people are excluded from such job oppor-

Unit: %

Shanghai

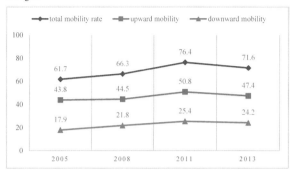

Japan

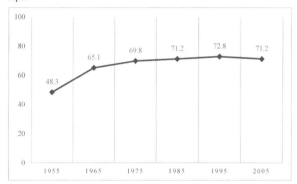

Figure 3-4: Shanghai's Total Mobility Rate

※Japanese data only shows total mobility rate for reference.

Source: arranged by the authors based on Shanghai Data from Chinese General Social Survey (CGSS) and Satoshi Miwa and Hiroshi Ishida (2008).

tunities. Second, housing expenses have risen during the 1980s and 1990s, forcing low-wage workers to move out of the cities. Therefore, mobilization for low-wage workers in the city has been reduced. Third, as new lifestyles were forming in cities, different areas became segregated according to land value. Fourth, segregation became emphasized as groups with cultural capital and groups without such capital began to live in separated areas. Based on these four factors, segregation within large cities like Shanghai are reinforced and opportunities of social mobility is reduced.

Although mobilization speed and prevalence were both reduced since the early 2000s, due to industrialization and urbanization from the 1980s and introduction of the capitalistic system, Shanghai's social stratification experienced numerous transitions. While occupations like managers, professionals and technicians, clerical support workers and service and sales workers increased greatly, workers in agricultural, forestry and fishery steadily declined in number. Figure 3-5 shows how occupational distribution changed in Shanghai from 1982 to 2015.

We can first look at the changes to occupations that are commonly tied to the middle class which are professionals, managers and technicians. As shown in figure 3-5, jobs in management fluctuated in numbers after 1982 but reached 5.3% of the total occupations in 2010 and 13.4% in 2015 according to Shanghai data. Although the 2015 data is from a survey carried out by Shanghai University and used different sampling methods and sample sizes compared to other surveys, we can still utilize it as reference to observe the trend of increasing jobs in management positions. In the case of professionals and technicians, there was an increase in their numbers from 10.7% in 1982 to 15% in 2010 and 17.6% in 2015; these occupations have shown steady rise for the past three

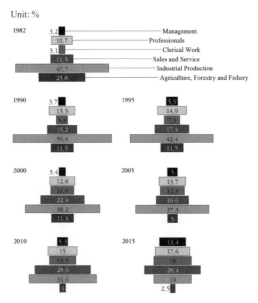

Figure 3-5: Shanghai's Occupational distribution
Source: 1982, 1990, 2000 and 2010 Shanghai Census Data; 1995 and 2005 data from the "Shanghai 1% of the Population Sample Survey"; 2015 data from the "Living Conditions of Urban Residents' Survey"

decades.

In the case of clerical and administrative workers, and service and sales workers, their numbers increased greatly during the post-industrial stages to 13.5% in 2010 for clerical and administrative workers and 28.6% in 2010 for sales and service workers. However, occupations that have existed before industrialization—including work in industrial production and equipment installment or jobs in agricultural, forestry and fishery that once took up 71.5% of jobs in the 1980s with 47.7% of jobs in production and equipment and 23.8% of jobs in agricultural, forestry and fishery—declined in number to almost half their past sizes. Overall, occupational distribution in Shanghai is slowly changing from an "inverted T-shaped structure" to a "pyramid-shaped structure" excluding the occupations in agriculture, forestry and fishery. This transition reflects the growing number of people in middle class with middle class occupations like professionals, technicians, clerical and administrative work, and sales and service work.

(3) Seoul: Low Expectation for Social Mobility

In Korea, from the early 1960s, there was a great increase of knowledge workers distinguished from manual laborers. These workers included those in management, professionals or technicians and those working administrative or clerical office jobs. According to nationwide data, from 1960 to 2010, people in professional or technical work increased from 2.4% to 19.4% and those in administrative or clerical office jobs increased from 2.6% to 16.3%. The increasing trends are more salient in Seoul. The percent increase for professional or technical work increased from 6.2% to 25.3% and for clerical and administrative work 10.2% to 20.2% in the past five decades. Since the advancement of industrialization from 1960, this new group of people working in new occupation types are concentrated in Seoul (see figure 3-6).

In order to compare mobilization in Korea with mobilization patterns of Japan and China, we utilized the results of analysis from Bongoh Kye and Sun-Jae Hwang (2016) who have based their study on Korean Educational Development Institute's "Education and Social Mobility Survey." The survey was carried out for three years between 2008 to 2011 on a sample size of 7,611 respondents born between years 1943 and 1986. Figure 3-7 shows the pattern of upward and downward mobility for sample size of 5,875 people with available data on personal occupation and their father's occupation.

Figure 3-7 categorizes mobilization patterns according to birth cohorts. For birth cohorts born between years 1943 and 1955, years they started work would

46

Unit: %
Nationwide

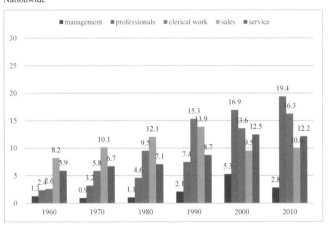

Seoul

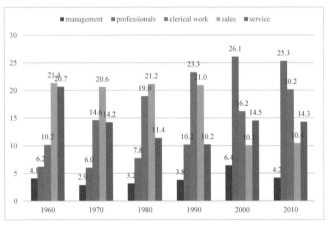

Figure 3-6: Occupational Breakdown for Korea and Seoul
Source: arranged by the authors based on annual data on employed individuals from the
"Population Census" by Statistics Korea.

range from mid-1960s to mid-1970s. For birth cohorts born between years
1976 to 1986, years they started work would range from mid-1990s to mid-
2000s.

Total mobility rate between mid-1960s and mid-2000s show that upward
mobility that had increased to 69.8% in mid-1990s declined for the first time to
67% in mid-2000s. On the other hand, from 1960s, downward mobility has

Unit: %
Korea

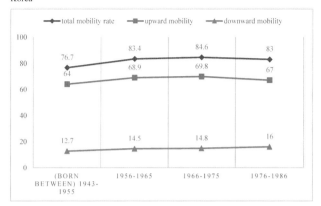

Japan

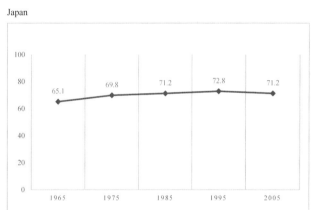

Figure 3-7: Total Mobility Rate by Korea's Birth Cohorts
Source: arranged by the authors based on data from Kye and Hwang (2016: 16)

steadily increased to reach 16% in the mid-2000s. Comparing this pattern to Japan's total mobility rate during the same period reveals intergenerational mobilization to be more active for Korea during the industrial and post-industrial stages.

Due to limitations existing in data, it is hard to calculate Seoul's total mobility rate during the same period. However, we can examine Seoul's attitudinal change on social mobility for the next generation during the past 15 years by utilizing the Statistics Korea's survey data.

Figure 3-8 shows ratio of responses to the question: "backed by a lifetime of

48

effort, how likely would it be for the next generation to improve their socioeconomic status?" Responses "very likely" and "somewhat likely" were labeled "likely" and responses "very unlikely" and "somewhat unlikely" were labeled "unlikely" in the figure.

Comparing men's attitudes on social mobility between nationwide data and Seoul data, we can see that the "likely" responses and "unlikely" responses cross over in 2011 to show an increase of the "unlikely" group. The attitudinal change is not drastically different between nationwide and Seoul data up until

Male

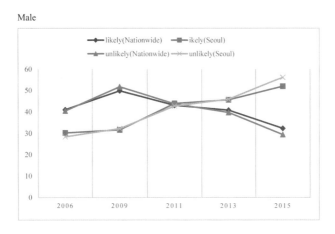

Female

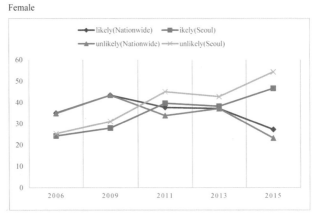

Figure 3-8: Attitudes on Intergenerational Mobility: Comparison between Korea and Seoul

Source: arranged by the authors based on "Social Survey: Mobilization for the Next Generation" by Statistics Korea.

2013 to show greater difference from 2015. The difference includes greater declining pattern of "likely" responses in Seoul compared to nationwide trend and smaller increase of "unlikely" responses in Seoul compared to Korea as a whole. This somewhat ironic pattern hints at two groups existing in Seoul: a group that still believes that mobilization is possible for the future generation backed by personal effort and another group that has given up on this possibility.

For women, mobilization attitude for the next generation shows different patterns for nationwide and Seoul samples. The general pattern of decreasing "likely" responses to possibility of mobilization for the next generation is consistent for both the nationwide and Seoul samples. However, the response of mobilization being unlikely is lower for Seoul and response for mobilization being likely is also lower for Seoul. We see a polarization of attitudes on the possibility of mobility for future generations.

3. CONCLUSION

This chapter examined three cities that are experiencing large-scale population mobility. We have looked at what kind of jobs are increasing and who fills those jobs. Also, by comparing occupations of people in the cities with occupations of their fathers, we decided to assess people's upward or downward mobility trends by utilizing the concept of social mobility. All three cities are attractive in a sense that they offer diverse jobs and relatively good employment opportunities. However, when these opportunities are reassessed and contextualized according to mobilization rates and intergenerational effects, the attraction level of the cities fluctuate depending on generations.

All three cities and three countries have experienced industrialization and post-industrialization albeit at slightly different times. The occupational changes and intergenerational mobility that followed economic structure changes took place around mid-1990s after the collapse of bubble economy for Japan. In Korea, these mobilization trends became weakened after the year 2000. On the other hand, mobilization remains active in China relative to other countries although its rate slowed down after 2000, following the trends shown in Japan and Korea.

Just by examining mobilization tendencies, it may look like the three cities are slowly turning into hopeless cities where occupation barriers are high for prestigious jobs in management or professional positions and low-skilled work is still being passed down generationally. However, if we view these trends as a characteristic of a changed job structure of a stabilized industrial and post-industrial societies as Kye and Hwang (2016) have contended, there are more research to be done. Hopeful factors include active mobilization of women in Japan despite the country's stall in total mobility rate. There is also the large-scale expansion of middle class for China.

What specific changes follow a society that has experienced reduced social mobility? What would that look like in the three cities? The next chapter will look at changing trends in occupational distribution by occupation and gender. It will also analyze the trends that show up in societies with reduced mobilization and retrace the factors of hope and despair that characterize the cities.

**An earlier version of this chapter was published in the *Development and Society* (Vol. 45 No.3, 2016).

REFERENCES

Bell, Daniel. (1976). *The Coming of Post-industrial Society.* New York, Basic Books. Translated in Korean by Park, Hyong-shin and Kim, Wong Dong, 2006. Seoul: Acanet.

Featherman, Jones and Hauser (1975).Assumptions of social mobility research in the U. S.: The case of occupational status. *Social Science Research*, 4(4), 329-360.

Hara, Junsuke and Seiyama, Kazuo. (1999). *Social Stratification in Japan: Inequality Amid Affluence (Shakai Kaiso: yutakasa no naka no fubyoudou).* Tokyo: Tokyo University Press. Translated in Korean by Jeong, Hyeon Suk, 2002. Seoul: Hanul.

Hong, Doo-Seung. (2005). *The Middle Classes in Korea.* Seoul: Seoul National University Press.

Hong, Doo-Seung and Koo, Hagen. (2008). *Social Stratification and Class* (2nd ed). Seoul: Dasan Books.

Korean Ministry of Employment and Labor. http://work.go.kr/

_____. *Korean Occupation Dictionary.* Available at: https://www.work.go.kr/consltJobCarpa/srch/jobDic/jobDicIntro.do

Kye, Bongoh and Hwang, Sung-Jae. (2016). Intergenerational Social Mobility of Korea: Cohort and Gender Comparisons of Occupational Mobility. *Korea Journal of Population Studies*, 39(3), 1-28.

Seymour Martin Lipset and Reinhard Bendix.(1959). *Social Mobility in Industrial Society.* Berkeley: University of California Press.

Li Qiang. (2016). *New Features and Trends of China's Social Structure and Social Stratification.* Beijing Daily. Version 15, May 30, 2016.

Miwa, Satoshi and Ishida, Hiroshi. (2008). Basic Analysis of Class Structure and Social Mobility in Postwar Japan (Sengo nihon no kaiso kozo to shakai ido ni kansuru kiso bunseki.) in Miwa, Satoshi and Kobayashi, Daisuke (Eds.). *Basic Analysis of 2005 SSM Survey in Japan (2005 nen SSM nihon chosa no kiso bunseki, 2005 nen SSM chosa shirizu* (1). Sendai:2005 nen SSM chosa kenkyukai.

Miyamoto, Taro. (2008). *Welfare Politics (Fukushi Seiji: nippon no seikatsu hosho to democracy).* Tokyo: Yuhikaku. Translated in Korean by Lim, Sung Keun, 2011. Seoul: Nonhyung.

National Bureau of Statistics. (1982 and 1990). Population Census.Available at: http://www.stats.

gov.cn /tjsj/pcsj/rkpc/ dscrkpc1/

National Bureau of Statistics. (1990). Population Census.Available at: http://www.stats.gov.cn /tjsj/ pcsj/rkpc/dscrkpc/

National Bureau of Statistics. (1995). 1% of the Population Sample Survey.Available at: https://data. stats.gov.cn/easyquery.htm?cn=C01&zb= A030601&sj=1995

National Bureau of Statistics. (2000). Population Census.Available at: http://www.stats.gov.cn/ tjsj/ pcsj/ rkpc/5rp/index.htm

National Bureau of Statistics. (2005). 1% of the Population Sample Survey.Available at: https://data. stats.gov.cn/easyquery.htm?cn=C01&zb=A0M0401&sj=2005

Sato, Toshiki. (2000). *Japan as Unequal Society: Good-bye to the Middle Class Society (Fubyōdō shakai nihon: sayonara sō-chūryū)*. Tokyo: Chuo Ko-ron New Books (Chūō kōron shinsha).

Shanghai Institute of Social Science Survey of Shanghai University.(2015). *Survey of Living Conditions of Residents in Megacities.*

Statistics Bureau of Japan. http://www.e-stat.go.jp/

_____. (2015). *Internal Migration in Japan derived from the Basic Resident Registration.* Available at: http://www.e-stat.go.jp/SG1/estat/List.do?lid=000001143175

Statistics Bureau of Shanghai. (2010). Shanghai Statistical Yearbook. Available at: http://tjj.sh.gov. cn/tjnj/20170629/0014-1000196.html

Statistics Bureau of Shanghai. (2016). *Shanghai Statistical Yearbook*. Available at: http://www.stats-sh.gov.cn/data/toTjnj.xhtml?y=2016

Statistics Korea. http://kosis.kr/

_____. *Migration Statistics by City and County.* Available at: http://kosis.kr/statisticsList/statis ticsList_01List.jsp?vwcd=MT_ZTITLE&parentId=A#SubCont

_____. *Population Census.* Available at: http://kosis.kr/statisticsList/statisticsList_01List.jsp?vwcd= MT_ZTITLE&parentId=A#SubCont

_____. *Social Survey: Movilization for the Next Generation.* Available at: http://kosis.kr/statHtml/ statHtml.do?orgId=101&tblId=DT_1SSSP243R

_____. *Working Population (ages 15 and above) by Gender, Age and Occupation.* Available at: http:// kosis.kr/statHtml/ statHtml.do?orgId=101&tblId=DT_1PC1010&conn_path=I3

Toffler, Alvin. (1980). *The Third Wave*. New York: William Morrow.

Wang, Chunguang. (2008). China's Urbanization and Changes in Social Structure. *Journal of China Agricultural University (Social Science Edition)*, 3.

4

Changes in Occupational Structure in Three Cities**

Hearan Koo
Yusuke Hayashi
Dingjun Weng
Jingqian Bi

People aspire to have good jobs. They believe jobs that are well-paid and stable are good jobs. If those jobs are what they want, they are considered to be even better. Unfortunately, according to the 2016 Gallup survey, only 4% of the 5 billion adult population in the world have jobs that fit the categories (Gallup, 2016). Reducing the qualification of good jobs to include people who might not like their work but are still employed in stable jobs with an adequate level of salary results in just 26%. The report also claims 30% of workers in Korea had such jobs and a slightly higher 33% for Japan. What is surprising is that this percentage is up to 48% for Sweden. These large gaps across countries indicate that finding a good job may have a close association with employment and labor market conditions and policies across countries.

Over the last century, industrialization and modernization have changed the job structure and characteristics of workers in the labor market. Although there may be country variations, many developed countries are likely to go through similar pathways of industrialization and transitions in job structure. At the risk of oversimplification, the changes in job structure accompanied by industrialization process can be summarized as follows. In the early stage, as technology advances, the manufacturing industry booms and generates massive demand for regular skilled labor. This leads to the growth of skilled workers who gain middle incomes and job security. They demand various services in education, health, housing, and quality public services. Consequently, the service sectors increase and the expansion of higher education and active participation of women in labor market serve to fill newly created service jobs.

As technology progresses further, service sector employment continues to grow with a corresponding drop in manufacturing employment. This stage is called a post-industrial phase of development. Technological advancement and automation reduce the number of semi-skilled jobs. On the other hand, the need for high-skilled and knowledge service workers increase. The workers displaced from manufacturing sectors, however, face challenges in transferring into skill-biased sectors, as they lack the appropriate knowledge and skills. Technological advancements not only threaten manufacturing sectors but white-collar, middle class service works. Computerization replaces routine tasks of medium-skilled service workers such as office clerks (Frey and Osborne, 2013). The middle income work that has increased in number in the beginning phase of industrialization becomes polarized into high-skilled and low-skilled jobs.

In fact, the impact of technological evolution and industrialization on the labor market and job structure is disputable. Until the late 1990s, there seemed to be a consensus favoring the positive impact of technology on job structure (Bekman et al., 1998). Researchers expected the increased demand for skilled labor induced by technological advancement could lead to the overall improvement of job structure. Since the early 2000s, however, concerns were raised to how the development of technology encroaches on routine tasks mainly performed by semi-skilled service workers while expanding non-routine high-skilled jobs and low-skilled jobs such as care or cleaning services (Autor and David, 2013; Goos and Manning, 2007; Wright and Dwyer, 2003). Scholars with such concerns argue that job polarization will only worsen over time.

Job polarization is not confined to developed economies. According to the World Development Report in 2016, developing countries, where the industrialization is still in progress, also experience polarization of their industries and jobs. As Rodrik (2015) argues, the discrepancy between high and low-skilled jobs in countries like China or India has been aggravated due to their premature transition into the service economies without full maturity in manufacturing industry development. This coexistence of developed and underdeveloped sectors in economy, known as premature deindustrialization, paired with duality in the labor market is regarded as one of the factors that complicate the paths to development for the developing countries.

The impacts caused by industrialization or post-industrialization on the labor market and job structure are complex indeed. People think that timing and pace of industrial development, and national-level employment structure and labor market policies modify and complicate common development trajectories shown in other developed countries. Recently, the economy and labor markets in East Asia are in the midst of dramatic structural changes. Particularly Japan,

China, and Korea have been undergoing different phases of economic development and are faced with various challenges in their economic future. What will the patterns look like for the three cities of Korea, China and Japan that have undergone industrialization and post-industrialization at different time periods then?

We are especially interested in cities because it is at the local labor market that job exploration and expansion of employment opportunities occur. Researchers often assume that overall structural changes at the local level are not so different from those at the national level. However national level labor market changes alone have limited effects on local labor markets. It is partly because the experience and impacts of global structural changes may well vary per local labor market, employment and other situations specific to the region.

Most cities have divergent local characteristics and institutional arrangements in terms of economy, labor market and welfare which condition the development of cities. These local specificities enforce cities to follow different routes within the context of state-level economic transitions. Successful policies that can increase productivity and sustainability in the local labor market, therefore, need to consider the characteristics of local labor markets and employment shifts.

This chapter explores patterns of recent changes in job structure tied to transition in industrial structures for three different cities of Korea, Japan and Japan. First, we will examine the similarities as well as the peculiarities of the three countries in their industrial stages. Second, we will look at the structural transformations in three cities and describe how they differ from national-level changes and go on to analyze the emergence and disappearance of jobs within demographic, economic and social structures. We will pay special attention to the characteristics of the workers who are filling up emerging job positions. Lastly, we will summarize the findings and discuss policy implications.

1. POST-INDUSTRIALIZATION AND KEY FEATURES OF THREE COUNTRIES

With advancements in industrialization, China, Japan and Korea have experienced shifting of labor from the manufacturing to service sectors. In 1980, the employment share of the service industry was 54% in Japan, 37% in Korea and 13% in China (World Bank, "World Development Indicators"). It shows that the service sectors in Korea and China were yet to develop during this time. On the contrary, Japan has already reached a stable phase of post-industrialization in the mid-1980s. Japan's manufacturing industry peaked around 1973 and then gradually declined thereafter (see Figure 4-1). Japan's employment numbers in service sectors continued to increase, instead. On the other hand, Korea retained a significant share of employment in the primary industry even during the 1970s, with more than 40% of the total employment condensed in farming and fishing. Only around the mid-1980s, employment in the manufacturing sector exceeded that of the agricultural sector, and continued to rise till 1991. From the beginning of 1990s, the manufacturing jobs have decreased sharply, signaling the advancement of post-industrialization. In the case of China, industrialization began in the late-1980s, the latest among the three countries. Although the primary industry still accounted for one third of the share of employment in 2015, during the 1990s, employment in the manufacturing and service sectors arose and primary industry jobs were reduced. These changes in China were instigated by the large migration movement as the manufacturing and construction industries boomed. In the mid-1990s, the employment in the service industry finally surpassed that of the manufacturing and the gap widened since then. As of 2015, 7 out of 10 workers in both Korea and Japan, and 4 out of 10 in China are employed by the service sectors.

The service industry can be divided into two groups in terms of skill level: the low-skilled service sectors which include personal and social services, wholesale and retail services, and restaurant and hotel services and the high-skilled sectors with more added value including work in finance, insurance, real estates and business. In general, the share of employment in high-skilled and high value-added sectors rise as the service industry matures. As shown in Figure 4-1, Japan's low skilled service sectors increased along with manufacturing. It, then, dropped significantly since the late-1990s. Instead, the number of employment in the high-skilled service sectors such as finance, insurance and business services exhibit gradual increments. Korea displays similar patterns: an increase of employment in traditional low-skilled service sectors with the growth of manufacturing up until the mid-1990s and the subsequent increase of employment in high-skilled service sectors. However, unlike Japan, Korea's employment in wholesale, retail, hotel and restaurant sectors still occupied one third of the total service sector employment in 2010. In China, while employment in various service sectors has expanded since the 1990s, high-skilled and value-added service sectors are yet to grow. Most of the service-related jobs expanded were mainly those in low-skilled sectors such as social and personal services.

Examining the transition of employment from manufacturing to service sec-

Unit: 1,000 persons

———— agriculture, forestry and fishery

———— mining

———— manufacturing

•••••• construction

•••••• sales, restaurants and hotels

·········· transportation, storage and communications

— — — finance, insurance, real estate and business service

— — — government service

— — — social and personal service

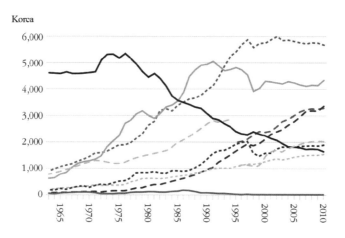

Korea

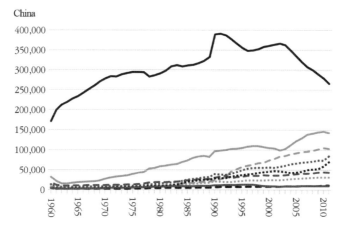

China

Japan

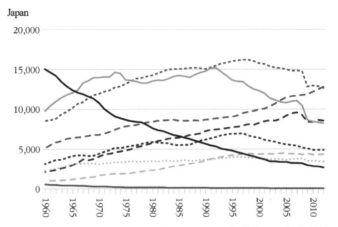

Figure 4-1: Change in the Number of Employments by Industry, 1960-2010
※Until 1994 in Korea, government service was included in community, social and personal services.Source: Groningen Growth and Development Center, "10-Sector Database"

Unit: %

Construction and Manufacturing Sector
■ Value-Added Cahnge ▢ Employment Change
Service Sector
▨ Value-Added Cahnge ▩ Employment Change

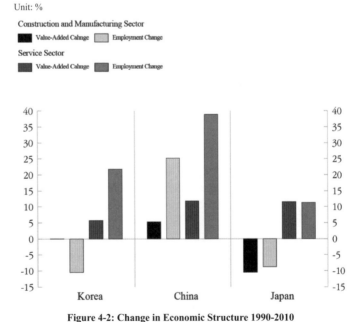

Figure 4-2: Change in Economic Structure 1990-2010
※value-add (% of GDP), employment (% of total employment)
Source: World Bank, "World Development Indicators."

tors, we can observe an interesting difference between Korea and Japan. Manufacturing employment in Japan was maintained for a considerable period of time during the transition period, avoided a sharp decline, while it declined dramatically in Korea. For a decade after the beginning of the post-industrial era, Japan's employment share in the manufacturing sector has declined by 5.6% (from 1973 to 1983), compared to the decline of 14.1% for Korea (from 1991 to 2000). If we compare the changes in output shares of economic sectors as of GDP and their employment shares of total employment (see Figure 4-2), we can see that the shifts of output shares have kept pace with that of employment shares in Japan. On the contrary, there is a large gap between employment growth and output growth in Korea and China. In the case of Korea, while the employment share of manufacturing industry has declined significantly, its share in value added remains unchanged. On the other hand, the change in service sector employment has risen faster than its output share of GDP. In China, the growth of value added both in manufacturing and service industries outpaced that of employment. These facts imply that three countries have experienced quite different transitions toward service economies. That is, Japan has experienced a relatively smooth transition to the high-valued service economy, while Korea and China have gone abrupt and imbalanced development of post-industrialization.

Such differences in post-industrial employment evolution among the three countries had significant impacts on their labor markets and job structures. During the economic transition period, the key to secure quality jobs depends on how the laborers displaced from the manufacturing sector are absorbed in the service sectors. It demands two conditions; first, the service sectors, especially high valued service sectors, should provide sufficient job opportunities to workforces in order to stabilize the labor transition and absorb the displaced labor forces. Second, the institutions should support the labor transition through adequate institutional arrangements and policies. The superseded workers need time and economic resources to accumulate new knowledge and skills appropriate to the high-skilled industry (Kim 2006: 9-10). When lack in these conditions, unemployment and underemployment would intensify along with the job quality decline.

The rapid growth of employment share in the service sectors and a remarkably slower increase in its share of GDP indicates that the service sector has absorbed primarily those workers who are unable to find high-paid employment in face of the structural transformation in Korea and China. This has led many of those workers to end up in marginal, low-productivity, low-wage services jobs.

It has often been noted that the speed of adjustment to employment shifts is closely related to the level of welfare support especially employment protection (Nickell et al. 2008; Pertold-Gebicka 2012). Automation of manufacturing or globalization of production is tightly controlled in countries with higher employment protection. However, it expands much faster in countries with lower protection and higher labor market flexibility. According to OECD statistics, from the 1980s, Japan has protected regular workers during its economic fluidity period but relaxed protection for temporary workers (OECD. Stat). These uneven protection policies have been criticized for preventing the entrance of socially vulnerable groups like women or the youth into the primary segment of the labor market, eventually deepening the duality in the Japanese labor structure. (Kambayashi and Kato 2013). Nonetheless, these social protections have served to secure the employment status of Japanese regular workers at least. In addition, due to employment protection law[1] executed in 1974, the relatively high rates of unemployment insurance coverage and income replacement ratio have provided workers with adequate support in their job transitions. Unlike Japan, however, Korea has loosen its labor regulations both on regular and temporary workers, leaving workers without comprehensive social protection for the growing unemployment during its high economic fluidity. Employment insurance was introduced to Korea in 1995 and expanded to 1998 but coverage and income replacement ratio were very low. Due to these institutional weaknesses, Korea failed to support the unemployed workers' transition into new industries. Those displaced were left with limited options and mainly absorbed into low-wage service jobs.

In the case of China, rapid industrialization and urbanization have mobilized migration within the country. The 'floating population', which denotes temporary migrants, has doubled from 79.0 million in 2000 to 170.6 million in 2010. However, China's household registration or the *hukou* system restricted migrant workers from access to, and opportunities of certain jobs, particularly jobs with higher pay and security in the cities. Because of the discriminated access of the migrants to local welfare benefits including educational opportunities, the low educated migrant workers have little chance to obtain higher level education in urban areas. According to Zhang and Wu (2013), migrant laborers in the city are mainly engaged in low-wage service jobs or self-employed and such institutional barriers in the city produced occupational segregation between the migrants and the local residents.

As we have seen, three countries have critically different characteristics in economic and labor market structures. Then, how do jobs and occupational changes in the cities reflect these differences in the national macro-economic changes and institutional systems? In order to answer this question, we examine industrial and job structures in addition to the demographic characteristics of workers in Seoul, Tokyo and Shanghai.

2. LABOR MARKET CHARACTERISTICS OF THREE CITIES

Tokyo and Seoul have long been the political, economic and cultural hubs in their countries. As of 2014, 34% of information-telecommunication business is located in Tokyo followed by 18.8% of R&D businesses (Bureau of Industrial and Labor Affairs, Tokyo Metropolitan Government, 2016). The city has also attracted various high value-added sectors such as finance and research development sectors. Similarly, Seoul has been at the core of various high value-added service sectors. Seoul is home to 55.7% of the information and media firms, 39% of the science and technology service, 27.1% of the business support service, and 25.3% of the finance and insurance companies in Korea as of 2014 (Statistics Korea, 2016).

Shanghai has long been the traditional industrial capital in China. Partly due to this traditional function, industry sectors still hold relatively high share of total employment while the development of service industry was relatively weak up until the 1990s. With the state's Open and Reform Policy and the development of the Pudong district as a commercial center, however, its service industry has expanded dramatically. The local government played a critical role in boosting the service industry in Shanghai. In 1992, the Shanghai government announced its public plans, prioritizing the growth of the service sector. And in 2001, the state implemented the "Master City Plan of Shanghai," which served as a blueprint for economic development through the invigoration of international finance, trade and shipping and the information-technology sectors (Kim, 2015: 138). Consequently, the growth of service sectors and employment has accelerated in Shanghai.

As such, the service sector is not only the core industry but also a strategic sector of development for their economies in all three cities. The majority of workers in the three cities are employed in the service sector: 81.5% in Tokyo, 84.0% in Seoul and 61.8% in Shanghai. These ratios are all higher than the national average. The share of service employment in Shanghai is notably 20% higher than that of the national level. Particularly, the employment ratio of high value-added sectors including finance, insurance, business service and real estate are all higher in the cities compared to the nationwide average. All three cities play leading roles in the development of high value-added service sectors in their countries so to speak.

However, when we examine workers' composition of the service industry in detail using the latest available data, we find significant differences across the three cities. The number of wholesale and retail employment accounts for the largest employment share in both Tokyo and Seoul. But the second largest share of service industry employment differs between Tokyo and Seoul. In Tokyo, medical care (8.8%) and information-telecommunication sector (7.8%) account for second and third highest employment shares. In Seoul, employment in restaurant and hotel sector (8.6%) ranks second, followed by employment in the education sector (8.3%). As for Shanghai, the strong tradition of manufacturing industry manifests, explaining for the 26.8% of the total employment concentrated in this sector as of 2014 followed by employment in wholesale, retail and real estate. In terms of the service sector employment, Tokyo has clearly established employment in high value-added service industries, Seoul shows employment concentration in both high value and low added value sectors and Shanghai still resembles an earlier stage of traditional service economy.

Recent changes in the industrial structures hint at the future directions for economic transitions for these three cities. If we compare that of the year 2007, we can see that Tokyo has experienced a decline in the wholesale and retail share (-1.8%) juxtaposed to the increase in the medical care sector (+1.7%). Additionally, employment shares in the science and technology sector as well as the public administration sector have grown. In Seoul, the shares of science and technology, health and social care, and business support services have expanded to great degrees while employment shares in manufacturing and service work in hotels and restaurants have stagnated. Lastly in Shanghai, employment in most industries has increased except for in agricultural, repair and personal service sectors. Specifically, rental, business service and construction sectors have witnessed the largest increments in Shanghai: rental service share increased from 5.3% in 2005 to 9.2% in 2014, and the share for the construction sector increased from 4.8% in 2005 to 8.1% in 2014, almost doubling the share in 2005. While the number of manufacturing workers has expanded in Shanghai, their total share has diminished with the growth of other industries from 31.9% in 2005 to 26.8% in 2014. The share for the repair and personal service sector experienced about a 6.5% drop from 9.1% in 2005 to 2.6% in 2014.

In sum, service sectors compose a relatively high share of employment in all three cities. However, the nature of the main service sectors differs critically. The general growth in high value-added service sectors are witnessed in Tokyo and Seoul. For both cities, the employment shares in information-telecommunication, finance and insurance, and science-technology sectors together account for more than 18% of total employment. On the other hand, except for employment in wholesale, retail and rental services, the overall share of service sectors is not so big in Shanghai. This is due to the fact that the high value added service sectors are yet to develop in Shanghai as well as the fact that the manufacturing industry still predominates. Employment share in high-skilled core service sectors including information-telecommunication, finance and insurance, and science-technology amount to only 9% in Shanghai, which is about half the ratio of the other two cities.

3. DEMOGRAPHIC COMPOSITION OF LABOR FORCES

Now let's look at the characteristics of the workers in the three cities. According to the Labor Force Survey conducted by the Ministry of Internal Affairs in 2015, 64.4% of the Tokyo residents aged 15 or older are economically active, meaning they have jobs or are seeking jobs and 62.1% of them are employed, consisting of 5.5% of the self-employed, 32.8% of regular workers and 18.9% of non-regular workers. In Seoul, 62.6% of the population 15 and older are economically active and 60% are currently working where 13.1% are self-employed, 32.1% hold regular jobs and 14.8% are non-regular workers. According to the 2010 Shanghai census data, about 5 out of 10 people aged 15 and above are currently working. The employment rate in Shanghai is 55.6%, which is significantly lower than Tokyo and Seoul.

If we compare the age distribution of working population 15 and older between cities, we can find that Tokyo has comparatively more workers who are 55 and older, corresponding to population aging experienced earlier than the other two cities (see Figure 4-3). Interestingly, the labor forces in Seoul have aged rapidly since 2005. Of the working population, 22.5% is aged 55 or older in 2015, compared with 13.7% in 2005. In contrast, the share of prime-age workers has shrunk significantly while Tokyo's working population between ages 25 and 54 has been reduced only slightly. This results in an increase in workers' average age in Seoul. This can be problematic in that it may contribute to lower economic productivity of Seoul. On the other hand, Shanghai's working population is relatively young with a large share of young workers between ages 15 and 24. Workers aged 55 and older account for only 6.5% of the total

64

Unit: %

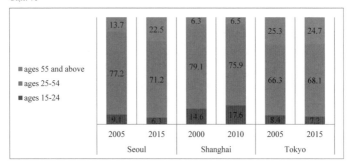

Figure 4-3: Age Distribution of Labor Force (% of total working population aged 15 and older)

Source: Statistics Korea, Economically active Population Survey (Seoul); Statistics Bureau of Shanghai, Shanghai Statistics Yearbook (shanghai); Statistics Bureau of Japan, Employment Status Survey (Tokyo)

working population in Shanghai. This could pose as a problem in a different sense. In China, workers retire when they are 55 years or older. This makes up a bigger portion of non-working population in Shanghai compared to the other two cities. According to the 2010 Shanghai census data, only 6% of the population who are between ages 55 and 64 are working. This may impose a burden on social security spending in Shanghai.

We now compare Seoul and Tokyo's working population shifts. Labor market vitality depends on several factors including continuous growth of population, active participation of population in the labor market, and high rate of employment. Figure 4-4 displays indicators measuring the vitality of the labor market in Tokyo and Seoul. We find that Seoul exhibits slower growth than Tokyo in all three indicators. If the number of population aged 15 and older in 2005 is given a value of 100, it is 105.5 in 2015, which is lower than that of Tokyo (108.9). In addition, the growth of the economically active population in Seoul is relatively small and is less than that of the population aged 15 years and older. In Tokyo, on the contrary, the growth of the economically active and employed population exceeds that of the population aged 15 and over. This means that an increasing number of people over the age of 15 in Seoul are neither working nor looking for jobs.

The non-working youth, known as "Not in Employment, Education and Training" or NEET, emerged as a social problem in Japan in the early 2000s. As Ohta poses, it is no longer a pressing issue in Japan (Ohta 2016). The NEET

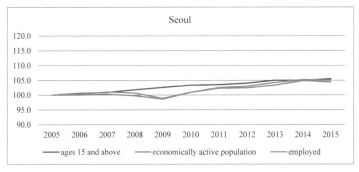

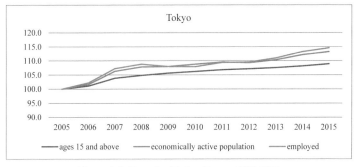

Figure 4-4: Growth of Labor Forces, 2005-2015

Source: Statistics Korea, Economically active Population Survey (Seoul); Statistics Bureau of Japan, Employment Status Survey (Tokyo)

problem is now more concerning in Korea, particularly in Seoul where the youth population continues to shrink but NEETs are increasing. According to Nam and Kim (2013), the size of youth NEETs between ages 15 and 34 in Korea have already surpassed 1 million in 2001. The NEETs in Seoul is emerging as a much more serious problem in that high-educated people take up a large proportion of NEETs.[2] It is also a critical problem in that it contributes to lower the productivity of local economy by combining with the low fertility rate and aging population in Seoul.

Comparing the changes in economic activity labor force participation rates, employment rates, and unemployment rates in Seoul and Tokyo (see Table 4-1), it can be clearly seen that the labor market in Seoul is stagnating. Tokyo's labor force participation rate was 64.4% in 2015 and employment rate was 62.1%, both showing an increase over a decade. On the other hand, Seoul was found to exhibit a decline in both labor force participation rate and employment rate.

Table 4-1: Employment Shifts by Gender in Seoul and Tokyo (2005, 2015)

Unit: %

		Total			Male			Female		
		2005	2015	Changes	2005	2015	Changes	2005	2015	Changes
Seoul	Labor Force Participation Rate	63.3	62.6	−0.7	75.3	72.9	−2.4	52	53.2	1.2
	Employment Rate	60.3	60	−0.3	71.5	69.8	−1.7	49.6	51	1.4
	Unemployment Rate	4.8	4.2	−0.6	4.9	4.3	−0.6	4.6	4.1	−0.5
Tokyo	Labor Force Participation Rate	61.9	64.4	2.5	74.5	75.2	0.7	49.5	53.9	4.4
	Employment Rate	59	62.1	3.1	71	72.3	1.3	47.2	52.2	5
	Unemployment Rate	4.7	3.6	−1.1	4.7	3.8	−0.9	4.7	3.2	−1.5

Source: Statistics Korea, Economically Active Population Survey (Seoul); Statistics Bureau of Japan, Labor Force Survey (Tokyo)

When examined by gender, employment indexes improved for both men and women in Tokyo. Notably, women's labor force participation rate and employment rate showed vast improvements. However, for Seoul, men's situation in the labor market has worsened while improving for women. The improvement for women in Seoul, however, is much less than for women in Tokyo. Since the collapse of the bubble economy in the early 1990s, Japan has infamously undergone long fluctuations in employment and economy, so called the "lost decades." Nevertheless, these numbers suggest that Tokyo hasn't lost it all, as the labor market seems to be returning positive figures.

Nevertheless, Tokyo still needs to resolve the disparity between its labor market and economic growth. The gross regional domestic product (GRDP) in Tokyo has declined considerably: if GRDP in 2007 is given a value of 100, it decreased to a value of 94.9 in 2012 (OECD Regional Database). In fact, Tokyo's GRDP has never recovered to its 2007 level. This shows the city is experiencing so-called a long-term "employment without growth." For Seoul, if GRDP in 2007 is given a value of 100, the city's GRDP was a value of 112 in 2012 and continues to rise. It means the city is experiencing "growth without employment." On which scenario is better for the economy is left to discussion. "Employment without growth" tends to lower the average wage of the workers despite growing job opportunities, which then threatens worker productivity and job quality. On the other hand, "growth without employment" aggravates income inequality and unemployment, particularly among the youth. After all, in a situation where labor market performance and economic growth is being decoupled, creating a virtuous cycle of growth and employment remains as a future task for the two cities.

4. EMERGING JOBS AND THEIR NUMBERS

In this section, we describe employment shifts in three cities since the year 2000.[3] Breaking down employment changes by wage can help us distinguish changes between "good" jobs and "bad" jobs.[4] Figure 4-5 shows which jobs have increased or decreased. The horizontal axis shows an increase of the employment share of each occupations. The vertical axis shows wage estimates of occupations. The size of circles shows employment shares of occupation types as of 2015.

Let's look at the sizes of each occupation category in the three cities first. The largest occupation share in Tokyo is the clerks, accounting for 24.3% of total employment, followed by professionals, sales workers and service workers. In Seoul, the size of the professionals is the largest (26.6%) followed by clerks. Shanghai that has a large manufacturing sector in the city shows the greatest number of workers in maintenance and production (34.6%) followed by workers in the service workers.

We can now look at what recent changes have taken place in the cities. Between 2007 and 2012, Tokyo has lost about 154,000 jobs and gained about 300,000 jobs. In Seoul, about 390,000 jobs have been created while losing 160,000 jobs between 2008 and 2015. During this period, professionals have increased the most in both cities—186,000 in Tokyo and 183,000 in Seoul, each amounting to 61% and 47% of new jobs created. For Tokyo, the next largest growth was found in service workers. About 38,000 new jobs (12% of the total increase in jobs) were created in this occupation. In Seoul, clerks have increased the second most in number. Between 2008 and 2015, 182,000 new employment positions were created in this occupation. 94% of new jobs created in Seoul were jobs for professionals and clerks.

Regarding employment reduction, jobs as managers have declined significantly in Tokyo, recording 28.6% of the total job loss, succeeded by manufacturing process workers, and construction and mining workers consecutively. In Seoul, service workers have declined the most recording about 35% of the total reduction, followed by technicians and craftsmen.

Figure 4-5 details the rise and fall of occupations in Tokyo: the rising trends are led by professionals, security workers, clerks and service workers, and low-skilled laborers while the falling trends include managers, transportation and machine operators, production workers, workers in construction and mining, and agricultural workers. Between 2007 and 2012, jobs for professionals have increased by 15% while jobs for managers have decreased by 17%. By connect-

68

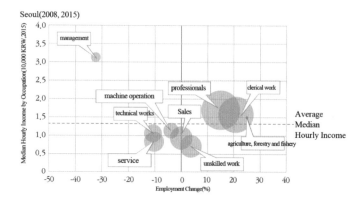

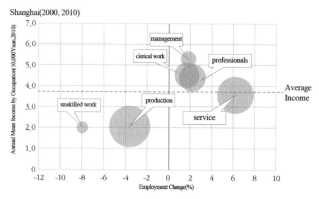

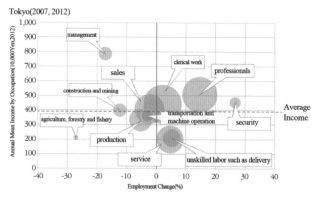

Figure 4-5: Ratio of employment Change by Occupation

Source: Statistics Korea, Local Area Labor force Survey (Seoul); Statistics Bureau of Shanghai, Shanghai Sixth National Census (Shanghai); Statistic Bureau of Japan, Employment Status Survey (Tokyo)

ing these changes to wage estimates, we can see that most jobs that have been reduced are middle-income jobs except jobs in management. Most jobs that have increased are concentrated in high (professionals, security-related workers and clerks) and low-income (service workers and unskilled workers) tiers. This indicates the polarization of high and low-paying jobs in Tokyo since 2007.

In Seoul, when comparing 2008 and 2015, new jobs have been created for professionals, clerks and unskilled workers. The number of clerks has notably expanded by 21%. On the other hand, jobs for managers and technicians, machine operators and service workers have been reduced in number. When matched to income, jobs of upper middle to high wages have expanded while jobs in the lower middle to low wages have shrunk, implying an overall improvement in job structure for Seoul. However, although not to the extent shown in Tokyo, there appears some sign of slight polarization in Seoul as the unskilled jobs have increased by 3.6% since 2008.

Unit: 10,000 Persons

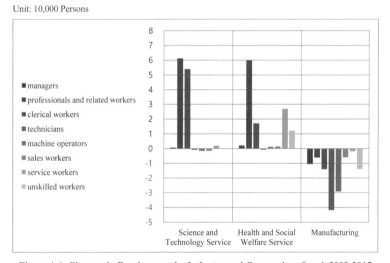

Figure 4-6: Changes in Employment by Industry and Occupation: Seoul, 2008-2015

The findings demonstrate that with the reduction of manufacturing jobs, middle-income jobs have been reduced to show a polarization of the job structure in Tokyo and Seoul. Job polarization is comparatively more deepened in Tokyo, reflecting its more mature industrial structure. Seoul shows a pattern of polarized upgrading with most job growth for high-paying occupations and some growth for low-paying jobs as well. In order to check the industry variation in job shifts, we break down industries into occupations and see in which industries, job shifts are happening in Seoul (see Figure 4-6). The results show that most employment growth in science and technology services are for professionals and clerks who are middle to high-paid workers. On the other hand, job growth in medical welfare service is concentrated both for middle to high-paid workers and middle to low-paid workers. It would seem that the job polarization in the health and social welfare services industry contributes to the polarization of the job structure. In the manufacturing sector, since the most reduction of jobs are concentrated in middle-income jobs such as technicians and machine operators rather than for jobs in management and simple labor, this industry also contributes to job polarization to some degree.

Since Shanghai data only conveys the proportion of occupational changes and exclude information on the actual number of employment and other details unlike data of the other two cities, direct comparison is not feasible. However, we can still observe and compare the overall trends of occupational changes in Shanghai. Between 2000 and 2010, the number of jobs in Shanghai has increased in all industries except in the manufacturing and agricultural sectors. According to the Shanghai government, over 600,000 new jobs are created each year, mainly in the service sector. Jobs with relatively higher wages like clerks, professionals and managers increased in their shares while low-wage job positions in agricultural and product-line work decreased. Overall, the middle to high income jobs have continued to replace lower wage jobs. Industrialization in Shanghai and job structure transition from the manufacturing sector to the service sector seem to have improved the overall job structure for the city.

Taking these results together, it can be seen that while all three cities are dominated by the increase in jobs at the upper-middle and high wage level, the characteristics of the change in the job structure are slightly different depending on the increase in the number of jobs at the lower and middle wage levels. In Tokyo, the number of good jobs increased in 2012 compared to 2007, but the job structure tends to be polarized as the number of middle-paid jobs decreased and low-paid jobs such as unskilled workers and service workers increased. In Seoul, good jobs, such as professional and white-collar jobs, generally drove job growth, and compared to Tokyo, lower-paid jobs such as service and sales did not increase, so it can be said that the job structure was generally improved. However, the slight increase in unskilled labor can be read as a sign of polarization of jobs. In Shanghai, it can be seen that the shrinking of the manufacturing sector has resulted in a decrease in the number of low-wage manufacturing workers and an increase in the middle to the upper-middle class of jobs, which clearly increases the number of good jobs. In sum, in Tokyo and Seoul, there is a trend of polarization amid the improvement or upgrade of the job structure, and in Shanghai, the improvement of the job structure is the dominant trend.

5. PATTERNS OF EMPLOYMENT SHIFTS AND WORKFORCE CHARACTERISTICS

Changes in the job structures work favorably or unfavorably for certain workers depending on the characteristics of workers in the labor market. For example, workers with relatively high skills and knowledge can benefit from the increase in high-skilled, high-wage jobs, but those who do not meet qualification may have a hard time finding a job.

A worker's characteristics such as gender, age or current employment status are typical attributes that cause discriminatory treatment in obtaining a specific job. Depending on gender, age and employment status, access to certain occupational groups may be allowed or limited. Then, who filled the increased jobs? Are there any structured differences between the three cities? Observing the distribution of gender, age and job status across employment changes may give us answers.

Looking at employment shifts between 2007 and 2012 in Tokyo based on gender and employment status, we can see that half of the jobs for professionals were filled by male regular workers (see figure 4-7). Regular male workers have declined in middle to lower middle-wage jobs in the production process and transportation sectors. Growth in regular employment for men was confined to upper middle to high-paying occupations such as professionals and security-related workers. On the other hand, non-regular employment for men filled some positions in professional fields and clerical work, but it appeared that they mainly filled the increased jobs of simple labor jobs including transportation and cleaning. In the case of women, while most regular jobs are concentrated in newly created jobs in professional and clerical work sectors, non-regular female workers have experienced the largest job share growth in low-wage jobs such as service and sales jobs although they have limited access to professionals and clerical work. Half of the newly created unskilled jobs were also filled by non-regular female workers.

We can find three points here. First, the newly created jobs are mainly non-regular positions except for jobs related to security jobs. Second, in the Tokyo labor market, jobs filled by regular and non-regular workers are separat-

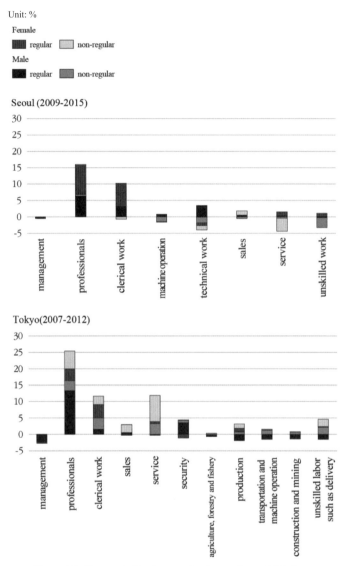

Figure 4-7: Changes in Employment by Occupation and Job Status

ed. While jobs increased in high-wage occupations such as professional and white-collar jobs were mostly filled with regular workers, jobs increased in service and simple labor jobs were almost filled with male and female irregular workers. Third, the proportion of female non-regular workers in service, sales, and simple labor jobs is larger than that of male non-regular workers. These characteristics can lead to income and social inequality between regular and non-regular workers, and between male and female non-regular workers.

Similar to Tokyo, most professional and white-collar clerical jobs created in Seoul were filled by regular workers. Notably, the number of jobs increased in this occupation was filled by female regular workers more than male regular workers. Intriguingly, however, female regular workers have also gained a growing share of employment in low-wage jobs such as service and simple labor occupations. Overall, in Seoul, we can see a decreasing share of employment in non- regular employment for lower middle to middle-wage positions. Except for jobs in service sectors, we can attribute most of these changes to the decline of non-regular male workers.

Next, we examine the age distribution of occupational shifts in the cities. This analysis is useful to provide answers to growing concerns over intergenerational job conflicts. First of all, looking at Tokyo, it demonstrates growth in the prime-age workforce population between ages 24 and 54 in most occupations. Particularly, this workforce accounts for many high-wage jobs as professionals and clerks as well as the low-paying service and sales jobs. On the other hand, jobs for the younger workers between ages 15 and 25 and the older workers aged 55 and older have not increased except for in the professional sector. According to this trend, we can conjecture that competition for newly created jobs between the years 2007 and 2012 is usually within prime-age workers rather than between younger and older workers.

Quite the contrary trend appears in Seoul between 2008 and 2015. The employment shares among the aged workers have expanded, while the prime-age workers retracted. Occupations for older workers aged 55 and older are concentrated in lower middle-wage positions while workers between ages 25 and 54 are increasingly employed in high-paid jobs as professionals and clerks. Other occupations for the prime-age workforce shows declining patterns. These findings evidenced age-related occupational segregation and job polarization in Seoul. It shows that in the midst of job competitiveness in Seoul, employers for lower middle to low-paying jobs might be hiring older workers in place of younger workers. This raises concerns about intergenerational competition over employment.

Since the data on the demographic composition occupation remain inaccessible in Shanghai, we are not able to perform a similar level of analysis for Shanghai. However, the previous studies that have noted occupational segregation between migrant workers and residents within the city provide an import-

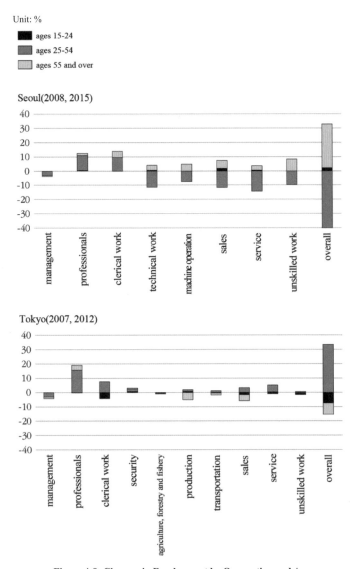

Figure 4-8: Changes in Employment by Occupation and Age

ant clue for understanding the situation in Shanghai. For example, Zhang and Wu (2013) argue that the widening gap in income between residents and migrant workers in the city is mainly due to occupational segregation between them rather than the unequal wage distribution. They also posit that these differences are associated with the education levels of the two groups.

In 2010, Shanghai has recorded about 9 million migrations, a three-fold growth from 2000. The migrant workers amount to almost half (47%) of the total working population (men between ages 15 and 59 and women between ages 15 and 54) in Shanghai. They are mainly young and women. Of the migrant workers between ages 20 and 34, 57.7% hold residency in a city other than Shanghai (Shanghai Statistic Bureau, 2011). They form the majority of the labor force in the traditional service sectors including production, wholesale and retail, and hotel and restaurant services. Of the total migrant population, 41.3% work for the manufacturing sectors compared to 28.9% of the resident local working population. Particularly, female migrant workers are mainly engaged in low-skilled service jobs due to their low education levels. In this respect, Shanghai experiences occupational polarization based on household registration status That is, most new jobs in high value-added service sectors are filled by registered Shanghai residents and low-skilled service jobs and manufacturing jobs are filled by migrant workers.

6. ARE IMPROVEMENTS SUSTAINABLE?

We have now seen how the cities are characterized by different industrial stages and how these dissimilarities lead to contrasting employment shifts. Further, employment shifts have been disproportionately distributed among the working population in the cities. With the advancement of industrialization, high-wage jobs have increased in all three cities. Yet, the job structures have rapidly polarized noticeably in Tokyo where middle-wage jobs have been reduced and low-wage jobs have increased. Most newly created jobs in Seoul are concentrated in good jobs, but expansion of public welfare and medical and social welfare services targeting the old has led to an increase of low-wage jobs. Shanghai continues to experience an increase of quality jobs that can improve job structure.

What jobs are created is closely linked to the industrial transition of the city. For example, the declining manufactures have also decreased the share of the middle-tier jobs, polarizing the job structure. In addition, job upgrading is often concentrated in particular industrial sectors. Today, many expect the high value-added industries to produce more quality job opportunities and contribute to economic growth. Yet this is not always the case as observed by examples shown in Seoul. The expansion of scientific and technical service sectors has led to the rise of slightly better jobs such as professionals and clerks but the expansion of health and social welfare service sectors has led to the increase of low-paying jobs in simple and unskilled service jobs.

The case in Tokyo exemplifies the expansions in the high value-added service sectors do not necessarily result in the upgrading of jobs. In fact, most developed countries have shown that it only intensifies job polarization. Therefore, it requires policy makers to take careful consideration of both industrial sectors and occupational forms in order to create quality jobs.

Recently in Korea, a growing fear of "growth without employment" has led to increased attention in social services known to create new jobs at a rapid pace. In fact, demographic shifts fostered by low birth rates and aging population create demands for new social services. However, if we approach the creation of social service jobs to solve employment problems, it is likely to create low quality jobs and lead to further polarization in job structure. In order to create new jobs that can eventually lead to job quality enhancement in job structure, well-coordinated policies are needed.

In order to sustain productivity and inclusiveness of labor markets, we need to consider the quality as well as quantity of jobs and their distribution (Hurley, Fernandez-Macias and Storrie, 2013). As detailed above, good jobs tend to be usually reserved for men, regular workers and prime-age workers. Newly created low-paid jobs are filled by non-regular workers and women in Tokyo, older workers in Seoul and migrant workers in Shanghai. The city's labor market differentiates between insiders and outsiders and limits opportunities for those without resources. There needs to be a policy implementation to lower such barriers. Without alleviating this dual structure in the labor market, equal distribution of good jobs become impossible.

Future policy design for occupational and economic upgrading should integrate and carefully coordinate related policies in industry, employment and welfare. The city should support new industries that can create more job opportunities in middle-tier jobs to balance out job demands. Employment policies should promote job qualities rather than quantities and focus on reducing inequalities and low-wage jobs. To add, welfare policies should be in place to support low-skilled and unemployed workers.

Last but not least, we would like to point out the importance of an effective governance system for implementing employment policies. The performance of labor markets in cities is largely influenced by a complex set of policies at the national and city level. Due to the traditionally strong authority of a national government, there has been little room for city government to implement policies on its own. Recently, however, policy makers have become aware of the importance of the local dimension of labor market policy and the need to cooperate with local government entities in order to promote effective policy outputs. For instance, OECD's Programme on Local Economic and Employment Development (LEED) and European Union's URBACT program show efforts to incorporate local needs. It becomes crucial to create an effective governance system that builds on both the central government and the local government. The effectiveness of local-level employment policies depends heavily on how the central government, local governments, and local labor market actors communicate to each other, and how to coordinate their interests in policy measures.

Scholars have already predicted that 47% of current jobs in the United States will be gone due to the advancements in automation and the digital revolution (Frey and Osborne, 2013). The U.K. expects the development of artificial intelligence will displace 35% of the current jobs (Diloitte, 2014). And the World Economic Forum (WEF, 2016) expects about 5 million jobs around the world to disappear within the next 5 years. All these predictions lead us to believe that labor market and industrial structure transitions are immediate concerns globally. A recent prophecy that the Third World War would be 'jobs war' (Clifton, 2015) only highlights the already growing fear of the imminent future. Are we well prepared for these changes? This question still remains unanswered.

**An earlier version of this chapter was published in the *Development and Society* (Vol. 45 No.3, 2016).

NOTES

1   Employment insurance is a form of social insurance that provides cash benefits, employment services and employment security support for the unemployed and training programs for the employed.

2   According to 2016 OECD Employment Outlook Report, Korea's high-skilled NEET ratio is 42.5% of the total NEET population. This is twice more than the 16.5% OECD average. On the other hand, Japan's ratio is 21.7%.

3   In order to examine the structural shifts in jobs, it requires the longitudinal data of representative and sizable sample. We utilized the Local Area Labor Force Survey (LLFS) collected by the National Bureau of Statistics in 2008 and 2015 for Seoul, and the Japanese Employment Status Survey (JESS) of 2007 and 2012 for Tokyo. Method of estimating income levels of each occupational category is as follows. The income level by occupations is calculated via monthly salary answered by wage workers for Seoul. For Tokyo, the estimation is based on the number of employees in each occupation per different wage ranges provided by the Japanese Statistic Bureau. In the case of Shanghai, since obtaining large size sample data was not feasible, the Shanghai census report (2011) was utilized with income level by occupation as outlined in the Survey of Living Conditions of Residents in Shanghai Megacities (2010). Although these crude approx-

imations may not provide accurate estimates, they may help to identify patterns of shifts that happened since 2000.

4   One caveat we would like to mention is whether income level can be a relevant indicator of job quality. Many scholars argue the wage level of a job does not always represent its quality. However, there have been numerous findings which reveal high correlation of wage with job stability, satisfaction, and the overall quality of its working environment. As this analysis aims to explore the overall trends in the occupational transitions in each city, we have thus considered the wage as the representative variable of its job quality. The validity of the wage as the representative of job quality remains to be scrutinized in further studies.

REFERENCES

Autor, David H. and Dorn, David. (2013). The Growth of Low-Skill Service Jobs and the Polari zation of the US Labor Market. *American Economic Review*, 103(5), 1553-1597.

Berman, Eli, Bound, John and Machin, Stephen. (1998). Implications of Skill-biased Technolog ical Change: International Evidence. *Quarterly Journal of Economics*, 113, 1245-1279.

Bureau of Industrial and Labor Affairs, Tokyo Metropolitan Government. (2016). *Industry and Employment in Tokyo: A Graphic Overview 2016.*

Clifton, Jim. (2011). *The Coming Jobs War: What every leader must know about the future of job creation.* New York, NY: Gallup Press. Translated in Korean by Jung, Junhee, 2015. Seoul: Booksnut.

Deloitte LPP. (2014). *London Futures Agiletown: The Relentless March of Technology and London's Response.* Available at: https://www2.deloitte.com/content/dam/Deloitte/uk/Documents/uk-futures/london-futures-agiletown.Pdf

Frey, Carl B. and Osborne, Michael A. (2013). The Future of Employment: How Susceptible are Jobs to Computerization?. *Oxford Martin School Programmes on the Impacts of Future Technology.*

Gallup. (2016). *2016 Global Great Jobs Report.* Gallup Inc. Available at: http://www.gallup.com/services/190922/gallup-global-report-great-jobs-2016.aspx

Goos, Maarten and Manning, Alan. (2007). Lousy and Lovely Jobs: The Rising Polarization of Work in Britain. *Review of Economics and Statistics,* 89, 118-133.

Groningen Growth and Development Center (GGDC). *10-Sector Database.* Available at: http://www.rug.nl/ggdc/productivity/10-sector/

Hurley, John, Fernández-Macías, Enrique and Storrie, Donald (2013). *Employment Polarization and Job Quality in the Crisis: European Jobs Monitor 2013.* Available at: http://www.eurofound.europa.eu/publications/report/2013/labour-market-business/employment-polarisation-and-job-quality-in-the-crisis-european-jobs-monitor-2013

Institute of Social Science Survey. (2010). Survey of Living Conditions of Residents in Shanghai Megacities. Shanghai University.

Kambayashi, Ryo and Kato, Takao. (2013). Good Jobs, Bad Jobs, and the Great Recession: Lessons from Japan's Lost Decade. *Center for EconomicInstitutions Working Paper Series*, 2013-01. Hitotsubashi University.

Kim, Hye-jin. (2015). Research on Structural Change of Shanghai's Labor Market in the Process of Deindustrialization. *The Journal of Chinese Studies*, 72.

Kim, Jong Il. (2006). Structural Change and Employment Problem of Korea since the 1900s. *Journal of Korean Economic Analysis*, 12(2): 1-48.

Nam, Jaeryang and Kim, Se-um. (2013). *Korean NEETs: Characteristics and Labor Market Performance.* Korea Labor Institute.

National Bureau of Statistical China. 2015. *China Statistical Yearbook 2015.* Available at: http://www.stats.gov.cn/tjsj/ndsj/2015/indexeh.htm

Nickell, Stephen, Redding, Stephen and Swaffield, Joanna. (2008). The Uneven Pace of Deindustrialisation in the OECD. *The World Economy*, 31(9), 1154-1184.

OECD. (2016). *OECD Employment Outlook 2016.*

_____. *OECD Regional Database.* Available at: https://stats.oecd.org/Index.aspx?Data Set-Code=REG_DEMO_TL2

Ohta, Souichi. (2016). Employment Trend and Outlook for Japanese Youth. *International Labor Brief*, May 2016.

Pertold-Gebicka, Barbara. (2012). Job Market Polarization and Employment Protection in Europe. *Economics Working Papers 2012-13*, Aarhus University.

Rodrik, Dani. (2015). Premature Deindustrialization. *NBER Working Paper,* No. 20935.

Statistics Bureau of Japan. (2010). *Employment Status Survey.* Available at: http://www.stat.go.jp/english/data/shugyou/

Statistics Korea. (2016). *2014 Report of the Census on Establishments.*

_____. *Economically Active Population Survey.* Available at: http://kosis.kr/

_____. *Regional Employment Survey.* Available at: http://kosis.kr/

Statistics Bureau of Shanghai. (2011). *Shanghai's Labor Resources and Employment Situation, The Ninth Series of Analysis Data of the Sixth National Census in Shanghai.* Available at: http://www.stats-sh.gov.cn/ fxbg/201111/235037.html

Timmer, Marcel, de Vries, Gaaitzen and de Vries, Klaas. (2015). Patterns of Structural Change in Developing Countries. In Weiss, John and Tribe, Michael (Eds.), *Routledge Handbook of Industry and Development.* London: Routledge.

World Bank. (2016). *World Development Report 2016.* World Bank Group.

_____. *World Development Indicators.* Available at: http://databank.worldbank.org/data/reports.aspx?source=world-development-indicators.

World Economic Forum. (2016). The Future of Jobs: Employment, skills and Workforce Strategy for the Fourth Industrial Revolution. *Global Challenge Insight Report.*

Wright, Erik Olin and Dwyer, Rachel. (2003). The Patterns of Job Expansions in the USA: A Comparison of the 1960s and 1990s. *Socio-Economic Review*, 1, 289-325.

Zhang, Zhuoni and Wu, Xiaogang. (2013). Registration Status, Occupational Segregation, and Rural Migrants in Urban China. *Population Studies Center Research Reports*, University of Michigan.

5

Work and Family Boundaries in Three Cities: Surviving as Working Mothers in "Tiger Mother" Generation**

Hyunji Kwon
Junko Nishimura
Meng Chen

(1) Seoul's Working Mothers in 2016

"How will I join moms' network?" This is one of the main worries of a working mother residing in Seoul raising a fourth grader. She had thought everyday was all about surviving during the years her child was not attending school yet. Now she realizes life was simpler back then. It was a matter of sending her child to a daycare center, preparing meals on time, providing entertainment and putting the child to bed. Now that her child is in upper elementary covering difficult school material, the working mom's worries are escalating. In order to protect her pride as a parent and her child's future, a Seoul mom needs to build up her child's competitive edge starting from primary school. This would ensure that a child makes it to a prestigious college in the future. For the mom, it would mean finding a relatively better center that is willing to foster various skills for children and not just "take care" of them after school. Having more information grants moms more power. However, you cannot come out on top without knowing other moms in the network. Many times, there is no place for "free riding" working moms at the cafes where stay-at-home mothers sit in groups sharing school and cram school information after dropping off their children at school. Since no one else can network in place of working mothers, some moms go to great lengths to try to participate in the network. One working mom shared her story on a newspaper interview: "I took a leave of absence from work when my kid was in first grade to participate in all the mom group meet-ups and was finally able to make some friends there." Yet another mom working as a medical doctor said that "one of my strategies was to help out an influential mom in the group on some administrative matters when she visited my hospital just to get connected." (JoongAng Ilbo, 2016).

Trying to balance household chores while attending school open houses, finding the right cram schools, giving children rides, securing educational tips, making educated guesses about future college application trends and keeping up with group chat room conversations with other moms are all part of a busy schedule for stay-at-home mothers. For working moms, there is the added pressure they receive at work as people question how long they will stay at the company. For many—and this includes both moms and their children—maybe it would be much easier to give up on being in the queue for competitive education. "Success in studying depends not on the child and her own efforts but on the mother" is a popular 2016 saying in Seoul.

Motherhood is not an inherent quality but a socially constructed one. Just two to three decades ago, the roles and images of mothers held some commonalities. Moms were those who cooked warm meals numerous times a day, dressed the children, provided emotional stability with generous warm hugs, waited home for family's return and remained as that one person who truly cared. In the 21st century—where many people are left with lasting trauma from the 20th century's fierce competition of liberalism and still trying to survive as families—the image of middle-class moms look quite different. One news journalist has used the word "evolved" to describe the change (eToday, 2011). "Helicopter moms" who manage daily events of their children are old news. Now, labels for moms have evolved into "educational coaches" or "manager moms." Mothers create educational curriculums and manage school grades for their children. Some would oppose generalizing all moms in Korea this way and argue that this trend is limited to the Gangnam area. However, we contend that middle-class Seoul moms are never completely free from this trend. The concept of motherhood has evolved and working mothers in Seoul are burdened further. To add, the term "work-life balance" that has gained popularity in the city is yet to be achieved in Seoul. Finding success as either a stay-at-home mom or as a working mom seem hard to achieve. Mothers in Seoul are still juggling the pros and cons of the situation they are in. They wonder if declaring "all-in" for their children is the right path. Also they worry if the success of their lives will depend on the success of their children. Working moms wonder if they can strike a between work and family when society seems to imply that it is not even guaranteed to succeed either one. Within this context, taking time to ponder about one's own existence or personal identity becomes a luxury for working mothers. The middle-class life supported by family income has been continuously threatened in Korea (Ku, 2011; Lee, 2014). There has been growing concerns about job and income security for ordinary middle-class male-breadwinner families. With the average of 400,000 Korean won spent on a child's private education (Ministry of Education, 2015), mortgage loan payments, middle class spending habits and retirement funding, it becomes hard for mothers to solely rely on husband's income especially when social trends have shown that relatively young workers in their late 40s and early 50s in high-level positions are at risk of layoffs.

(2) Lives of Mothers in Three Cities: Similarities and Differences

The conflict-filled lives of working moms are not limited to Seoul. Middle-class mothers' lives in global East Asian cities, Tokyo and Shanghai, are also ridden with concerns for educational achievement of their children. Mothers of all three East Asian cities carry the burden of educating their children. They share common values and experiences: that educational attainment has led nation's success, and that there are numerous[HK2] cases around them where social status was achieved and maintained through education. They also lived through a collective experience of compressed development. The Japanese TV series like the *Mother Game* broadcasted by TBS that deals with troubles of working moms and the Chinese TV series *Tiger Mom* broadcasted by Dragon Television and Tianjin TV display similar stories to middle class moms' experiences in Seoul. Although the stages and paths of developments diverged at some levels, the three cities share their roots in patriarchy and familialism. Now, middle class mothers are sharing the conflicts that rise between work and family spheres.

Would things look different in China due to its socialist experience? The recent trend of labor market exits for urban middle class women in their 30s reveal an increased competition brought on by the expansion of capitalism. The added educational fervor to this trend might be enough to push Chinese women to curtail their career. At least these trends are not visibly present at the moment. Under Mao Zedong's slogan "women can hold up half the sky," China has included gender equality to be one of its socialist values. Different from Seoul and Tokyo, Shanghai shows a decent employment pattern for women, which is not very different from men's in the city—the pattern is a"∩" shape, meaning that women will not experience a drastic curve in employment during their prime years.

Seoul and Tokyo's so-called "M-shaped curve" for women's employment pattern deviates from the global pattern and limits women to specific labor market positions. However, during the few decades after the bursting of Japan's bubble economy, employment rate and pattern for women in Japan went through major shifts. There was a high increase in the employment rate for women and the stark M-shaped curve became alleviated. These changes show that women's roles have changed; before the collapse of the bubble economy, women's expected primary role was to be stay-at-home mothers. In Japan, the foundation of strong patriarchy and remaining ties between family and corporations have remained. Despite ongoing debates in the past two decades, it is hard to find supporting evidence for the end of male-centered long-term employment practices. Although the foundation of past systems is still engrained, it is maintained through shifts in specific practices including wage freeze over the past two decades. These changes in the Japanese male dominant labor market affect women's workplace and family responsibilities. Often, lowered men's wage requires additional household income from another adult member of the family. To add, demographic changes request shifts to women's roles. With the lack of labor force entering an aging or super-aging society, social expectation for women's labor has increased. As a result, various policy initiatives have been imposed to encourage labor market participation for women in Japan. For the last two decades, women's labor participation has been sought by the state, families and companies to use as a supplement to reduced workforce and to balance out the lowered wage of men. Unfortunately though, expectations placed on women to become wage earners did not ease expectations for their family responsibilities. Attitudes on viewing women's primary role as being within the family still persists. These changes caused a shift in a particular direction: from women as stay-at-home mothers—at least for mothers with younger children—to women as part-time workers. During the past decades after the burst of the bubble economy, Japan has supported the transition to a "1.5 breadwinner model." As a result, the steep dip shown in the M-shaped employment ratio curve has been raised as in addition to the overall employment rate. We would like to emphasize that despite recent changes, Japanese social structures have maintained the building blocks of patriarchy and expected gender roles within families. For this reason, it would be hard to claim that gender equality has made great advancements in Japan. Unlike the West, the expectations held for men to work long hours have remained the same. This work norm would not be placed on middle-class education mothers (教育マ, きょういくママ Kyōiku mama) who are primarily in charge of children's education at least until middle school.

Within the context of greater emphasis placed on mother's role in managing academic success for children, Seoul women are facing great hardships caught between work and managing education paths for their children. Contrary to women in Tokyo, mothers in Seoul do not seem to think of part-time employment as a viable option although the employmen type has been rapidly increasing. Social attitude on part-time work remains negative in Korea and most part-time options do not provide the level of income needed for the family (Jung, 2002; Chang, 2016). It is common practice for mothers in Seoul to choose one out of the two options: to stay at work or exit the labor market to become stay-at-home mothers. This is one of the reasons why the M-shaped curve shows a bigger dip in Seoul. The recent instability of men's employment and wage further deprived lower class mothers from freedom to concentrate on child-rearing. It is hard for lower class families to rely on grandparents or other family members for child-care. Nearly 80% of working-class mothers work full-time after childbirth. The employment rate for middle class mothers returning to work is also increasing but remains lower than working class mothers, and even lower for those coming back after career breaks (Jung, 2014). For these reasons, roles and activities for mothers in Seoul are seen to be differentiated by class.

This chapter attempts to explain women's employment patterns in three cities through the mechanisms underlying work and family shifts. We especially focus on how mother's role expansion to become income earners and education mothers particularly among the middle class mothers have influenced women's employment patterns. We also look at how this women's role expansion affects their work-life balance or conflict. Lastly, we compare the relationship between people's attitudes toward work and family in three cities and their life satisfaction. This chapter will serve as an opportunity to observe the effects of expectations placed on women regarding work and family and effects of mother's decisions made in reaction to these expectations.

1. EMPLOYMENT PATTERNS FOR MOTHERS WITH YOUNG CHILDREN IN THREE CITIES

We have emphasized previously that more burden was added to mothers as mother's role of educating their children was reinforced. This section examines employment patterns of women at the national-level for Korea, China and Japan. Based on these observations, we move on to discuss city-level trends.[1] Finally, we investigate whether differences in employment procedures and gender norms within families serve as mechanisms to affect women's labor market participation.

(1) Historical Context: Patriarchal Familism, Post-traditionalism and Women's Positions

The three cities of analytical interest are economically thriving cities within their countries. This also means labor market participation in these cities including women's participation is very active. Although these cities are still under the influence of Confucian gender norms and traditional social values (Ochiai, 2014; Cho, 2011), they are also characterized to be furthest away from older values due to earlier urbanization and marketization influences they experienced compared to other peripheral cities. The cities were also on the front lines of merging with global economies and experiencing economic shifts to either socialistic or capitalistic systems. However, the break away from traditionalism happened at different times and in different ways for each city. For example, Shanghai and Tokyo shifted away from traditionalism relatively early on to interact with modern cultural values from the West. For Japan in the past, there have been periodic efforts to recruit women's labor such as in times of war but the traditional gender norms of a breadwinning husband and stay-at-home wife have been institutionalized in major social spheres including the state, society, workplaces and families (Osawa, 2007). On attitudes on marriage, divorce, cohabitation and gender roles, Tokyo men and women show the most post-traditional and open-minded attitudes (Eun and Lee, 2005) but show high traditional values on division of gender roles in families. In that regard, Tokyo shows a high discrepancy between gender role attitudes and gender role fulfillment. This trend, along with recent demographic transitions and economic recession caused by the burst of the bubble economy, is influencing many social patterns such as marriage, childbirth and women's labor market participation.

Shanghai, a city that experienced a compressed transition into post-traditionalism through a socialist revolution, has gone through a starkly different trajectory from that of Seoul and Tokyo. From 1949, a high number of women in Shanghai have participated in the labor market consistent with the values of open-door policy pursued by the central government. Women's liberation was emphasized as one of the main policy goals of the national socialist state. In building up the state, the government requested labor participation of women under the pretense of upholding gender equality and women's liberation values. Up until the economic reform and opening of China, women in China were pulled into labor force as part of the gender equality movement and state-feminism discourse (Wu, 2015; Zuo, 2005). Shanghai, a coastal city located at the geographically and economically prime spot of Yangtze River Delta, is a city that has actively transitioned into a market economy since the reform and opening of China in late 1970s. Women in Shanghai have lived through many transitions in society. These transitions include the state's urbanization and shift to market economy to join the global market in the 2000s around the time China became a member of WTO. Shanghai women are experiencing firsthand a unique balance game between the labor market and family that are being molded by the recent transitions and the remaining legacy of socialist values.

On the other hand, Seoul experienced post-traditionalism much later compared to the other two cities. Labor market participation for Seoul women has always and continues to be the lowest among the three cities. To add, intergenerational gap remains widest in Seoul. For the past 70 years, women's economic activity has been a hidden and not a missing puzzle piece of Korea's modern economy. Korean families have frequently experienced absence of fathers during the struggling times such as during colonial times and war, leaving responsibilities of child nurturing and management of household economy to mothers. Unofficial labor at home carried out by mothers were never properly recorded or recognized. During the planned economy period in Korea, women's role became even more important. In the 1960s and 1970s, young women who have migrated to cities from rural areas were lured into low-paid jobs in clothing, sewing and other exporting industry sectors (Ku, 2001). Not only did these women play a critical role in contributing to the economic development by providing labor force during the beginning of industrial stages but they also built up the economy in a different sense by having an important role for families such as taking care of families in rural settings or supporting siblings to attend schools (Kwon, 2016; Chang, 2015). As the cores of industrialization and export moved over to the heavy chemical industry in the 1980s, women's economic role was forgotten and became less valued. Based on the new social expectations, an image of a sacrificial wife and mother leading a middle-class nuclear family replaced the former image of a sacrificial daughter raising up a family. Since then, Korean women have been excluded from the official economic scenes. In the 1980s, Seoul experienced a compressed post-traditionalism fueled by delayed social movements and women's movement. Seoul can be characterized as a city that holds both values that are still traditional as well as strong oppositional values that have been formed rapidly. Among the cities, Seoul faces the fiercest conflict between the differing social values. As a result, Seoul women's position within the workplace or in family is still very unstable; the conflict between work and family spheres have only been intensified (Oshio, Nozaki and Kobayashi, 2013). Neither the conflict between generations nor the conflict between work and family have been aligned or mediated. These conflicting relationships are facing new frontiers that arrived during the turn of the century including globalization, free market economy, demographic changes and expansion of education.

Women's labor market participation patterns are constantly interacting and shifting with social, economic and political contexts and national policies. Based on these complex interactions, roles and positions of mothers are also shifting.

(2) Women's Life Course Employment Patterns in Korea, Japan and China: A national Comparison

Before examining economic activity trends of mothers in three cities, we can note general trends by referring to official national-level statistics. We first notice two peaks and a dip when looking at employment patterns for prime age working women. This is the M-shaped curve that is also well known in the West but has now become a rare trend. The dip is created by the high employed numbers of women in their early to mid-20s and 40s and the dip of low employment rate for women in their 30s. This pattern reflects the diverging life courses of men and women. The career break created by the dip increased application rejections for women returning to work, turning them over to lower-quality jobs. The common East Asian social expectations held for women regarding marriage, childbirth and child-care have stripped away career goals of women who have been in the labor force since their 20s. But recently, there have been considerable quantitative changes in women's employment patterns for Korea and Japan. Although the M-shaped curve still exists due to effects of career breaks, more women who are between ages 25 and 39 are now participating in the labor market.

Although these features are shared, trends in women's employment in Korea and Japan have diverged over the past few decades. First, Japanese women's employment rate for women in their late 20s and early to mid-30s is much higher. In fact, the employment rate for women was already high from the late 1980s in Japan where seven out of ten women in their early 20s and 40s were employed. Except for the employment rate that falls below 50% for women in their late 20s and early to mid-30s, Japan's employment rate for women is increasing along with the trends followed by other major developed countries in the west. By contrast, even in the early 2000s, the employment rate for women in their early 20s and 40s barely hit 60% in Korea.

Second, the change in ratio is faster and greater in Japan. In Japan, the employment rate for women in their 40s is nearing 75% and over 65% for any age group. The dip has also been significantly weakened. This implies that after childbirth, more women in Japan now either stay at work or return to work after taking a brief time away from work. We also notice a pattern where women are flexibly choosing their times of marriage and childbirth, deviating from the traditional pattern of women giving birth in their mid to late 20s. These changes are also noted in Korea but the dip in employment pattern for women in their 30s is still more salient compared to Japan as shown in figure 5-1.

On the other hand, women's employment in China looks different from Korea and Japan. The M-shaped curve does not show in China. Women of most ages in China's statistics show high employment rates. 2010 demographic survey data shows 80% employment rate for women between ages 25 and 44 with some low rate for women in early 20s and late 40s. More than half of women nearing age 60 are also participating in the labor market. The employment pattern of women by life stage is comparable to men's bell-shaped (∩) curve. This reflects the decades-long socialist tradition of women participating in labor. Historically, women in China have stayed at work despite giving birth and raising children. The highest peak in employment rate shown by the traditionally child-raising age group (ages 25 to 39) reveals an opposite trend from the dip shown in Korea and Japan. The tradition of working women—which have existed before China's reform and open-door policies—is still maintained in modern society backed by the expectation that women need to contribute to the household economy.

Recently, however, labor market statistics of China show a slightly different trend. Unlike Korea and Japan where employment rates are steadily increasing, employment rates have declined between years 2001 and 2010 across all age groups. Reasons for this phenomenon should be different across age groups. First, we can look at the high school expansion policy initiatives. Since these policies were first carried out in 1999, the reduced population of women between ages 15 and 24 seem to be associated with the growing size of students in middle school and higher. However, a more noticeable pattern is the decline in the working population size of women between ages 25 and 39. This is the age group we are paying closer attention to since employment patterns shown in Korea and Japan for this age group are deviating from patterns shown in other Western countries. Will the recent change in China eventually lead to more working mothers leaving the labor force? We will try to address this question by comparing the three cities—Seoul, Shanghai and Tokyo—that have fewer discrepancies in social contexts and economic developments among each

Unit: %

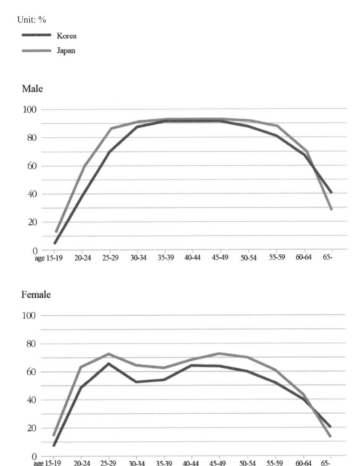

Figure 5-1: Employment Rate in Korea and Japan by Age and Gender (2014)
Source: OECD, "LFS by sex and age-indicators."

other compared to country comparisons.

(3) Women's Employment Patterns in Seoul, Tokyo and Shanghai: A city comparison

City-level employment patterns for women are not drastically different from national-level statistics. Figure 5-2 shows the employment rates for women in Seoul, Tokyo and Shanghai by age. [2] As observed at the national-level data, the M-shaped curves are also observed for Seoul and Tokyo. Women's employ-

Unit: %

Seoul

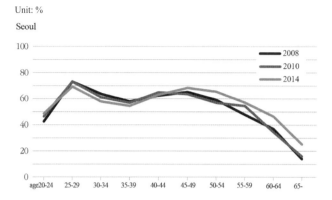

Shanghai

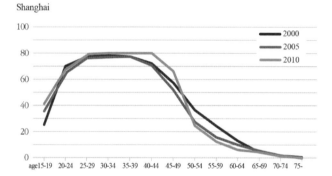

Tokyo

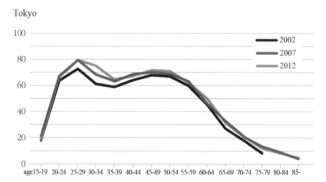

Figure 5-2: Employment Rate for Women in Seoul, Tokyo and Shanghai by Age
Source: Statistics Korea, "Economically Active Population Survey"(Seoul); National
Bureau of Statistics of China, "Fifth National Population Census", "2005 1% Nation-
al Population Survey Census Data", "Tenth National Population Census"(Shanghai);
Statistics Bureau of Japan, "Employment Status Survey"(Tokyo)

ment rate in Seoul is lower than Japan's, matching the national-level patterns. However, the gap has continued to grow between the two cities. As emphasized earlier, the employment rates for Tokyo women between ages 25 and 34 have drastically increased between years 2008 and 2014 but those for women in Seoul between ages 25 and 44 have declined during the same period. The reason for the average high employment rate of Tokyo women is the contribution of the high employment rate for women aged 45 and over. These statistics only intensify our curiosity towards the previously formed questions on the employment pattern of women in Seoul. Why are women with young children in Seoul not coming back to work despite the expansion of child-care facilities and increase of high school graduates among women?

As Seoul and Tokyo trends reflect patterns shown at national-levels, Shanghai's pattern also reflects trends shown in China excluding those in retirement age 55 and older. For Shanghai, the employment pattern is observed to be a perfect bell-shape. Women's employment rate in Shanghai have increased between the years 2005 and 2010 although not to the degree shown in Tokyo. Women's labor market participation shows similar trends in the Survey of Women. According to this survey, women's employment rate in Shanghai has started to increase again after past declines. This is a contrasting pattern from the nationwide trend.

Let's now narrow down our focus to working mothers. Figure 5-1 shows that in contrast to the previously mentioned rising the employment rate for women in Shanghai, the employment rate is actually declining for young mothers. Between the years 2013 and 2015, employment rate fell from 70.6% to 45.8% for mothers with children below 6 years old and from 77.8% to 51.7% for mothers with children between the ages 6 and 14. This is a contrasting pattern from the rising employment rates for mothers in Seoul and Tokyo. According to a study on gender discrimination, Chinese mothers were found to feel most discriminated by wage gap (Zhang and Hannum, 2015). This figure may reflect the level of discrimination present in China. What we really want to focus on however, is the pressure placed on mothers regarding education. The declining employment rates for women in Shanghai may convey the existing turbulent balance between work and family for mothers as they feel the burden of educating their children. If what scholars are saying is true in that wage for mothers are lower than wage for women without children, there is a great likelihood for mothers in China to shift toward child rearing similar to mothers in Korea and Japan.

Table 5-1: Employment Rate for Women with Children Below 6 Years and Children Between Ages 6 and 14

① Employment Rate for Women with children Below 6 Years

	2007	2008	2010	2012	2013	2014	2015
Seoul		26.99	41.13			41.32	
Shanghai					70.60		45.80
Tokyo	37.4			45.7			

② Employment Rate for Women with Children Between Ages 6 and 14

	2007	2008	2010	2012	2013	2014	2015
Seoul		44.33	48.73			48.01	
Shanghai					77.80		51.70
Tokyo	37.4			62.0			

Source: Research Group of Shanghai Social Research Center (2013); Liang and Zhang (2015);

One other thing to note is the changing ratios of working mothers in Seoul and Tokyo depending on the age of their children. While employment rates between Seoul mothers who have children below 6 years old and those who have children between ages 6 and 14 do not show great variance, there is stark difference shown for Tokyo mothers. This difference seems to be based on the contrasting education trends between the two cities which will be discussed in the next section.

The divergences between cities are rooted in contrasting employment processes and labor market structures of the cities. Among three cities, Shanghai has the lowest wage gap between men and women with women's median monthly wage being 83% of men's. By contrast, Seoul's median monthly wage for women is 60% of men's. Such wage disparity prevents educated women in Seoul to participate in the labor market. Another important difference between the cities is the employment type of women: most women in Seoul and Shanghai are pressured to either work full-time or not work at all whereas a high number of women in Tokyo choose to work part-time. Part-time employment is widespread among low-wage work or low-skilled service work. However, income women earn from these jobs usually become a good source of additional household income. Meanwhile, part-time positions are increasing in Seoul due to government policies but most are concentrated in low-wage sectors. Median monthly earnings for part-time work is only 20 to 30% of full-time monthly earnings. Also, part-time jobs in Korea are commonly filled by very young or elderly workers. These jobs are not attractive enough to middle class educated mothers who are returning to the labor force. What is evident is that for Seoul and Tokyo mothers, once they exit the labor market to commit to family responsibilities, it becomes difficult to secure the same level of job they had.

Overall, employment situations for women in the three cities are similar in some ways and diverging in other ways. Seoul and Tokyo share more similarities while Shanghai has more divergences due to its distinct political and economic development tracks. Although Seoul and Tokyo have many commonalities, there are increasing differences in women's work patterns and in the ways and degrees mothers find work. To add, although Shanghai has many distinct characteristics, current trends show that there is rising possibility Shanghai mothers who have young children could exit the labor force.

Next section will emphasize that gender conflicts arise from the complex relationship shared between public and private spheres. In order to understand women's labor market participation in their various forms, we need to examine the similarities and differences of public policies related to child-care, family values and women's roles in families.

2. CAN DIVERGING CHILD-CARE POLICIES EXPLAIN EMPLOYMENT PATTERN AND EMPLOYMENT RATE DIFFERENCES?

Previously, we have noted past similarities and recent divergences between the employment patterns of Seoul and Tokyo. One of the recent differences involve women who have given birth and taken care of their young children. For this group of women, labor market participation is lower for Seoul mothers compared to mothers in Tokyo. How can this difference be explained? Figure 5-3 shows OECD data on child-care or daycare facility use combined with Korea's trends from years 1995, 2003, 2007, 2010 and 2012 (Chang, 2016). A rapid quantitative improvement can be noted for Korea's daycare facilities. The number of facilities doubled between the years 2007 and 2012. Also, daycare use for Korea is higher than Japan in 2012. Based on quantitative measures, Korea's index is comparable to Denmark, a country known to have achieved the highest level of the public child-care facilities.

However, there have been numerous concerns regarding the quality aspect of child-care facilities or centers. The problem lies in the quality discrepancies between the facilities. Most parents in Korea wish to send their children to public centers. The next preference is usually large daycare centers known to

Unit: %

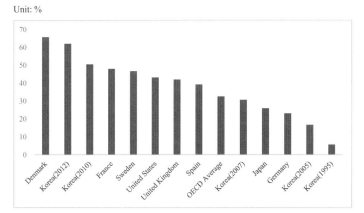

Figure 5-3: Daycare Use Trend in OECD Countries Including Japan and Korea
Source: OECD(2012); Chang(2016)

provide quality child-care services. However, commonly preferred centers are already full and have long queues. The waiting time to be admitted to such centers can last up to several years creating an ironic juxtaposition to the 60% daycare use rate. On the other hand, daycare centers that are home-based and privately certified and usually located within apartment complexes are not faring well despite making up half the total child-care facilities in Korea. Around 7% of these centers recently shut down in the span of two years. In 2012, the implementation of free child-care for children between ages 0 and 2 led to a rapid expansion of daycare centers. The excess surplus of centers paired with lowered birth rate led to these centers going out of business. Although the increase in supply seems to be tied to market mechanisms, this policy is a clear example of market failure. This is because the primary goal of this policy— which was to solve the problem of low birth rate through providing child-care support—was not achieved. The prevailing distrusting attitude of working moms toward daycare centers and increasing number of women quitting work to care for their children also show this to be a market failure. An excerpt from a newspaper article further supports this reality.

A 32 year-old working mom (residing in Yongsan district) after a year-long parental leave has placed her child's name down for a number of child-care facilities near home but the shortest waitlist showed 79 children already in the queue. [..] She tried placing her child in a home-based child-care center in her apartment complex but felt uncomfortable with the twenty children gathered in a home space of about 1,000 square feet. "I worry that my child might get hurt in that small space..I think of quitting work to stay at home because I can't concentrate thinking that my child may contract a disease at the center." (EDAILY, 2016)

This reveals a side effect of overly depending on the market for child-care services. In contrast, the Japanese government approached the same issue with the mindset that the state is primarily responsible for providing child-care. The problem was different from Korea in that supply could not match the demands. While Korea relied on quick expansion of child-care centers by depending on the market, which resulted in too many centers that did not measure up to the quality expected from parents, Japan made efforts to expand public facilities and control quality through license systems. However, it failed to provide an adequate number of services to match increasing demands. Bigger cities with more population like Tokyo experienced such shortcomings with more force. With continued increase of demands, long queues were formed at child-care facilities in Japan. It is reported that 8,466 children are on the waitlist in Japan to get into child-care facilities as of July 2016 (Tokyo Metropolitan Government, 2016).

The state's approach to solve this problem was similar in Japan. From 2001, Tokyo started opening more certified daycare centers. The qualifications for these centers were much more lenient than the public daycare centers. Similar to Korea, these centers could be home-based in apartment complexes near bus or subway stations, did not need to have an outdoor playground and required a smaller space per child than what's required as a national standard. The Japanese government encouraged joint-stock companies and other entities to become involved in daycare businesses. As a result, in 2016, one out of ten child-care centers in Tokyo were certified daycare centers, leading to a quick expansion of daycare services. However, it was still not enough to match the growing demands. Also, like Seoul, quality concerns over the daycare centers were raised. The discrepancy in quality between the different centers was noted by the public (Hoikuen wo Kangaeru Oya no Kai, 2006). However, compared to Seoul, where home-based daycare centers make up close to half of all centers and the number of children attending these centers are more than 20% of the total number of children in daycare, Tokyo's child-care system seems to have more control over managing quality between the daycares.

A comparison of the child-care systems between Seoul and Tokyo reveals that Seoul mainly faces problems in quality control while Tokyo's main struggle lies in trying to increase number of daycare facilities. In both Seoul and Tokyo characterized by high population levels with an average age that is younger than other cities, women who have young children are failing to stay in the labor market. It is undeniable that some of the fault lies in the government's failed investment and policy directions. However, there are other areas that are still unexplainable. For instance, the higher ratio of Korean mothers who choose to become stay-at-home mothers cannot be explained by child-care policies alone.

In order to explore other explanations, we compare child-care support systems between the two countries, paying special attention to parental leave policies. This area has received a wide array of attention from feminists, policy-makers and scholars. In Japan, the Childcare Leave Act, enacted in 1991 and amended several times since, requires all businesses to allow their employees to take one-year parental leave (leave can be extended up to 18 months in case of inability to find a place at a daycare center by the time the child is one year old). In the case where both parents take paid leave, parental leave can be extended up to one year until the child is 14 months old. Since 2004, fixed-term employees, most of whom are non-regular employees, became eligible to take parental leave. From 2017, parental leave qualifications will become relaxed. Monetary benefits tied to parental leave have improved as well; from 2014, 67% of the wage received just before the start of leave is paid for the first 6 months and 50% for the remainder of the leave period.

In Korea, legislation of previous maternity protection laws came together in 2001, leading to an expansion of child-care centers and a full-scale policy formation targeting work-life balance for working mothers. Although the importance of child-care has been previously noted, most past policies were geared toward providing childbirth support. The progressive direction of the government in power also supported such policy shifts. In the early 2000s, gender mainstreaming was selected as a basic policy concept backed by the establishment of the Ministry of Gender Equality and Family. Since then, various child-care policies have been enacted. Recent Korean child-care-related policies seem to provide more benefits on child-care compared to policies in Japan. Both countries allow parental leave for both parents but for different lengths: parental leave covers 18 months of leave in Japan while both parent can separately apply for up to one year of parental leave per child aged 8 and below in Korea. To add, parents in Korea can also use the leave on a part-time basis or split the full eligible duration into two parts. Looking at policies alone, parental leave seems more flexible in Korea relative to Japan. However, income substitution in Korea falls short of parental leave monetary benefits in Japan. Korea's parental leave policies provide a fixed wage of five hundred thousand to one million Korean won during the leave period. A practice that is different from Japan that exists in Korea is post-payment of some part of the income substitution. This monetary benefit is awarded after six months of returning to work. This practice in Korea is in place to prevent a discontinuity in career. Even by examining parental leave differences, it is hard to explain the employment rate differences between mothers in Korea and Japan in its entirety.

We now turn to observe the related policies that directly support enactment of child-care policies. Namely, we observe whether policies are successfully implemented within the companies. We assume that there are more barriers to proper implementation in Seoul. For instance, in Korea, parental leave is only eligible for those who have worked for over 180 days and are covered by the employment insurance. In 2015, only 42% of non-regular employees were covered by the employment insurance. Considering the high rate of non-regular workers in Korea, we can assume that qualifications for parental leave are highly selective. Also, most working women cannot afford to leave work for longer periods. A bigger problem lies in the fact that only half of the companies with parental leave policies were found to be actually applying them (Kwon, 2016). The effectiveness of parental leave policies is significantly reduced due to lack of implementation in companies and evidence that labor market participation of mothers is linked to social policies and institutional practices. In the case of Korea, related policies that can execute or not execute polices related to child-care are acting as a barrier to women's employment. Japanese companies are recognized to have more efficiency in carrying out parental leave policies but detailed comparisons are not provided in this chapter due to lack of directly comparable datasets. Other factors to consider for women's employment patterns and rates include the effect of family norms and change of mother's roles in Japan and Korea, which will be covered in the next section.

We have mentioned previously that employment experience for Shanghai women is very different from women in Seoul and Tokyo. Let's examine how the distinct characteristics we find in women in Shanghai is related to child-care policies. Due to the historical background of socialism in China, public child-care is more widely available compared to Korea and Japan. However, a large portion of children's education was left to the market after open-door policies. Daycare centers that existed from 1951 were reduced in number during the cultural revolution. State responsibility in child-care was further reduced with the collapse of the *danwei* system in 1990. Pubic responsibility for child-care decreased with policies prioritizing private kindergartens. Marketization effects can be shown by the reduction in public child-care service from 60 to 40 percent between the years 2001 and 2007 (Lee and Baek, 2012). The diversification of child-care services was fueled by marketization, leading to an increase of costly kindergartens, monetary bribes in daycare centers and advanced learning courses offered at kindergartens (Lee and Baek, 2012). Recently, however, there has been a rising trend emphasizing the public responsibility for children's education. According to the 2010 "Outline of Educational Policies," the government of China announced the need for universal education for preschool children and quantitative expansion of child-care facilities including plans to raise kindergarten enrollment rate from 50% to 95% for children between ages 3 and 6 (Lee and Baek, 2012). China's reevaluation of child-care as a public service led to recent advancements including: raising the qualification bar for opening kindergartens and hiring teachers; making amendments to teaching positions and wages; and managing administration and providing information to promote quality education. We can predict to some level the association between women's labor market participation and marketization and diversification of child-care education. However, it is too early on to predict the effect of the policy shifts that reclaimed child education to the public sphere.

How can we explain the low exit rate of working mothers with young children in Shanghai? With the past socialist development, the labor market participation of both genders became a social norm in China. What are the social policies that can actualize these norms then? The legal length of maternity leave in China is usually four months and sometimes five months in the case of complications (medical documents need to be presented) resulting from childbirth. This is a longer period than what is commonly allowed in Korea and Japan. It could be seen as a policy that encourages mothers to concentrate on the early stages of child rearing. However, this policy alone cannot explain for the other differences Shanghai has. A critical factor that distinguishes Shanghai from the rest of the cities is the role of grandparents in helping with child-care. Compared to other cities, there is an active division of labor between generations in Shanghai to the point that 90% of children under the age of three are said to be taken care of by grandparents (Chen, 2011). The institutionalized retirement age for women set at 55 years old, which is five years earlier than the retirement age set for men, reflects the reality and expectations for older women to perform familial duties. We can conjecture that child rearing by grandparents is socially accepted as a common norm and also institutionalized by supporting policies. Women in China including Shanghai have less pressure regarding child-care after birth as well as in balancing work and family duties. This does not mean they do not have pressure regarding their paid work. Also, recent trends indicate that the division of labor between generations has weakened in larger cities like Shanghai. With the growing education fever, more emphasis is now placed on the mother's role in educating their children. We will discuss this further in the succeeding section.

3. THE THREE CITIES: CHANGES TO MOTHER'S ROLES, FAMILY VALUES AND FAMILY HAPPINESS

This section will explore the similarities and differences of the three cities by focusing on family roles and norms and move on to discuss how each city's characteristics contribute to the mother's labor market participation. We will take close attention to observe the commonly accepted family norms and maternal roles as well as the recent transitions of these trends within the cities. First, we would like to emphasize the role of the "educating mom" to unravel the differences in the labor force participation that cannot be explained solely by child rearing practices. We first detail the expected mother's role that contributes to children's education in each city. Then, we will examine the city attitudes on mother's roles including attitudes on mothers's roles as stay-at-home mothers in charge of child-care and household work and their roles as economic providers. Lastly, we observe the levels of work-family conflict and family life satisfaction levels; we look at how women's work characteristics and family-related attitudes affect work and family spheres in the cities.

(1) Mother's Role as an Educating Mom

Mother's role in educating their children are recently been emphasized in three cities. The most reactive group is the mothers who are part of the middle class or higher and usually with richer educational experiences. The discussion below reflects to some degree this social context.

The fixation and active involvement middle class mothers show in children's education is shared by the three cities. However, when we look at the city contexts and education system of their states, we can see that educating mothers have different roles in each city. In Seoul, mothers have played an important role in prepping their children for college entrance for some time. Recently, this same trend has been extended. Now, mothers need to invest more years in guiding their children as special-purpose middle and high schools are now offering additional competitive edge for specific college entrances. Since the late-1990s, mother's roles have slowly changed to be in charge of investing and coaching their children's education paths. This trend was stronger among women with higher education levels and for those wanting to attain self-realization through such engagement (Ryoo, 2015).

Mother's role as educators is also emphasized in Tokyo where competition for select schools is extremely high. However, once a child reaches the age of twelve and enters the middle school to spend a lot more time in cram schools, mother's roles are considerably reduced.

In the case of Shanghai, there is rising competition for select high schools and even middle schools. In the past, there was high importance placed on the role of grandparents in child rearing. Recently, with a heavy emphasis placed on academic success, parental involvement, especially involvement of mothers, is being highlighted. For this reason, mothers are having more and more difficulty in balancing full-time work and child rearing. In the next section, we will examine in more detail mother's roles for each city and how they are shaped by educational realities and systems.

(2) Seoul

Educational opportunities have expanded greatly in Korea within the past four decades. Korea's high school education system can be characterized by the competitive college entrance exams. Colleges are strictly ranked and students are thrown into the competition from very early on. Since selection processes for competitive high schools are very complex in nature, mother's roles and their investment in time are emphasized. Special-purpose private and public middle and high schools form according to educational policy modifications. These schools provide quality preparation for prestigious colleges. The amount of years and time mothers spend on becoming an education coach for their children are being extended. Private cram schools and institutions open up daily and the most prestigious ones are centrally located in Gangnam, Seoul. The amount of effort and strategic role required of Seoul mothers are reinforced daily.

One of the most important factors that affect academic achievement and college applications in Seoul is "moms' network." These networks form among mothers starting from when children are attending elementary schools. Within this network, important information on education ranging from tips on private institutions and college entrances are shared. The network even influences school lives and social connections of children. Moms' network becomes especially important during the time when children are attending high school. Ever since the college application review process in Korea was broadened, mothers are expected to keep track of extracurricular activities of their children in addition to their scholastic achievements. Valuable information on high school activity clubs, writing contests and summer camps are exchanged within the network of mothers. A network that could gain the most recent information ahead of other networks become extremely powerful. This is one of the reasons why mothers prefer special-purpose high schools, autonomous private high schools and the reputable "8th school district" Gangnam high schools. Since admission rates to prestigious colleges differ even among autonomous private high schools and specialized high schools, the value of moms' networks has increased further. Mothers known as "Gangnam mothers" are especially recognized for their active engagement. The term is reserved for mothers who have children attending schools in Gangnam and are actively engaged in their children's academic achievements and college entrance preparations. These mothers spend great energy in forming networks and staying connected.

To add, since students need to be accepted to select schools like autonomous private schools or specialized schools to secure a more efficient track to prestigious colleges, emphasis is placed on the mother's role of strategically coaching their children from as early as elementary school. The news article that reported a ten-ford increase of false resident registration within a year supports this social trend (EBS News, 2016). There are also known cases of private elementary schools giving selective treatment to students from certain kindergartens. Selection of the "right schools" starting from very early on has now become one of many responsibilities expected of mothers. As the social environment stressing the importance of mothers' role on educational achievements of their children gets strengthened, more mothers are sacrificing their lives to fulfill those expectations. Working mothers are feeling additional pressure to balance work on top of the socially expected role of an educating mother.

(3) Tokyo

Like Seoul, Japan's society is characterized by fierce competition for college admissions. Japan is known to have entered an "all-incoming era" where number of admission spots surpass prospective students. However, paths to be admitted to top national schools are still very narrow. The starting age of entering this competitive scene is getting lower (Hirao, 2001) and social expectation for mothers to handle both emotional and academic needs of their children is getting higher.

Education fever is especially strong in large cities like Tokyo. There is a higher number of children aged below six in cities like Tokyo and a higher number of classes registered per child in large cities compared to smaller cities and suburbs (Hida, 2008). Top middle and high schools that are known to be college preparatory schools are concentrated in larger cities and add to the education fever. Since many students who graduate from these schools get admitted to top colleges, parents believe that sending their children to prestigious middle schools will boost academic success. From the late 1990s, select public schools were also changed to a joint middle school-high school system, further exacerbating the competition. Although private schools are distributed across the country, about 40% of them are located in Tokyo. For this reason, older elementary school students in Tokyo attend cram schools to prepare for middle school entrance exams. Entrance exams for prestigious middle schools are usually held on February 1st. It was once reported that over half of sixth graders attending schools in Tokyo's 23 wards missed school to take the middle school entrance exams (Ohta, 2012). Parents and their children together form a common front to prepare for middle school admission. Parental effort, especially that of mother's, is deemed essential. These efforts include selecting cram schools or exam preparatory academies, setting up study schedules at home and seeking ways to reduce stress and boredom for children from long study hours. Japan's enterprises and publication companies produce magazines targeting parents planning for their children's middle school admission. An article titled "Taking a middle school entrance exam is a parent's endeavor too" carried an advisory comment made by a lecturer of a cram school to parents.

Middle school selection is made by parents. If you want to let your kids select their own schools, the easiest and wisest way is to lay out candidates and have your children choose a school. [...] Parents need to manage the study schedule of their kids and prepare them for exams. The last few years in elementary school is a critical time of physical and mental development. [...] Even when kids enter a rebellious stage, parents need to guide them and continue to nurture their academic passion (Nihon Keizai Shinbun[NJ4], 2016).

Once the child enters middle school, however, mother's role in Japan becomes reduced to taking care of the child's physical and mental health. Direct academic involvement becomes unnecessary. Once a child enters a prestigious middle school that is already affiliated with a good high school, academic coaching is left to the schools and teachers. Public school curriculum in Japan is designated by the ministry of education but private schools can create their own curriculum. This is one of the reasons why students compete to get into a prestigious private school. Private schools can utilize more advanced material tied to college preparation and set apart more time on subjects like mathematics and English that have more weight in college entrance exams. Older high school students dedicate most of their school time in preparing for college admissions.

Japanese middle school students spend most of their time at school regardless of attending private or public schools, and regardless of going to school in small cities, large cities or in suburbs. The reason lies in the wide array of after-school extracurricular activities. These activities include sports clubs for basketball, soccer and tennis and cultural clubs like brass or other musical instrument bands. Most students partake in extracurricular activities after school until dinner time. Many clubs require weekend practices and commitment to enter competitive contests. Excluding a week of summer break, most students in Japan stay actively engaged in extracurricular activities.

Within this context, for mothers in Japan, responsibilities related to education are concentrated during children's elementary school years. Once a child enters middle school, parent-child time is considerably reduced and parental involvement becomes limited. This is one of the reasons why mothers in Tokyo consider returning to work at this stage of their life courses.

(4) Shanghai

In large-sized Chinese cities like Shanghai, education fever is increasing among families who have children attending schools. For instance, real estate prices for Haidian district, located close to three prestigious Chinese universities including Peking University, Renmin University and Tsinghua University, are skyrocketing. In a run-down residential area in Beijing called Futong, sublet advertisements for downtrodden homes reveal unexpectedly high prices. This is because a prestigious Beijing high school is located in this area. Since students can only attend schools and take college entrance exams in the district they are registered in, many families seek to establish residency to attend good schools. And since paths to prestigious universities are extremely narrow, competition to get into select colleges is increasing. The "tiger mom" term coined by the Chinese American Yale Law School professor became widely popular in China. The traditional value that sees child rearing as an activity extended to larger family networks still exists in China. However, modern parents who reside in larger cities seem to hold different values. Among these parents, there is consensus that grandparents can give help in child rearing but cannot fill the role of educating children. Therefore, there is growing pressure on parents to select right educational paths for their children. There is also growing awareness of how challenging it is to educate children when mothers have full-time jobs. This has led to the preference of stay-at-home mothers among young middle-class families. Some scholars have contended that the two-child policy implemented in 2016 has only added to the pressure for mothers to stay at home and focus on educating their children.

(5) Attitudes on Child Rearing

In this section, we will explore how the different educational roles of mothers in three cities affect attitudes on child rearing and child-care. Data used for analysis is the Family and Changing Gender Roles IV module from the 2012 (ISSP Research Group, 2016).

Figure 5-4-1 shows male and female responses to the question: "who is the main decision maker in child rearing?" All three cities show higher responses for females selecting "myself" as their responses. Notably, women in Seoul have a comparatively higher percentage of replying this way. The percentage is 56.1% for Seoul, 17.9% for Tokyo and 31.5% for Shanghai.

Figure 5-4 visualizes attitudes on child rearing. Figure 5-4-2 shows that the majority of men and women in the cities agree to the statement: "it is the greatest joy to see my child grow up." However, there are clear differences among cities for other child rearing attitudes. Compared to Tokyo and Shanghai, more women and men in Seoul agree to statements "having a child limits the freedom of parents (figure 5-4-3)," "it is a financial burden to raise a child (figure 5-4-4)," and "having a child limits occupational opportunities (figure 5-4-5)." The heavy burden of educating children in Seoul as detailed earlier seems to have made child rearing more difficult and an act of sacrifice.

(6) Colliding Expectations? Women as Stay-at-home Mothers and Income Earners

Next, we will look at the attitudes of city residents on expected roles for women and mothers. All three cities rated stay-at-home mothers highly albeit at different levels. Figure 5-5-1 shows city responses to the statement: "what most women want is family and children." 50% of men and 38.7% of women in Seoul and 59.1% of men and 44.7% of women in Shanghai agreed to this phrase. For Tokyo sample, 20% of men and women agreed while 40% of men and women neither agreed nor disagreed to the statement. Figure 5-5-2 shows

Unit: %

① Who is the main decision maker in child rearing?

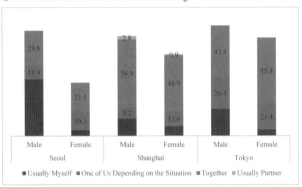

② It is the greatest joy to see my child grow up.

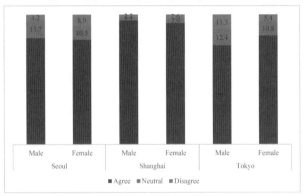

③ Having a child limits the freedom of parents.up.

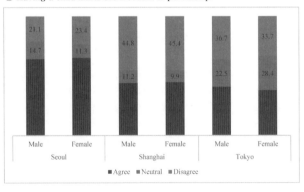

④ It is a financial burden to raise a child.

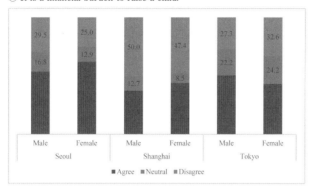

⑤ Having a child limits occupational opportunities.

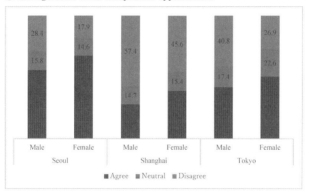

Figure 5-4: Comparison of Child Rearing Attitudes

that 70% of men and women in Tokyo and over 80% of respondents in Seoul agreed to the phrase: "there is same level of satisfaction for being a stay-at-home mother and working for income." Even in Shanghai, over 40% of respondents agreed to this attitudinal statement.

However, a positive attitude on the role of stay-at-home mothers does not necessarily mean people expect only the role of stay-at-home mothers for women. There are higher expectations for women's income earring role in Seoul and Shanghai compared to Tokyo. To the statement "both men and women need to contribute as income earners," only 40% of Tokyo respondents agreed compared to about 60% of Seoul respondents and 76% of men and 90% of women in Shanghai (figure 5-5-3). In the case when there is a preschool child or younger, 25% of men and 35% of women in Tokyo replied that it is good for mothers to work whether it be part-time or full-time work (see figure 5-5-4). On the other hand, around 50% of men and 65% of women in Seoul and 70% of men and over 80% of women in Shanghai agreed to this statement. As data shows, women in Seoul and Shanghai face high expectations as income earners even as mothers.

Ironically, there is a prevalent attitude among Seoul respondents that working mothers are not good for children who are preschool age and younger. This is an opposing attitude to the expectation placed on women as income earners. Figure 5-5-5 shows that about 70% of men and women in Seoul agree to the

Unit: %

① What most women want is family and children.

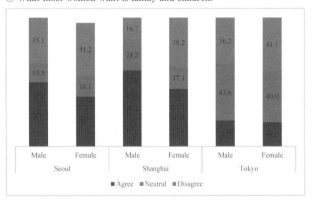

② There is same level of satisfaction for being a stay-at-home mother and working for income.

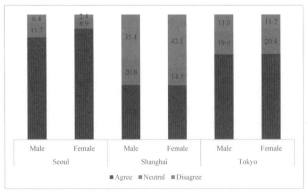

③ Both men and women need to contribute as income earners.

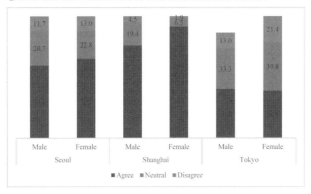

④ Work category of women who have children preschool age and younger.

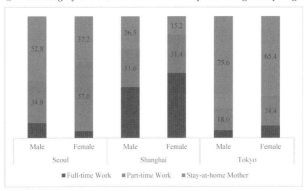

⑤ Children preschool age and younger face difficulties if their mothers are working.

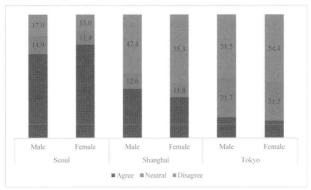

Figure 5-5: Comparison of Attitudes expected of Women and Mothers

statement "children preschool age and younger face difficulties if their mothers are working." By contrast, 30 to 40% of respondents in Shanghai and around 15% of respondents in Tokyo agree to this statement.

(7) Torn Between Work and Family

Within the three cities, there are similarities and differences in expectations held for women's diverse roles as educator, child-carer, income earner and stay-at-home mother. These differences and similarities seem to be based on each city's ways of promoting importance for work and family.

Studies on coexistence of family and work have commonly focused on for whom and under what conditions conflicts between work and families exit. On this topic, Frone and other scholars conceptually distinguished how family responsibilities hinder work and how work responsibilities hinder sacrifice for family (Frone et al., 1992). Conflict between work and family is tied to conflict in time management and work burden (Greenhaus and Beutell, 1985). This section compares conflicts around work and family and conflicts around time and work pressure for the three cities. We will then unravel the findings to discuss family life satisfaction levels.

Figure 5-6-1 shows levels of family conflict tied to long working hours. The responses display frequency of feeling difficulty of performing family responsibilities due to work hours. The levels of conflict differ between women in three countries. Compared to Shanghai women, women in Tokyo and Seoul feel more difficulty performing family responsibilities due to overworking. Women in Seoul are especially likely to feel a lack of time and conflict due to overworking. Meanwhile, all men from the three cities feel difficulty of performing family responsibilities due to long work hours. The level of conflict women in Seoul feel is comparable to these men. In that sense, we can say that group of comparison for Seoul women becomes men rather than women of Tokyo and Shanghai. Figure 5-6-2 illustrates yet another conflict rooted in work burden. Specifically, it shows the levels of conflict based on the statement: "it is hard to perform family responsibilities because work exhausts me." More people in Seoul agree to this statement compared to respondents in Shanghai and Tokyo.

Now, we can look at how family responsibilities place strain on work. Findings are not that different from the above results. Figure 5-6-3 shows that men and women in Seoul are more likely to agree to the statement "it is hard to concentrate at work due to family responsibilities" compared to respondents in Tokyo and Shanghai. Seoul respondents are also more likely to feel too ex-

Unit: %

① It is hard to perform family responsibilities due to long working hours.

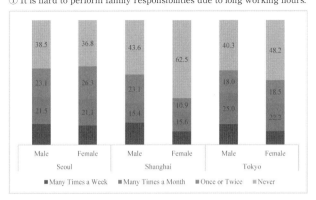

② It is hard to perform family responsibilities because work exhausts me.

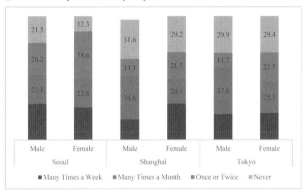

③ It is hard to concentrate at work due to family responsibilities.

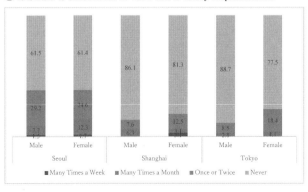

④ It is hard to concentrate at work because family responsibilities exhausts me.

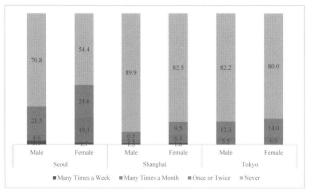

⑤ Family Life Satisfaction

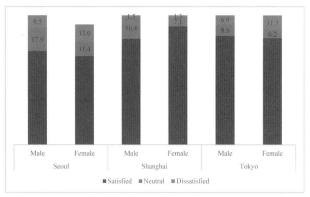

Figure 5-6: Work-Family Conflict and Family Life Satisfaction

hausted due to family responsibilities to concentrate at work compared to To-kyo and Shanghai counterparts as shown in figure 5-6-4. More Seoul women compared to men feel this way.

These circumstances affect the overall satisfaction of family life. Figure 5-6-5 shows that most respondents in three cities are satisfied with family life. However, positive responses are less for Seoul compared to Tokyo and Shanghai. Notably, Seoul women's satisfaction is the lowest out of all comparison groups. We have observed how the negative effect of overworking and work pressure was highest for Seoul and more so for women compared to men. The lowest family life satisfaction shown in Seoul especially for women supports the association of family life satisfaction and strain of working. As detailed previously, pressure of raising children can be another factor in reducing life satisfaction levels. This burden seems to be bigger and longer lasting in Seoul compared to Tokyo and Shanghai. Also, this element can greatly reduce life quality of parents. It is important to note that out of all groups, family life satisfaction is the lowest for women in Seoul. Reduced satisfaction in life is caused by a combination of these factors: the burden of educating children and the lengthened period to carry out this role; for those with a job, the added burden of working; and the ironic attitude people hold regarding mother's roles. The coexisting attitudes of people expecting mothers to work while believing working mothers can negatively affect children have burdened mothers in Seoul at many levels.

4. DISCUSSION AND CONCLUSION

According to the Global Gender Gap Report presented during the 2016 World Economic Forum, out of 144 countries, China placed 99th (total score 0.676), Japan placed 111th (total score 0.660) and Korea placed 116th (total score 0.649) on the gender gap. Noting that China is considered an upper-middle income country while Japan and Korea are considered high-income economies, we see a great mismatch between the gender gaps and economic levels for these countries. It was found that the major contribution to the high gender gap in China was based on low satisfaction levels of women in terms of health and survival while low rankings of Japan and Korea had to do with limited opportunities in economic participation for women.

This chapter observed coexisting spheres of work and family in the perspectives of working women in Seoul, Tokyo and Shanghai. We have first examined employment patterns. Then, we analyzed the influential factors including conditions of child rearing and child education, attitudes on work-family balance, forms of conflict between work, family and life satisfaction. Findings reveal that all factors interact together to mutually influence each other. We also find similarities and differences between the cities. The three cities share East Asian contexts but deviate from each other in institutional characteristics rooted in social, economic and political trajectories.

Many women in Seoul and Tokyo exit the labor force until their children have grown up to some degree before returning to work. In contrast to this employment trend, most Shanghai working women of all age groups maintain their work positions. This means that the labor market participation of women in Shanghai is not affected by marriage, childbirth and child rearing.

All women from the three cities are moving away from traditional gender roles due to globalization trends and exacerbated market competition. However, they are still under the influence of family-centered gender norms. In all three countries, social responsibilities are being more emphasized in the work-life spheres. As the importance of investment and management of education have been widely highlighted as social values, educating moms have become the newly expected role of mothers in three cities. Recently, the priority of mothers has become managing educational achievements of their children. This trend is especially salient among middle class families, adding more pressure to women in terms of labor force participation.

Within this new trend of emphasis placed on "education moms," there are divergences that exist in the three cities. Seoul mothers strategically educate their children as early as in elementary school. As a result, it was found that mothers in Seoul have the hardest time and feel the most conflict in balancing work and family life. In Shanghai, academic achievements of children have been highlighted as one of the most important ways to reduce anxiety of the recently expanding middle class. With heightened competition to enter prestigious colleges and rising passion of mothers to secure quality educational resources, more mothers in Shanghai are feeling the burden of staying as working mothers. Tokyo mothers experience similar hardships but once their children turn twelve, their stress levels are significantly reduced. However, for mothers who have left work for family duties, it becomes hard to secure the same occupational position they have left behind. This is because the longer mothers wait to return to work, the lower the job qualities become. This is a common experience shared by both Seoul and Tokyo mothers although it could be said that Tokyo mothers fare better due to the higher availability of part-time work. An important thing to take away is the current reality of existing high barriers to former jobs as well as the reality of being pushed to low-wage jobs for women in their late-30s and 40s returning to work. The two societies have yet to figure out a solution for mothers who have curtailed their careers to fill responsibilities for their families.

A large ratio of survey respondents of the three cities has agreed that an instinctive attitude formed on a mother's primary role involves family and children. Further, most respondents of all gender agree that for mothers with children not attending school yet, child rearing should be prioritized over work. The ratio of respondents who agree the most to that statement is the highest for Seoul. In Seoul, where roles of mothers as stay-at-home mothers and income earners are all highly emphasized, women's happiness levels have stayed low. Among the three cities, the ratio of families especially women who feel low satisfaction in life was the highest in Seoul. Women's role as expected by men and as normalized in women as gender norms are seen to collide with women's role and expectations as income earners of modernized families, brininging down satisfaction levels in both work and life spheres for women. This conflict that rises from social and economic development built on sacrifice of women will eventually weaken family stability. This is problematic for family stability lays the foundation for institutions of societies. The risk of weakened family stability is shown to be the highest in Seoul.

In short, women in Shanghai are characterized by high employment rates but are recently facing some changes that may disrupt this pattern in the future. Employment for mothers is slowly increasing in Tokyo and Seoul, which can be seen as hopeful signs. However, no big changes are recorded for women's employment positions, leaving room for improvement. Tokyo women are characterized by strong internalization of mother's roles in their families and having comparatively easy access to part-time jobs, thereby experiencing relatively less conflict between work and family life. In contrast, women in Seoul are facing the greatest dilemma stuck between the roles as income earners and stay-at-home mothers. Even though at different levels and in different forms, mothers of the three cities are experiencing some level of conflict between work and family spheres. Although these women are part of different systems, regulations and norms, they face the same clash between their goals and family expectations in their life course.

All countries of the three cities hold importance in emphasizing familial duties to societies by implementing policies. However, these policies all seem to fall short of integrating women and accommodating their needs. For instance, the newly fostered mother's role of educating their children is not reflected in policies. Also, as shown in the case of Korea, policies lack the power to change company procedures to help work and family life become compatible. Policies in Japan also seem to neglect gender discrimination rooted in internalization of gender roles. More than half of women in Japan become hired as part-time workers and it becomes extremely hard for married women to achieve same level of career success compared to men due to prevailing discrimination at the workplace. This is the reason why women's ratio of executives and management level positions are lower in Japan compared to Korea.

Each city's policies should focus on how women's happiness can be maintained in their personal and social lives apart from their family responsibilities.

All states need to realize that their decisions shape social institutions and public policies need to support a healthy balance of work and family. As mentioned previously, the implementation of these policies on company regulations is weak at most. Policies should not just target the growth of the total number of employments or employment rate for women but address employment quality, labor force discrimination and work-family conflicts. A policy enforcing gender equality within hiring practices to prevent concentration of women in specific work types or positions is necessary. In order to advance gender equality, however, more important than expansion of these policies is the actual implementation of these policies within the workplace.

Further, states need to evaluate social systems and policies to support early education of gender parity and raise social awareness that child rearing is not an assigned role to women but rather a responsibility of both parents and the society as a whole. Lengthening parental leave for women is not always considered a good policy because what matters most is to minimize the negative effect that comes from women leaving work due to child-care. Instead of lengthening time of leave, it would be more practical to expand various vacation leaves that can be used by both genders. Instead of curtailing labor participation of one gender and reinforcing traditional gender roles, what will be more beneficial is to reduce labor time for both genders and to provide child-care facilities that match demands. Since child-care facilities are domains that can be autonomously managed by local governments, future policy directions at each city-level should consider balancing demand and supply of child-care as well as quality and quantity to better support family lives.

Continued efforts to uplift the rationality of education resource allocation is needed for all three cities. In order to reduce the burden and anxiety faced by modern families and working women, states need to strengthen public education to support academic achievements for children coming from different backgrounds and give aid to overburdened parents. Local governments need to recognize that society is primarily responsible for children's education and support needed by parents to consider a wide array of perspectives including the life course of women and their families.

**An earlier version of this chapter was published in the *Development and Society* (Vol. 45 No.3, 2016).

ACKNOWLEDGEMENTS
We would like to thank the research assistants of The Institute for Social Development and Policy Research, Seoul National University, and the former master's students in Sociology, Seokyung Kim and In Choi who collected various data and harmonize them for the three cities for this chapter.

NOTES

1   Labor market statistics of the three countries, Korea, China and Japan, are managed by the central government. Publicly released data usually carry limitations in that they provide statistics at the national level and not at the city level. For this reason, nationwide statistics are used for comparisons. Later, we compare labor market participation of women with additional city-level data.
2   There are limitations of comparability due to the differences in time periods that each city datasets offer.

REFERENCES

Chang, Dukjin et al. (2015). *Archeology of Compressed Development.* Seoul: Hanul Books.

Chang, Ji Yeon. (2016). *A Gender Perspective on Employment Policy.* The 16th Korea-Japan Labor Forum Women's Employment Presentation.

Chen, Lin. (2015) Decisions for Institutionalization Among Nursing Home Residents and Their Children in Shanghai. *Qualitative Health Research*, 25(4), 458-469.

Chen, Shirley. *Should Shanghai Grandparents Be Left Holding the Baby?.* CNN. January 27, 2011.

Cho, Soon-kyung. (2011). *Labor Market Flexibility and Patriarchy.* Seoul: Prunsasang.

EBS News. *False Resident Registration Problems Surge in Major Cities..Twelve-fold Increase in One Year for Elementary Schools.* September 29, 2016.

EDAILY. *Boomerang Effect of Free Child Care: Daycares Closing Despite Long Wait Lists.* June 27, 2016.

eToday, July 19, 2011.

Eun, Gi-Su and Lee, Yun-Seok. (2005). Family Values in Korea from a Comparative Perspective. *Korea Journal of Population Studies*, 28(1), 107-132.

Frone, Michael R., Russell, Marcia, and Cooper, Mary Lynne. (1992). Antecedents and outcomes of work-family conflict: testing a model of the work-family interface. *Journal of Applied Psychology*, 77(1), 65.

Greenhaus, Jeffrey H. and Beutell, Nicholas J. (1985). Sources of Conflict Between Work and Family Roles. *Academy of Management Review*, 10(1), 76-88.

Herald Business. *Manager Mom Generation: Helicopter Moms Evolve into Manager Moms.* July 19, 2011.

Hida, Daijiro. (2008). Issues Related to Junior High School Selection on "The Age of Choice in Junior High School" (Chuugakkou Daisentakujidai no Chuugakkou Sentaku ni Kakawaru Shomonndai): *Research Report on Junior High School Selection* (Chuugakkou Sentaku ni Kansuru Chousa Houkokusho). *Research Institute Report (Kenkyu-sho Hou)*, 48, 16-21.

Hirao, Keiko. (2001). The Effect of Higher Education on the Rate of Labor-force Exit for Married Japanese Women. *International Journal of Comparative Sociology*, 42(5), 413-433.

JoongAng Ilbo. *Joining Mothers' Network: A Working Mother's Dilemma.* March 21, 2016.

Jung, Ee-hwan. (2002). A Comparison of the Characteristics of Non-Standard Workers in Korea and Japan. *Korean Journal of Sociology*, 36(1), 83-112.

Jung, Sung-Mi. (2014). The Women's Situation and its changes in the Labor Market Labor Market. *Labor Review*, 111(6), 5-19.

Schwab, Klaus et al. (2016). *The global gender gap report 2016*. World Economic Forum.

Koo, Hagen. (2001). *Korean Workers: The Culture and Politics of Class Formation*. Seoul: Changbi Publishers.

Koo, Hagen. (2012). Rethinking Korea's Middle Class. *The Quarterly Changbi*, 40(1). 403-421.

Korea Labor Institute. *Korean Labor and Income Panel Study*. Available at: https://www.kli.re.kr/klips/index.do

Kwon, Hyunji. (2016). Korean Women's Labor Market in the East Asian Context. *Women's Status and Women's Movement in the 21st century in North East Asia: North East Asia Forum Report*.

Lee, Yunjin and Paik, Mihwa. (2012). The Long-Term Early Childhood Education Reform in China and the Case of Shanghai. *Korean Journal of Child Care and Education Policy*, 33, 28-38.

Liang, Y., & Zhang, H. (2015). The Middle Class in Beijing, Shanghai, and Guangzhou. In P. Li, G. Chen, Y. Zhang, W. Li, & X. Xu (Eds.), Society of China Analysis and Forecast (2016) (pp. 189-218). Beijing: Social Sciences Academic Press (China).

Ministry of Education. (2015). *2015 Survey on Private Education Expenses*. Available at: https://www.moe.go.kr/

Ministry of Education of China. (2010). *The National Medium and Long-term Educational Reform and Development Outline 2010-2020*. Available at: http://www.moe.edu.cn/publicfiles/business/htmlfiles/moe/moe_838/201008/93704.html

National Bureau of Statistics of China. (2000). *Fifth National Population Census*. Available at: http://www.stats.gov.cn/tjsj/pcsj/rkpc/5rp/index.htm

_____. (2005). 2005 1% National Population Sample Survey Census Data. Available at: http://www.stats.gov.cn/ztjc/zdtjgz/cydc/

_____. (2010). *Tenth National Population Census*. Available at: http://www.stats.gov.cn/tjsj/pcsj/rkpc/6rp/indexch.htm

Nihon Keizai Shimbun, Inc (Ed.). (2016). *Nikkei Mook: The First Book to Read When Considering a Middle School Entrance Exam*. Tokyo: Nihon Keizai Shimbun,Inc..

Nishimura, Junko. (2016). *Motherhood and Work in Contemporary Japan*. Abingdon and New York: Routledge.

Nishimura, Junko and Kwon, Hyunji. (2016) Divergence in Women's Employment in Korea and Japan: What shapes the different patterns around childbirth?. *Development and Society*.

Ochiai, Emiko. (2011). Unsustainable Societies: The failure of familialism in East Asia's compressed modernity. *Historical Social Research/Historische Sozialforschung*, 219-245.

Ochiai, Emiko. (2014). Leaving the West, Rejoining the East? Gender and family in Japan's semi-compressed modernity. *International Sociology*, 29(3), 209-228.

OECD. (2012). *OECD Family Database*. Available at: http://www.oecd.org/social/family/database.htm

_____. (2014). *OECD Employment Rate*. Available at: https://data.oecd.org/emp/employment-rate.htm

_____. *LFS by sex and age-indicators*. Available at: https://stats.oecd.org/Index.aspx?DataSetCode=LFS_SEXAGE_I_R

Ohta, Toshimasa. (2012). *Choice Called Junior-High School Entrance Examination* (Chuugaku Jyuken to Iu Senntaku). Nikkei Premium Series. Tokyo: Nihon Keizai Shinbunsha.

Osawa, Mari. (2007). *Life Security System in Today's Japan: Coordinates and Courses* (Genndai Nihon no Seikatu Hoshou Sisutem: Zahyou to Yukue). Iwanami Shoten.

Oshio, Takashi, Nozaki, Kayo and Kobayashi, Miki. (2013). Division of Household Labor and Marital Satisfaction in China, Japan, and Korea. *Journal of Family and Economic Issues*, 34(2), 211-223.

Ryoo, Cheyon. (2015). Educating Mother As a Self-fulfillment (Jjko Jitsugenn Toshite no Kyouiku Suru Hana). *Family Sociology Research* (Kazoku Shakaigaku Kennkyu) 27(1), 7-19.

Research Group of Shanghai Social Research Center. (2013). Report on the Quality of the Social Development of Shanghai in 2013. *Scientific Development* (4), 104-112.

Statistics Bureau of Japan. *Employment Status Survey.* Available at: http://www.stat.go.jp/english/data/shugyou/

Statistics Korea. *Economically Active Population Survey.* Available at: http://kosis.kr/

The International Social Survey Programme(ISSP). (2012). *IV(Family and Changing Gender Roles IV).* Available at: http://www.issp.org/

Tokyo Metropolitan Government. (2016). *Social Welfare and Public Health in Tokyo.* Available at: http://www.fukushihoken.metro.tokyo.jp/joho/koho/tokyo_fukuho_e16.files/2016fukusi_eigo_1.pdf

Wu, Xiaoying. (2015). Ideological Debates behind the Family Policy. *Collection of Women's Studies*, 128(2) , 17-25.

Yee, Jaeyeol et al. (2014). The rise of civil Society and the declining middle class. *In Kang et al. Are You Middle Class?.* Seoul: BOOK21.

Zhang, Yuping and Hannum, Emily. (2015). Diverging fortunes: The evolution of gender wage gaps for singles, couples, and parents in China, 1989–2009. *Chinese Journal of Sociology*, 1 (1), 15-55.

Zuo, Jiping. (2014). Understanding Urban Women's Domestic-Role Orientation in Post-Mao China." *Critical Sociology*, 40(1), 111-133.

Zuo, Jiping, and Bian, Yanjie. (2005). Beyond Resources and Patriarchy: Marital Construction of Family Decision-making Power in Post-Mao Urban China. *Journal of Comparative Family Studies*, 36 (4), 601-622.

Hoikuen wo Kangaeru Oya no Kai (Parents' Association to Think about Daycare Center) (ed.). (2006). *A Parents' Guide to Starting a Daycare* (Hajimete no hoikuen). Tokyo: Shufu To Seikatsu Sha.

6

Lone Dwellers of the Three Cities

JiYoung Kim
Masako Ishii-Kuntz
Suping Huang

1. THE AGING STATE AND THE YOUNG CITY

(1) Demographic Changes in the Three Countries

Demographers commonly categorize population into three age groups: ages 0 to 14, ages 15-64 and ages 64 and older. Historically, for every state, the working age population—ages between 15 and 64—had taken up the largest ratio of the total population. Recently, we are facing an era where this common trait is starting to be challenged. A time has arrived where working age population has started shrinking. In the case of South Korea, this change has already begun in 2017. By 2018, South Korea will enter an era of aging society where the population ratio of the elderly will surpass 14% (Statistics Korea).

Social problems like low childbirth and aging society are not unique to South Korea. Japan has been struggling with the problem of aging society from 1995 and reduction of working age population from 2000, 17 years before South Korea. China, which had been fueling its economic development with cheap labor from the young working population, started facing a reduction in its working population from 2012. All in all, working age population is shrinking relative to "older-age" population in three countries. Within each country, however, big cities are the ones that attract young people more than other localities.

(2) Still a Vibrant City: Seoul, Tokyo and Shanghai

Scenes of Yeoido, Seoul, during a weekdayafternoon in October 2016 (picture on left) and Shinjuku, Tokyo, during a weekend afternoon in November 2016.

During weekday lunch hours, piles of young workers crowd the streets of Jongno, a district in Seoul with a high concentration of government offices and press agencies, and financial districts of Yeoido and Gangnam, central business districts in Seoul. The groups of twos and threes heading to restaurants and people scurrying to places with coffee in hand are common Seoul scenes where clusters of companies are located within the city's 25 districts.

Although South Korea as a whole is indeed facing an aging society with a dwindling number of the young, Seoul depicts a different picture. Out of Seoul's total population recorded to be 9.567 million in 2015, the ratio of the young in their 20s and 30s was 31.3%, which is higher than the national average of 27.8%. On the other hand, the ratio of the elderly (ages 65 and older) was 12.6% in Seoul, lower than the 13.2% national average. Compared to other South Korean cities, Seoul is a city that is "still young".

The difference in demographic structures between a state and its city becomes more apparent looking at Tokyo. Figure 6-1 shows population migration of Tokyo's major cities in years 2010 and 2015. When outflowing population and inflowing population are the same, net migration population is shown as zero. Because these cities are major cities, there are more population coming in than those leaving. For instance, Tokyo's 23 wards are receiving noticeably large number of migrants. Based on 2015 data, Tokyo's inflowing population was 70,000 more than the outflowing population and more than 90% of those moving to Tokyo were in their 20s.

Even for China that had suffered a dwindling of working age population from 2014, the city of Shanghai is growing. Shanghai's working age population recorded to be 67% of the city population in 1995 has continued to climb for the next twenty years to 73.5% in 2014.

Unit: Person

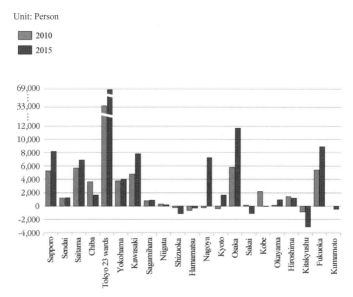

Figure 6-1: Population Relocated to Tokyo's 23 Wards
Source: Statistics Bureau of Japan (2015)

Age breakdown reveals Seoul, Tokyo and Shanghai to be very unique cities within their countries South Korea, Japan and China. A closer look at the "still young" cities' demographic structures inside the aging nations and the stories of people who reside alone in these three cities will compose the next sections of this chapter.

2. WHEN DOES A "NORMAL FAMILY" STOP BEING NORMAL?

(1) The Change to the Ratio of "Normal Families"

Historically, people have made great effort to protect and claim limited resources. In this sense, population increase is a threatening factor tied to conflict surrounding limited resources. In order to evade these conflicts and enhance life quality for citizens, state policy makers have drawn out agendas to control population known by the term population control policy.

State-level incentives to control population levels were introduced to achieve economic prosperity with limited resources. In South Korea, movement to reduce population and poverty levels started after the Korean War with state-level economic development plans. Japan has executed population control policies after finding out economic growth is not guaranteed through the 1973 oil crisis. One of the more common population control policies employed by the states is the birth control policy: a policy that controls the number of births and inevitably family structures.

South Korea instilled a family policy advocating for two children for families in the 1970s. This policy was changed to a one-child policy in the 1980s and then to a multi-child policy in 2000. China advocated for a two-child policy up until the 1970s and then a one-child policy from September of 1979.

This trend flipped in the late 1990s with Japan. After the 1990 "1.57 shock," a social reaction to Japan's lowest recorded birth rate, low birth rates and reduction in number of children started to become problematized. South Korea's birth rate also started to drop in the 1990s to dip into 1.5 and still lower after the 1997 IMF financial crisis. On the other hand, the Chinese one-child policy that was maintained for 35 years were loosened from 2015, allowing up to two children for married couples who had no siblings.

There have been changing trends in the "ideal" birth rate tied to an "ideal" family setting. The number of family members as portrayed on media that constitutes a "normal family" has been reduced as well. The normal family range advocated in the 1970s was a four-person household comprised of parents and two children. From the 1980s, promotional policies for family planning reduced the normal range to three-person households. For some time, the three-person household was known to be a nuclear family that could not be broken down further. However, in Seoul, Tokyo and Shanghai, these units have been further reduced to two-person households or single person households (SPHs).

(2) Single Person Households in the Three Cities

After family planning policies were executed in the 1970s, Seoul's family types became widely diverse. Figure 6-2 displays the ratio of "normal family" households in Seoul. At the time the policy rolled out, three-person or four-person households were uncommon, taking up barely 10% of the household types. In fact, more common households were those comprised of five or more household members. However, in 1990s after the two-child and one-child policy took effect, ratio of three-person or four-person households more than 40% and this family types became the "main category" for households in Seoul.

Figure 6-2 also highlights the heightened number of SPHs in comparison to number of "normal family" households. Like three-person and four-person

Unit: %

Seoul

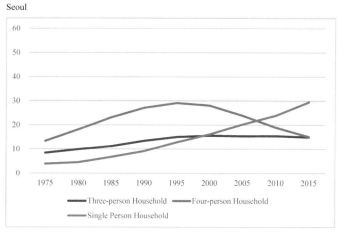

Shanghai

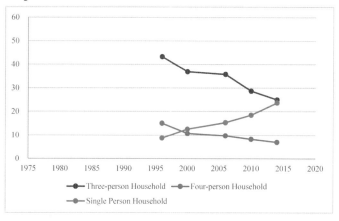

Tokyo

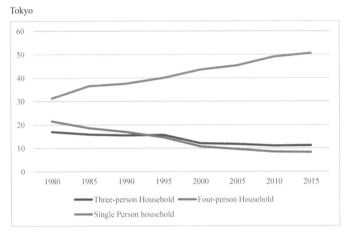

Figure 6-2: Changing Ration of "Normal Families" and "Single Person Household"

Source: Statistics Korea, "The Census (Seoul)'; National Bureau of Statistics of China, "Chinese Statistical Yearbook"(Shanghai); Statistics Bureau of Japan, "The Census" (Tokyo)

households, SPHs was a "minor category" in 1975. It was after year 2000 that number of SPHs surpassed that of three-person households and surpassed that of four-person households in 2010. By 2015, SPH became a "main category" of households taking up 29.5% of all Seoul households in Seoul. The number of SPHs increased steadily from 54,000 units in 1975 to more than 1,000,000 in 2015.

The contrasting trends shown in ratio changes of SPHs and "normal families" are also reflected in Tokyo and Shanghai. To graph out the comparisons of the two cities, Tokyo's national census and Shanghai data from the Chinese Statistical Yearbook were utilized. As shown in figure 6-2, Shanghai's three-person household ratio is the highest, which is a reflection of family structures formed by the one-child policy that was in place for 35 years. However, this ratio has steadily decreased to 25% by 2014. Four-person household ratio was merely 15% in 1996 and continued to dwindle to 7% by 2014. In contrast, the 8.7% ratio of SPHs in 1996 increased three-fold within two decades in Shanghai to be 23.7% in 2014.

In contrast to the two cities, Tokyo had a high number of SPHs for early on. As shown in figure 6-2, while SPHs in Seoul and Shanghai were much lower in count than "normal type households" in the 1980s and 1990s, Tokyo's SPH ratio was over 30%. In 2015, this number increased to 50.6%, making SPHs the main household type in the city.

SPHs in the three cities have increased greatly over the last two decades. It has already become the main type of household for Tokyo while Seoul and Shanghai are closely chasing this trend. What would the demographic characteristics of those who live in the cities by themselves look like? The next section will provide a closer look at their unique attributes.

3. EXAMINING SINGLE PERSON HOUSEHOLDS IN THE THREE CITIES

(1) Resemblances and Disparities

We can first look at the breakdown of gender, age and household distribution in the three cities (see figure 6-3). In Tokyo, where SPH ratio was already past 30% in 1980, this number escalated to 53.2% for males and 46.8% for females in 2010. The age breakdown of the male SPHs are as following: 14.5% for ages 25 to 29, 12.3% for ages 30 to 34, and 11% for ages 35 to 39. Together, among the male SPHs, men in their mid-twenties to late thirties make up the largest portion. For women, this ratio is lower but like men, the largest concentration of female SPHs are between ages 25 and 39. One difference is that unlike men, the number of women who live alone climbs again at the age range between 50 and 54. There is also a high concentration of women in SPHs over 65 years in age.

The high concentration of women among the young and high ratio of elderly women living alone reflect demographic scenes in Seoul as well. However, unlike Tokyo, 52.7% of total SPHs in Seoul are women, which is over 5% more than male SPHs. It is also unique to Seoul that 52.6% of these households are concentrated in the age group 25 to 39. The reason why there is such a high ratio of this age group is closely tied to Seoul's unique history of spatial formation and will be covered later in this chapter.

Shanghai, on the other hand, is comprised of 56.9% male SPHs and 43.1% female SPHs, statistics similar to Tokyo. In Shanghai, there is also a high concentration of young SPHs in their twenties and thirties and higher ratio of female SPHs aged 65 and above. The three cities resemble each other in the higher population of the young and higher SPH population for elderly women. What is unique about Shanghai is the high ratio of the very young—28.9% of the young households are between ages 20 and 24 and 8.3% in ages 19 and younger.

Unit: %

Seoul

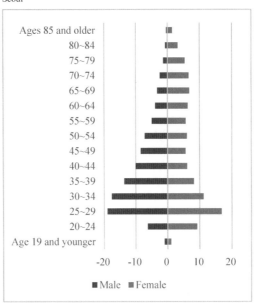

Shanghai

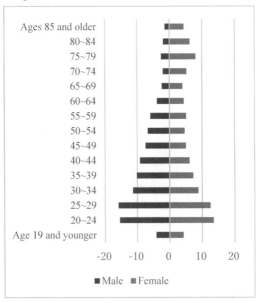

Tokyo 23 Wards

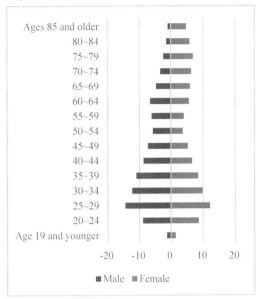

Figure 6-3: Distribution of Single Person Households by Age and Gender in 2010

Source: Statistics Korea, "The Census (Seoul)'; National Bureau of Statistics of China, "Chinese Statistical Yearbook"(Shanghai); Statistics Bureau of Japan, "The Census"(Tokyo)

(2) What Jobs Can Tell Us

A deeper examination of the three cities that both resemble and contrast each other can reveal even more interesting findings. A comparison of jobs held by the SPHs can categorize some of these findings. In order to carry out an even comparison, a systemic way to sort jobs of the three cities can be useful. However, a consistently even platform is unachievable; each city uses a distinct categorization of jobs that becomes untranslatable in other cities. Adding to this limitation is lack of data for Shanghai. Since China is newly facing a surge in SPHs, except for basic demographic characteristics like age and gender, data on SPHs is limited. In order to compensate for this lack of data, we decided to rely on employment data on SPHs from the Shanghai Survey (2015 Survey of Living Conditions of Residents in Shanghai Megacities).[1]

Table 6-1 shows which occupations are held by SPHs in Tokyo and Seoul. Since occupation categories of Tokyo and Seoul are dissimilar in the datasets utilized, occupation types for the two cities are separately ranked. The top occupation category in Tokyo is "clerical work" followed by "technology professional," ratios being 19.2% and 17.5%, respectively. Although 36.7% of SPHs in Tokyo hold occupations that are considered to be "white collar work," other occupation types include sales (10.2%) and service (8.1%). We can conjecture that economic backgrounds of SPHs in Tokyo are not uniform.

SPH characteristics reveal a higher concentration in certain occupation types in Seoul compared to Tokyo. For instance, 29.3% of Seoul residents have occupations in "professional or related work" and 19.6% are employed in "clerical work." The two occupation categories following are 13.2% in "sales" and 12.1% in "service." These categories are also ranked third and fourth in Japan.

Table 6-1: Occupations Breakdown of Single Person Households in Tokyo and Seoul, 2010

Tokyo 23 Wards		Seoul	
Clerial Workers	19.2%	Professionals	29.3%
Professionals	17.5%	Clerial Workers	19.6%
Sales Workers	10.2%	Sales Workers	13.2%
Service Workers	8.1%	Service Workers	12.1%
Production Workers	4.6%	Unskilled Workers	10.8%
Transportation, Cleaning, Wrapping Workers	4.2%	Technicians	7.1%
Freight, Machine Operator	2.4%	Machine Operator	4.9%
Consturction, Mining Workers	1.8%	Managers	2.7%
Managers	1.7%		

※Ratio reflects percentage of employed SPHs within occupational category.
※Ratios do not add up to 100% due to selection of major occupational categories.
Source: Statistics Korea, "The Census"(Seoul); Statistics Bureau of Japan, "The Census"(Tokyo)

According to the 2015 Shanghai Survey, occupational categories SPHs in Shanghai are in are as following: 20.3% in "professional," 15.7% in "sales," 15% in "clerical or administrative work" and 11.8% in "service work." In Shanghai, those categorized as a professional or as a clerical worker consist of 35.3% of the total households in the city. To add, those employed in work related to either sales or service include 27.5% of the city residents. This means that majority of the Shanghai residents are broadly employed in four occupational categories.

We can conjecture that in Tokyo, Seoul and Shanghai, SPHs can be broadly categorized as either high paying professionals, clerical workers or as low paying professions in sales and service work among others. However, noting group disparity between high paying and low paying SPHs is just the beginning of analysis. There also is limitation in data for the analytic sample does not include those without a job. Understanding that occupational status is positively associated with household income, we can conjecture disparity in financial resources will exist between those employed and unemployed. We can then ask the following question: how will employment and unemployment rates differ between SPHs of the cities?

A closer look at the ages of people residing in SPHs can reveal more on household economy. As outlined previously, relative to other regions, the young age group ratio is higher in all three cities, notably from ages 25 to 39. If most of these people were employed, young SPHs won't be considered "problematic" in our society at least from the financial side of things.

In order to further compare SPH economic activities between Tokyo and Seoul, we decided to categorize the employed and unemployed separately. The employment category includes hourly paid labor and temporary work while the unemployment category includes those who are not economically active and unemployed. The economically inactive group consists of those who are at school, raising children, keeping house, or suffering from physical or mental conditions that prevent them from working. Figure 6-4 illustrates the ratio of unemployed among SPHs by gender and ratio of unemployed between the ages 25 and 39 by gender.

Seoul's unemployment or economically inactive group ratio of SPHs is 31% for men and 45.5% for women. These ratios are much higher in comparison to

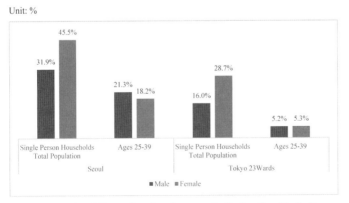

Figure 6-4: Ratio of Unemployed and economically inactive Single Person Households (2010)

Source: Statistics Korea, "The Census"(Seoul); Statistics Bureau of Japan (Tokyo)

Tokyo's where it is 16% for men and 28.7% for women. This difference is underscored when specifically looking at ages 25 to 39: where 21.3% of men and 18.2% of women in this age group are unemployed or economically inactive in Seoul, merely 5.2% of men and 5.3% of women are unemployed or economically inactive in Tokyo.

In this sense, there exists some differences between financial situations of SPHs in Seoul and Tokyo. Although the top four occupational categories—professional, clerical work, sales and service—align for the two cities, employment ratio is much lower in Seoul relative to Tokyo. Further, the ratio of unemployed economically inactive for the age group 25 to 39 are also higher in Seoul.

(3) Housing Situation of Single Person Households

In addition to analyzing occupational distribution, housing occupancy index of SPHs can further unravel the economic standing of these households. Figure 6-5 compares how the SPHs of the three cities own or occupy housing.

Although limitations exist due to different ways of categorizing occupancy status in the three cities, we can still draw some conclusions. In Tokyo, where one out of two households are occupied by single person residents based on 2010 statistics, 24.9% of SPHs live in homes they own. The majority of the residents, however, pay monthly rent for private housing with a deposit of two to three month's rent. Because Japan does not have South Korea's *jeonse* system and tenants do not receive back full amount of deposit after the end of sublease, initial cost of finding housing can be expensive. Out of every two non-SPHs, only one SPH are homeowners and number of SPHs that pay month-

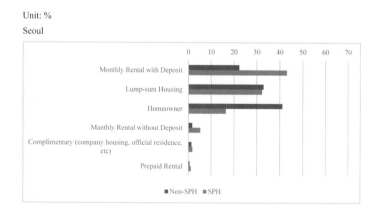

Unit: %

Seoul

Shanghai

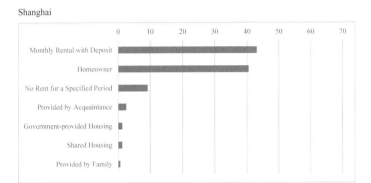

Tokyo

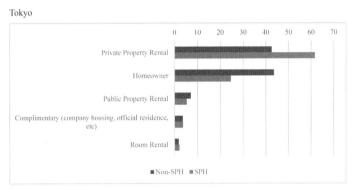

Figure 6-5: Housing Occupancy Status of single Person Households
※Tokyo and Seoul, 2010 statistics; Shanghai, 2015 statistics.
Source: Statistics Korea, "The Census"(Seoul); 2015 Shanghai Survey (Shanghai); Statistical Bureau of Japan (Tokyo)

ly rent for private housing is also 20% higher compared to non-SPHs. In this way, housing cost burden rests more heavily for a SPH.

How will things look similar or different in Seoul? 2010 statistics reveal that out of three non-SPHs, there is one SPH in Seoul. Of the SPHs, 43.1% pay monthly rent with prepaid deposit, 32.3% live under the *jeonse* system and 16.4% live in their own homes. The percentage of homeowners is about 8% lower than Tokyo. Also, while there are 41.1% homeowners among non-SPHs, homeowner ratio among SPHs is less than half of that. 22.3% of non-SPHs live on monthly rent with deposit compared to 43.1% of SPHs. 1.7% of non-SPHs live on monthly rent without deposit compared to 5.3% of SPHs.

2015 Shanghai data reveals that among SPHs in Shanghai, 40.5% are home-owners, which is the highest ratio among the three cities. According to South

Korea's classification, those who live on monthly rent without deposit consists of 43.1% of SPH population. In order to understand the high homeownership among SPHs in Shanghai, we need to consider two factors. The first factor is the high number of Shanghai *hukou,* or registered households, revealed in 2015 Shanghai data. The *hukou* system was originally initiated to oversee travel between regions. Historically, people registered in Shanghai had a higher probability of being more affluent compared to those registered in rural districts. The second factor is China's 1998 labor structure's unit change. With work unit change, housing that was once owned by state administrative units were allowed to be privately owned by citizens, resulting in high ratio of homeownership among SPHs. China's household registration system and structure change have influenced Shanghai's current residential state of SPHs.

Generally, among the SPHs in the three cities, there is a higher ratio of people who rent their housing in a form of monthly rental or *jeonse* (in the case of South Korea) compared to those who own their homes. For SPHs, the ratio of renting homes is 20% higher than non-SPHs. We can conjecture that many SPHs are constrained financially in order to pay for their housing. We can also try to find out whether SPHs are able to obtain quality lives in the type of housing they are most likely residing in. Figures were drawn using Seoul's data on housing status of SPHs.

Figure 6-6 compares Seoul's residential changes for SPHs for those aged 25 to 39 between years 2010 and 2015. For this group, "house" was the most common housing type they were residing in for both years. One thing to note is the

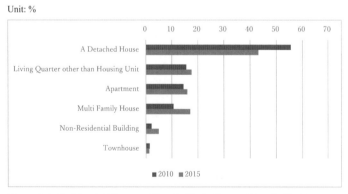

Figure 6-6: Residential Change of Seoul's Single Person Households (Ages 25~39)

Source: Statistics Korea, "The Census"

decline in this ratio from 55.6% to 43.1% over the 5 years. This means that SPHs that used to reside in houses have moved to different housing types. Residential changes show a rise in other housing types including "non-house residence," "apartment," "multi-family house" and "non-residential housing," housing, all housing types that are relatively cheaper than houses except apartments.

The next common housing category after "house" that SPHs in Seoul reside in is the "non-house residence" defined by Statistics of Korea as residence falling short of housing standards. Statistics of Korea includes in this category the following house types: officetels (a multi-purpose building with combined residential and commercial units), rooms in motels or other lodgings, dormitory or social facilities and *goshiwon* or small room rentals. The ratio of SPHs in ages 25 to 39 who reside in "non-house residence" has increased from 15.6% in 2010 to 17.6% in 2015. To add, ratio of those who reside in multi-family housing buildings—commonly buildings that are below four stories high and smaller than 660 square meters—increased from 10.7% in 2010 to 17.1% in 2015. Also, ratio of those who live in non-residential buildings commonly used for commercial purposes also increased from 2.2% to 4.9% from year 2010 to 2015.

As the numbers suggest, among SPHs in Seoul, there are many more households burdened by monthly rent than those who live in homes they own. To add, SPHs aged 25 to 39, which is 35.8% of the total SPH population, are increasingly dwelling in lower quality housing like multi-family houses and non-residential housing.

4. WHY SHOULD WE FOCUS ON THOSE WHO LIVE ALONE?

Up until now, we have analyzed SPHs in Seoul, Tokyo and Shanghai based on their gender, age, economic activity and their residential environment. As detailed earlier in this chapter, Korea, Japan and China have come face to face with a "new" demographic setting in the form of aging population with reduction in working population, albeit at slightly different times, and this trend will only accelerate in the future. However, the cities that this book focuses on offer a slightly different perspective than the respective countries they are located in. Seoul, Tokyo and Shanghai are "young" cities that continue to attract young people seeking new opportunities and as more of these people reside alone, such mode of residential arrangements are becoming the norm for the residents in these cities.

The reason why this chapter focuses on SPHs in the three cities is not simply due to sudden increase in the number of such households. Rather, it is because this trend seems to be an accurate portrayal of the dramatic change in modern society the three countries are facing. The change, mentioned in this context, can be understood through a concept termed *individualization* first coined by Ulrich Beck (1986), recognizing that the formation of SPHs is more than a mere reflection of personal decisions and choices.

Midori Ito (2008) interpreted Beck's notion of individualization to include following three aspects: changes brought to conventional social structures and relationships, greater amount of decision-making responsibilities given to individuals needing to make increasing number of life decisions on their own, and lastly, the need for individuals to effectively address various life situations and problems. Therefore, individualization implies increase in individual responsibility to handle personal problems by oneself as conventional social buffers, such as influences from family, professional, and local community ties have waned. However, as Beck has contended, the weakening of such relationship ties in traditional relationship settings not only "forces" burden on individuals to make more decisions on their own but also "liberates" those individuals to make autonomous decisions, free from collective judgement.

In short, the onset of individualization implies the need for individuals to actively engage in life problems and changes on their own compared to the previous generations. Interpreting the rise of SPHs within the context of Beck's notion of individualization shows that increase in such households implies transition in collective bond ties centered around conventional form of households to a single household form, and can be seen as the junction where new generation of individuals, free from the constraints of conventional family structures, are born. In particular, the fact that SPHs of the three cities are comprised mainly of younger population ranging from ages 25 to 39, where 91% of individuals residing in Seoul in this age group are unmarried, and among them 37.5% of the individuals in their twenties and 43.5% in their thirties have reported to view marriage as either an option or being unnecessary (The Seoul Institute, 2015), shows that the rise in SPHs in these cities is not just a temporary trend. Thus, SPHs cannot be overlooked as they have become a type of household distinct from the conventional ones, have emphasized individual autonomy and responsibility, and will have prolonged impact on the understanding of collective bond ties in these cities.

Another reason to focus on SPHs is due to potential problems that may rise when an individual from this household of maximized responsibility and autonomy faces a threat that cannot be handled or solved single-handedly. Shogo Takegawa (2004) observed three areas of individualization including individualization in family, career and local community. In particular, he brought attention to how previous welfare and social care systems that had been provided by family, company and local community have shrunk in size and influence, relinquishing all risk and burden on individuals. Takegawa contends since societal security system adheres to traditional family units, previous structures are unable to keep up with the changing pace of dissolution and weakening of traditional groups, which can result in various side effects. Within this context, since SPHs have a higher ratio of unemployed or non-economic participants and higher housing instability compared to traditional households, they may suffer from not having enough resources to offset their disadvantaged conditions. This highlights the point brought up by Myungwoo Noh (2018) who has contended that the real problem behind SPHs is the lack of economic and relational resources which are necessary assets to enable individuals with complete independent lives.

We have decided to focus on SPHs because as it is becoming more apparent, they visibly portray the trends and problems that come with individualization. We will go on to discuss major SPHs in the three cities to observe what changes they are facing and what risks they are living through.

5. SINGLE PERSON HOUSEHOLD'S FAILURE TO RESPOND TO OR CONTROL DANGER

(1) Young Single Person Households Who Delay Their Life Course

It is important to take note that there is a high number of SPHs in Seoul that are very young—between ages 25 to 39—and that high unemployment or economically inactive group rate is recorded for that age group. This is problematic for this age group consists of new graduates and eligible young workers. This puzzling phenomenon might make more sense by looking at the areas where this group is concentrated in (see figure 6-7).

Figure 6-7 also shows the increase of SPH population between 2010 and 2015 in Seoul's 25 districts. The ratio of increase is displayed for each district where darker the color, higher the increase. In Seoul, the darkest-colored districts are Gwanak-gu and Gangseo-gu. Although the rate of increase of SPH population is high in Gangseo-gu with its population recorded at 56,990, it is only about half of Gwanak-gu's SPH population of 100,320. Within a five-year span, there's been a 242.8% increase in SPH population in Gwanak-gu, 53%

these households being between ages 25 and 39.

Unit: %

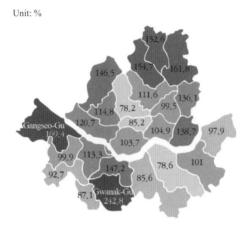

Figure 6-7: Growth Rate of SPHs in Seoul (2010 and 2015)
Source: Statistical Geographic Information Service (SGIS)
Created by the author based on the SGIS data (http://sgis.kostat.go.kr/)

The area in Sillim-dong, Gwanak-gu, commonly called *goshichon is* where SPHs in Seoul are concentrated in. It is a popular off-campus housing ground for college students. SPH population first increased in Sillim-dong when the campus of Seoul National University in 1975 moved to this area. The resulting influx of student boarders and college graduates populated Sillim-dong. The neighborhood officially became a *goshichon* with close to 50 *gosiwons* that opened in the 1980s. As the state bar exam in South Korea abolished the age limit and increased appointment of new public officials to 1,000 annually, population continued to climb in this area (Seoul Museum of History, 2015: 14).

Since a big portion of SPH population in Sillim-dong are those preparing for the national judicial and public official examinations, residents are usually economically inactive group and live in *gosiwons. Gosiwons* are categorized as housing that falls below average residential quality. Therefore, SPH living in Gwanak-gu closely matches the financial and living conditions of Seoul's SPHs between ages 25 and 39. The increase in number of the young preparing for state exams is both due to the change in the exam system and the attraction of stable government jobs highlighted after the 1997 IMF financial crisis. Considering that not everyone will land a government position even after the 2 to 10 years spent in preparing for the exam, we may conjecture that delayed life course are common patterns displayed among SPHs starting from 1990s.

SPHs in Sillim-dong faced yet another turn of events post-2008 when the South Korean government approved opening of law schools, greatly decreasing the number of bar examination preparers. Population of SPHs in Gwanak-gu have continued to increase from 2000 but the ratio of those preparing for the national bar exams has gone down. The rooms left behind by the bar exam preparers were soon filled by college students, those applying for work, young workers and day laborers. In addition to studios and *gosiwons* in Sillim-dong, rooms known as "room to just sleep in" have been increasing in number as well.

Seoul Museum of History (2015) contends that those burdened by unemployment or unstable working conditions, as well as those struggling financially as students or looking for career opportunities, have tended to gravitate to Sillim-dong where cost of living is relatively cheap. Although people have landed in Sillim-dong for various reasons, most residents think of their neighborhood as a "temporary place" they wish to move away from once prospects improve. As the sheer number of increase in Sillim-dong's population from 20,900 to over 100,000 over fifteen years hints, employment and housing cost problems for the young will remain as social issues for the time being.

↑↑Real estate agency and advertisement of *goshiwon* rental in Sillim-dong (October, 2016)

↑view of a *goshiwon* room in Sillim-dong occupied by a male tenant in his late thirties (October, 2016)

(2) Elderly Single Person Households Exposed to Danger

Unlike the high population of unemployed or economically inactive, 95% of SPHs in 23 wards of Tokyo between the ages 25 and 39 hold jobs. In Tokyo, the "social problem" lies somewhere else: there is an increased elderly population, one of the byproducts of an aging society.

As shown in figure 6-8, households including an elderly person aged 65 and above have continued to rise from the 1980s. 24.2% of SPHs in Japan and 29.9% of married two-person households include an elderly person in the household. This ratio is slightly different in Tokyo: it is 26.2% for the two-person households and 36.5% for the SPHs. We can see that the two-person household ratio is below the national average while the ratio for SPHs is 12% higher.

Japan

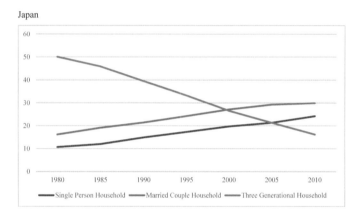

Tokyo 23 wards

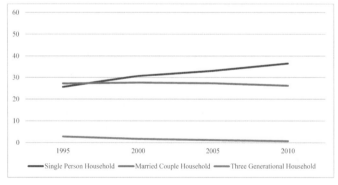

Figure 6-8: Transition of Ages 65 and older Household Composition

Source: Cabinet Office, "Annual Report on the Aging Society"(Japan); Tokyo Metropolis, "Population of Tokyo"(estimated) (Tokyo 23 wards)

A noticeable increase in middle-aged SPHs is a distinct pattern to take note of in the midst of Tokyo's SPH population increase. According to the National Institute of Population and Social Security (2016), Tokyo's "lifetime non-marriage rate" or ratio of those never married until 50 was 2.6% for men and 4.45% for women in 1980 and 20.14% and 10.61% for men and women respectively in 2010. These findings forecast a continued increase of the elderly SPH population including those who have never married.

The elderly SPH population is a group that will benefit from daily caregiving and medical assistance. A future increase of unmarried elderly population—set apart from the elderly SPHs who are divorced or living apart from family—calls for an increased need for state and local-level attention and support. In the same vein, the increase of unmarried middle-aged SPHs is also cause for concern for they will eventually become part of the elderly SPH population to create a high-risk group.

The problems faced by the elderly SPHs in Tokyo exist at multiple levels. According to the 2013 survey from Japan's Ministry of Health, Labor and Welfare, the ratio of those among elderly SPHs who receive caretaking provided by professional services rest at 40%. This ratio is a lot higher than the ratio (below 10%) for the elderly population cohabitating with a spouse or other family members. It is estimated that 70,000 care workers would be needed to provide caretaking services for the rapidly increasing elderly SPHs (Mizuho Financial Group, Inc., 2016). However, in a city where the working population is shrinking and society is aging, it would be difficult to pull together a large work force concentrated in care work.

Further, whereas there is a high portion of young SPHs that are working in Tokyo, majority of elderly SPHs are either unemployed or economically inactive. If relative poverty is defined as lacking minimum income to fund basic necessities in life, 29.3% of male SPHs and 44.6% of female SPHs who are 65 years and older are in relative poverty (Abe, 2014). In comparison to the average relative poverty ratio among elderly population in Japan—which is 15.1% for elderly men and 22.1% for elderly women—the ratio of relative poverty is almost twice as high for the SPHs.

It thus becomes hard for the financially struggling elderly SPHs to receive proper caretaking. According to the 2016 Tokyo metropolis reports, 48.3% of the elderly SPHs are non-homeowners paying monthly rent. This percentage has continued to increase from the time of first survey in 2010. The high ratio of non-homeowners is tied to the high population of unmarried SPHs. Because the unmarried SPHs have never married or had children, they experienced lack of opportunities or motivation to purchase their own homes. In Japan, rather than pre-purchasing apartments or multi-family houses, vast majority of people first purchase land before building their houses. Then, the house building is financed through long term loans provided by companies to employees. We may conjecture that the motivation to take out loans to fund a future family house would be low for SPHs. To add, for single persons, barriers exist in applying for long term loans since these loans are usually set apart for family units. As the ratio of non-married SPHs continues to increase, SPH ratio who do not own their own homes is expected to increase as well.

(3) Newly Formed Single Person Households

We have discussed our findings using the term single person households or SPHs for those living alone in the three cities. This term is quite a recent development in literature. In Japan, where the ratio of SPHs had surpassed 30% back in the 1980s, the term that had been designated to those living alone was "single household" and for the elderly, "elderly single household." In South Korea statistics, the term "single person household" had been in use to label those living alone but had been used interchangeably with term "single household" introduced in the 1990s. From 2005, "single person household" became the official term to describe households consisting of single persons residing alone.

In Shanghai, despite its delayed emergence of single person households in respect to Seoul and Tokyo, the term "single person household" was incorporated into the national 2002 census. The term was utilized before South Korea but it was only after 2010 that SPHs and related issues were made aware through media exposure.

The recent attention to SPHs in Shanghai is testament to the recent surge of SPH population. The underlying reason for the comparatively small number of SPHs in Shanghai lies in the aforementioned *hukou* system. This system was first introduced in 1958 to restrict migration to cities with a state goal to keep city population levels below 20%. Before *hukou* system was reformed, it was not feasible for someone not registered under the Shanghai city system to find a job and house in the city.

The *hukou* system that had strictly banned moves between cities was first scrutinized for reform in mid-1990s when a large number of migrant workers flocked to an administrative region located at a rural-urban fringe called *jin.* The discourse for reform became widespread among small and mid-sized cities. When China became a member of WTO in 2001, the state reformed The *hukou* system for big cities like Shanghai to lure talented individuals to the cities. From 20005, public educational opportunities were given to rural migrant workers' children in Shanghai (Sungkyun Institute of China Studies, 2014).

Due to the effect of the *hukou* reform, from 2000, there has been an increased number of foreigners moving to Shanghai in addition to migrants arriving from rural areas of the country. According to the Shanghai Census 2010, 60.1% of SPHs in Shanghai are foreign-born. An even higher ratio of foreign-born is recorded among younger SPHs—92.2% in ages between 15 and 19, 90.2% in ages between 20 and 24 and 77.7% in ages between 25 and 29.

Unit: %

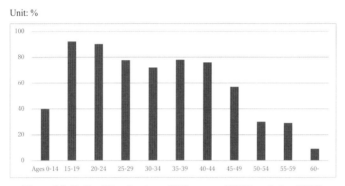

Figure 6-9: Ratio of Foreign-born SPHs among SPH Population (2010)
Source: Statistics Bureau of Shanghai (2011)

An important factor to consider when observing SPHs in Shanghai is the housing price. Among those registered under the city household system, there is a high ratio of homeowners. However, things are different for those who were not originally part of the city. Often these people do not have the full requirements to qualify for housing purchase or simply can't afford the steep price. People who relocate to Shanghai commonly sublease temporary housing at six-month intervals. In order to purchase a house, residents need proof of tax payment for at least two years. Even after providing such documents, people are deterred from buying a house in Shanghai for the housing price is higher than other Chinese cities.

To add, Shanghai's housing price is on the rise. According to the Fang Holdings Limited, the biggest real estate portal service (fang.com) in China, there was a 41.4% pricing increase on newly constructed houses and 45.5% for previously listed houses between years 2014 and 2016. Although locating to the city has become possible with the reformed *hukou* system, the high housing price still serves as an obstacle to SPHs. Hence, there is great likelihood that the city will become divided into two groups: the small group of professionals and white-collar workers who have moved to the city for economic opportunities and the group of economically inactive international students and low-income workers who struggle to maintain their lives in the city.

6. SINGLE PERSON HOUSEHOLDS: PROCESS AND OUTCOMES

We have taken time to draw comparisons between the quickly rising SPHs in the three cities taking to consideration their demographic and household characteristics. Our interest lies further than just the sheer increase in the SPH population. Rather, our focus is on the underlying social contexts that accompany SPHs in the cities. It is critical to understand the past developments in the three cities: city dwellers have shifted from traditional relationships and networks whence they used to receive and reciprocate resources from family, work and communities. Now, they are making decisions and resolving problems on their own, represented by the stark "individualization" reflected in SPHs.

SPHs have now become a main family type surpassing traditional "normal families." SPHs encompass both the professionals and white-collar workers and the low-wage workers in industries like service and sales. Breakdown of SPH economic activities in Seoul and Tokyo reveal that compared to Tokyo, SPHs between ages 25 and 39 living in Seoul have a 15% higher percentage of unemployed and non-working population. A conclusion can be drawn that in

Real estate agency in Shanghai displaying housing prices (October, 2016)

Seoul, there exists a high portion of SPH population that are not equipped with adequate financial resources fitting a city life. We can also assume that they do not possess sufficient resources or protection from the state to face unexpected obstacles in their life course.

The hopeful elements of the three cities are the continuous inflow of young people and a good supply of diverse jobs relative to other cities. However, when looking at places like Sillim-dong overcrowded by *goshichons,* a grim reality of the young delaying their life course to find "stable jobs" settles in. Only when the households consisting of lone dwellers of the city are able to gain their independence paired with quality life, we can reinterpret their existence as based on "hope" rather than "despair."

NOTE

1   The Shanghai Survey was carried out in October 2015 by Shanghai University. A two-step random sampling was utilized—multistage cluster sampling followed by an adaptive cluster sampling. A final sample group of 2002 was selected for analysis, 1004 from first sampling and 998 from second sampling.

REFERENCES

Beck, Ulrich. (1986). *Risk Society: Towards a New Modernity (Risikogesellschaft: Auf dem Weg in eine andere Moderne).* Frankfurt am Main: Suhrkamp Verlag. Translated in Korean by Hong, Seong-Tae, 1997. Seoul: Saemulgyul.

Cabinet Office, *Annual Report on the Aging Society Japanese.* Available at: http://www8.cao.go.jp/kourei/whitepaper/index-w.html

Global Future Research Center, The Seoul Institute. (2015). *Policy Response Research to Seoul's Single Person Households.* Seoul Metropolitan Center

Ito Midori. (2008). *The Concept of Ulrich Beck's Individualization: Individual and society in reflexive modernity.* Japanese Sociological Review 59(2): 316-330.

Kito, Hiroshi. (1983). *Japanese History (in Demography) (Jinkokara Yomu Nihonno Rekishi).* Tokyo: Kodansya. Translated in Korean by Choi, Hea-Joo and Son Byung Giu, 2009. Seoul: AMHBook.

Mizuho Bank, Ltd. Industrial Research Department. (2016). *Mizuho Industry Survey*, 54(1). Available at: http://www.mizuhobank.co.jp/corporate/bizinfo/industry/sangyou/pdf/1054_04_05.pdf#search= '高齢者単独世帯の社会的リスク'

National Archives of Korea. *Population Policy, Yesterday and Today.* Available at: http://theme.archives.go.kr/next/populationPolicy/viewPolicy.do

National Bureau of Statistics of China. *Chinese Statistical Yearbook.* Available at: http://www.stats.gov.cn/ENGLISH/Statisticaldata/AnnualData/

National Institute of Population and Social Security Research. (2016). *Demographic Statistics, 2016.* Available at: http://www.ipss.go.jp/syoushika/tohkei/Popular/P_Detail2016.asp?fname=T06-23. htm

Nho, Myungwoo. (2013). *About Living Alone: Sociology for Isolated People.* Seoul: April Books.

Poverty Statistics. Available at: http://www.hinkonstat.net/貧困率の長期的動向-国民生活基礎調

146

査を用いて/

Seoul Museum of History. (2015). *Sillim-dong Youth: Goshiwon Lives*. Seoul: Seoul Museum of History.

Shanghai Jingrong Information Technology Co., Ltd. Available at: http://sh.fang.com/

Sungkyun Institute of China Studies. (2014). *China Handbook: A Handy Volume of China*. Seoul: Gimmyoung.

Statistical Geographic Information Service (SGIS) Available at: https://sgis.kostat.go.kr/view/thematicMap/thematicMapMain?stat_thema_map_id=oqrEJzwryv201601211158069778qDoxqxpMF&theme=CTGR_001&mapType=04

Statistics Bureau of Shanghai. (2011). *Analysis on the Characteristics of Shanghai Population Family: Sixth Series of Analysis Data of Shanghai's Sixth National Census*. http://www.stats-sh.gov.cn/fxbg/201111/234552.html

Statistics Bureau of Japan. http://www.e-stat.go.jp/

_____. *Population Census*. Available at: http://www.e-stat.go.jp/SG1/estat/GL02100104.do? tocd =00200521

_____. (2012). *Population Census, 2010*. Available at: http://www.e-stat.go.jp/SG1/estat/GL08020103.do?_toGL08020103_&tclassID=000001043904&cycleCode=0&requestSender=-search

_____. (2015). *Internal migration in Japan derived from the basic resident registration*. Available at: http://www.e-stat.go.jp/SG1/estat/List.do?lid=000001143175

_____. (2015). *Summary of the Results of Internal Migration in 2014*. Available at: http://www.stat.go.jp/english/data/idou/2014np/index.htm

Statistics Korea. http://kosis.kr/

_____. *Population Census*. Available at: http://kosis.kr/statisticsList/statisticsList_01List.jsp?vwcd= MT_ZTITLE&parentId=A#SubCont

Takegawa, Shogo. (2004). *Welfare State and Individualization*. Japanese Sociological Review 54(4): 322-340.

Tokyo Metropolis. "Population of Tokyo(estimated)" Available at: http://www.toukei.metro.tokyo.jp/jsuikei/js-index2.htm

Shanghai Center for Social Science Survey of Shanghai University (2015). *Survey on the Living Condition of Megacities' Residents*

7

The Transformation of Social Ties and Communities in the Three Cities

Byeong-Eun Cheong
Hao Yuan
Tetsuo Mizukami

The aim of this chapter is to describe and explain how people in Seoul, Tokyo and Shanghai respond to trends of social changes and carry on their lives. All people are social beings. People get together with others, have meaningful interactions, share emotional bonds and help one another for survival. The patterns and attributes of such human relations have varied on the basis of social circumstances. In the formation and development of the modern society, the factors that greatly influenced people's social bond are urbanization and recently, individualization.

Urbanization refers to the phenomenon of population concentration into urban areas for jobs, education and other opportunities. There are two contrary views regarding urbanization: while some express concerns over disappearance of community and weakening of social bond, others insist that communities are not disappearing but in fact bonding in a new way. Unlike the western societies that went ahead with industrialization and modernization, Korea, Japan and China demonstrate different paths and progress of modernization. Also, the major cities of Korea, Japan and China, which are Seoul, Tokyo and Shanghai, have differing urban development goals and contexts among themselves. There is a need to analyze how these cities share general traits of urbanization while focusing on different forms of social bonds in each city.

Another change that has influenced urban population and social bond is individualism, a social trend which puts more emphasis on individuals over collective group. Particularly, at a time when diminishing public welfare system puts individuals in social threat, individualization, where individuals are responsible for one's own life career, is an important trend to note. In Korea, Japan and China, family or enterprises have often been in charge of welfare. To add, hierarchical groups have been prioritized over autonomous individuals. Thus, individualization of these countries appears to be different from that of Western countries.

Urbanization and individualization have produced a tragic bypass known as "lonely deaths." This phenomenon evidences how the social bond of modern urban population has been either extremely weakened or cut off. In a society with increased number of solitude deaths, witness of deaths without dignity often becomes a threat to one's own dignity. The number of "myself generation" (people who prefer spending time alone over socializing with others) have also increased. People who are part of this group form bonds in a unique way. Myself generation's way of living is often portrayed as lives in isolation and loneliness and as precursor to social disintegration. Yet, there is a need to examine if this pessimistic stance towards myself generation is valid. A hopeful angle to myself generation portrays the bonds as restorative to communities and personal relationships. Further, a new approach of forming relationships between strangers have been noted. Since people are social beings, it is too early to conclude that spread of individualization in metropolises have caused dismantled societies. Instead, this new social phenomenon can hint a possibility to an alternative community.

1. URBANIZATION: ANONYMITY OF RELATIONSHIP AND HIGH MOBILITY

(1) Indifferent Encounters and Anonymous Relationships

In a pre-modern society, the city functioned in a way that reflected people's lifestyles and daily routines. For example, community facilities like traditional markets enabled making of social ties, such as personal interactions, information exchange, formation of public opinion and credit-based transaction. In addition, community facility also brought formation of social capital. City streets were not just where people passed through, but places where neighbors greeted each other and carried on everyday conversations. Notably, residential streets of an old city was virtually a "small society" where children played with peers, interacted with elders of the village and accomplished socialization in a natural way.

On the other side, modern urban living can be portrayed as living as one of the many unspecified general. This is unlike a traditional society based on intimate relationships. People who pursue their personal space away from a community are reluctant to let others in their space including people they share close ties with. These people prefer a closed and separate space and wish maintain a certain distance with others. This distance and indifference toward others is a way to achieve their own comfort by respecting others' space in return.

In an urban life with great emphasis on privacy, people follow a behavioral rule: that they should stay out of each other's lives. Goffman referred to this rule as "civil inattention," an invisible rule that refrains people from having too much interest in others. Rather than ignoring others, civil inattention is about acknowledging their presence through unobtrusive gestures. For instance, not meeting others if possible and negligent meetings between people at convenience stores are regarded as an advantage. According to such feature of urban life, people try not to invest their time in others. Knowledge and relationships with others remain superficial.

These indifferent meetings are expanded through infrastructures such as convenience stores and apartment structures among others (Jun, 2014). As for Korea, apartment complex style of residence was extensively popularized during 1970s and 1980s when Gangnam region of Seoul started to develop on a full-scale. An apartment complex is usually separated from its surroundings and is equipped with shops, playground, kindergarten, and other common living facilities. Apartment was preferred among people who neither wanted to violate others' privacy nor wanted to be violated of their own privacy. It provided security and protection of privacy to those people. It became common for people to keep their introductions and interactions limited or cut off from neighbors. There existed a social pressure of not wanting to start unwelcome conversations.

On the other side, there is an argument that despite such anonymity, urbanization does not bring about social disintegration and individual isolation. Individuals with rich economic and human resources are found to prefer living in urban areas, building and expanding networks (Fischer, 1982). In this sense, urbanization do not alienate nor isolate people but build different forms of personal relationship. An example of this relationship could be a working married couple living near their family or relatives to receive childrearing support (Chung, 2007). Neighborhood effects in a metropolises have been observed (Sampson, 2012) where apartment communities create social ties based on similarities of income, occupation, and educational levels among others (Jun, 2009).

(2) Mobile Life in the Cities

Recently, the contemporary society has been termed a "new nomadic society" characterized by nomadic lifestyles of people. In this society, groups, organizations, and permanent settlement are losing significance and individuals prefer great mobility in life. People are mobilizing and not limited by geographical, occupational, and hierarchical limits. Off-line and online mobilization have also become fluid. Boundaries for states, governments, corporates, and NGOs have become obscured. The new nomadic society was precipitated by the IT/Digital revolution bringing to invention the Internet, laptops, cellphones, MP3, and other digital products. Today, people freely move beyond cities and borders with constant access to their digital devices. People living in the mobile era with no physical and spatial boundaries are referred to as "homo nomad" or "homo mobilicus" (Jun, 2014).

Table 7-1 compares the residential period shown in years for current residents from the three countries and their cities. Based on the residential period in the countries, people who are living in Korea reported the shortest residential period while those living in Japan reported the longest. On the city-level, the result is a little bit different. The residential period was shortest in Shanghai, then Seoul, and longest in Tokyo. Of the three countries, Korea has the highest mobility and of the three cities, Shanghai has the highest mobility.

Table 7-1: Period of Residence Shown in Years at Current Address /
The comparison of living period at same place

Year	country			city		
	China	Japan	Korea	Shanghi	Toyko	Seoul
Under 3	10.5	7.6	12.2	14.4	9.1	11.9
3-5	7.4	4.3	8.1	10.8	5.5	8.7
5-10	12.9	10.2	13.0	19.8	12.8	16.0
10-23	21.8	17.7	20.0	29.3	18.9	17.4
Over 20	35.9	44.6	38.4	16.8	41.3	38.4
Since birth	11.5	16.7	8.3	9.0	12.5	7.8

Source: East Asia Social Survey Data Archive (2012)

The mobility of Koreans is quite high even on international level. This is shown through residential mobility, the percentage of households that moved its residence in two years. Korea's residential mobility was 37.5% in 2006, 35.2% in 2008, 35.2% in 2010 and continued to drop until 32.2% in 2012, then increased to 36.6% in 2014. Residential mobility of Seoul is higher, reported to be 43.6% in 2006, 39.9% in 2008, 38.8% in 2010, 32.3% in 2012 and 40.5% in 2014 (Kang et al., 2014).[1] This is far higher than the average of OECD countries, which is 16% (Sánchez and Andrews, 2011). This also means that potentially a region could be repopulated with newcomers within the span of 5 to 6 years, forming a "society of strangers." Finally, according to data, regardless of occupancy type, middle to higher income households and city residents moved more frequently compared to lower income households and rural residents, respectively.

The high mobility in South Korea is the result of the efforts made by middle class and some lower class sector to move up in class by purchasing their own housing by utilizing state's housing policies. Classes that can afford to accumulate wealth view houses in Korea as something to invest in rather than live in. Construction companies take advantage of this social pattern and advertise apartments as a popular commodity. Preference of apartments is not usually based on fundamental elements, such as comfort level of the house, but based on other factors such as proximity to preferred school district, transportation, as well as how likely the housing prices will increase. In Korea, large apartment complexes were built in several places destroying small streets and alleys. Residents develop a strong sense of ownership over their apartment and share a common interest to raise economic value for their premises (Kim, 2016). In such circumstances, non-homeowners resort to frequent moves, unable to afford rent rising at a higher rate than paychecks. Homeowners also stay mobile, seeking to invest in a home that is bigger, more profitable and fitting the educational needs for their children. From the 2000s, when apartment became the dominant type of residence, a mixture of "nomads" could be spotted in Korea: nomads kicked out of their housing due to residence development plans and nomads on the search for a better apartment (Jin, 2012).

The phenomenon of residential change centered around apartments is also witnessed in China's east coast cities. These cities are characterized by rapid developments spurred by state's economic reform and open policies. China is undergoing a rapid urbanization and expansion of major infrastructure, such as housing and roads. However, this pace is still slower than the urban population growth. Shanghai had already been receiving an inflow of around 200,000 people annually until mid-1950s, and with additional agricultural population flowing in, the city had been experiencing an explosive growth. In order to regulate this population, China executed the registry system in 1958, but it turned out to be ineffective. There would be people registering in rural areas and moving to cities. This caused a problem of some population being excluded from social security and public services. With the installment of the Pudong development project as one of the steps to economic reform and opening in 1990s, urban scenes in Shanghai changed as well. The city witnessed a comprehensive construction of houses and roads, demolition of old buildings in downtown and mass construction of high-rise apartment buildings. As a result, even residents of Shanghai would remark that "the city is changing so rapidly that some places are hard to find unless you buy a map every year." (Lee, 2012)

On the contrary, in Japan, smaller firms were more involved in urban development than larger enterprises. This led to an increased construction of smaller apartments and single-family houses rather than larger apartments. Single-family houses take up more than 50% of annual construction of residence buildings, and they are built separately rather than in a large complex. Single-family houses are built on designated fields and often region-based, being processed by small housing firms, carpenters or government offices (Park, 2014). Also, due to the development of regional organization and formation of regional bonds, residents tend to stay longer in their residence. Many residents live in the same region for decades, further strengthening the interaction and bond between neighbors. To add, because of these regional bonds, it becomes easier for residents to never leave their region (Jin, 2012).

2. EAST ASIA'S SOCIAL CHANGES AND INDIVIDUALIZATION

(1) Individualization or "Surviving Alone"

Modern welfare states emerged from the prosperity accrued in postwar capitalist economy and enjoyed the golden age of the labor market with full employment up to early 1970s. However, the foundation of welfare states was rapidly weakened by the changes following the first oil shock. After the initial oil shock, socialist states collapsed, the digital revolution took place, knowledge-based economy emerged and the world started to globalize. Neo-liberalism started spreading in early 1980s but it opposed government's intervention in market mechanism and weakened the public welfare system. Labor market became more flexible in a way of increasing irregular and precarious jobs. Disadvantaged groups like teenagers, women, and the elderly were either discriminated with wages, job security, and social security, or excluded altogether. The traditional system regarding family, relatives, marriage, and local communities eventually weakened and social network shrank. On top of that, public welfare that used to function as a social safety net also diminished. As a result, individuals were burdened and anxious from the uncertain realities. By facing the times when unemployment and unstable work conditions became structurally embedded, individuals lost traditional bonds and network. They were forced to embrace a state of individualization where surviving hardships embedded in daily life and in labor markets became extremely personal. Individuals are to live life freely making their own decisions to actualize their dreams but they are also expected to survive on their own. Each decision and risk taken became the sole responsibility of an individual.

The concept of individualization here is the process of macro and structural alteration which is tied to an increased opportunity for an individual to choose his or her life. But at the same time, individualization is also forcing the individuals to choose their lives (Beck, 1986). The social structure is framed to compel people to be individuals and to be responsible for their own life. This forces individuals to make yet more decisions. People in such a society need to free themselves from restraints tied to family, relatives, and social positions to become responsible for their own survival amidst various risks. Although people have been released from past traditions and restrictions from communities, they are now burdened to seek and pursue meaningful lives on their own. They are disintegrated from existing norms and values. Individuals no longer find identity in class, race, or other social groups and are reluctant to sacrifice for a collective outcome (Shim, 2013).

Individualization discourse within the context of East Asia is different from that in the West. Individualization in the West took place during the transition to Thatcherism-dominated states that emphasized individuality and the belief "there is no more a society". Before the transition, the West consisted of total welfare states that took care of their people "from the cradle to the grave." This is where historical difference needs to be considered between East Asian countries and Western countries. Korea has not experienced a welfare state, Japan is supported by a strong company welfare and China is a socialist state. "Individualization without individualism" (Chang and Song, 2010), "family-oriented individualization" (Shim and Han, 2010), "marketized individualization" (Shin, 2013), and "compressed individualization" (Hong, 2015) demonstrate the traits of East Asian individualization. "Individualization without individualism" focuses on individualization in people's family and life patterns accompanied by unawareness or lack of actualization of individualism for individuals. For example, in Korea, there has been an increase in single person households and preference for individualistic lifestyles, but that does not mean familism was completely taken over by individualism.

Individuals in Japan and China also face the burden of being solely responsible for one's survival as individuals are separated from traditional or modern welfare (Suzuki, et al., 2010; Yan, 2010). However, individuals are unable to make decisions or survive adequately when life patterns and family matters intervene. For example, the influence of parents on their children's big life decisions is increasing in China. Young generations who live competitively are still unable to choose how to live their life and stay overly dependent on their parents. "Family-oriented individualization" has much stronger collective elements than individualistic elements, and from this aspect is distinct from Western individualization and found only in East Asian countries like Korea (Shim, 2011).

(2) Digitalization and Individualization

The steps of individualization are also related to the digital revolution and the following network era. The information age or the network era is a society where individualism became the new social operating system (Kim, 2015). The information age emerged from digitalization often characterized by invention of personal computers and cellphones. The focus of the network era is on individuals rather than groups or organizations. Individuals stay connected, and communicate and organize among themselves. Recently, private online spaces are getting popular as web media individualizes. Collective community (such as online cafés or groups) are converting to an individual-oriented network (such as blogs) and web media seems to be advancing to become more individual-centered (Nho and Yun, 2008).

Wang and Wellman explain how individualized network was formed from three series of revolutions: the social network revolution, the Internet revolution, and the mobile revolution. In an individualized network, an individual's normal relations are individualized differently from the traditional way yet individuals stay connected to community in a new way (recitation from Jo and Kang, 2015). According to this perspective, social network revolution increases individual's desire for autonomy and at the same time, stretches one's mobility. Furthermore, as communication technology improved, people became connected more broadly and different social relations became specialized and unofficial making boundaries between groups less distinct. The use of the Internet made online communication more convenient and long distance communication became smoother. Friendly internet language used over the web became positive reinforcements to create more interactions. For example, American adults' usage of the Internet did not cut people off from others but transformed their relationships to be tied to an individualized network. In the meantime, with the spread of mobile smartphones, social media became more popular, and both physical limits in space and time were reduced. Through increased frequency in online interactions, reinforcement of non-physical communication and real-time access to media, each individual's life became atomized into single units.

Digital friendly generations are familiarized with the Internet and mobile smartphones from early on and become inseparable from such technology. Different forms of digital media have provided these generations with new communication characterized by vibrant conversation and interaction. The new generations grow up to be digital beings who continuously communicate and express themselves on smartphones, instant messengers and other platforms. These gadgets popular among teenagers have also started spreading to the middle-aged and elderly, increasing the volume of text communication. Text communications can be freely exchanged according to an individual's situation and are limitless in time and space. Contrary to telephones, this text-based communication allows flexible interactions where full attention is not mandatory. This technology allows an individual to freely choose and become the subject of one's life, furthering recent individualization trends.

(3) Traits of Individualization and Social Bond in East Asia

Within the context of what was discussed previously, individualization in the three East Asian countries can be divided into "structural individualization" and "avoidant individualization." Structural individualization refers to the phenomenon that appeared as social structure and system based on modern rationality were weakened or dissolved. Global economic crisis and low economic growth triggered economic justification. This in turn fragmentized individual's career by creating labor market flexibility. In addition, in dealing with mass unemployment and the working poor, the size of regular workers who had power over the labor union was cut down. In an age where a lifetime career is never a guarantee, workers switch back and forth between permanent and temporary work positions. This instability in employment condition impacted stability of families.

In Korea, the initial policy for labor market flexibility was introduced in mid-1990s. During the 1997 IMF economic crisis, there was a large-scale lay-offs and the fundamental condition for social reproduction collapsed. Labor market, due to its distinct segmented dual structure, grants a low possibility for low ranked workers to move up. For example, Korea recorded 25.1% on the incidence of low pay, 4.71 on deciles distribution ratio and 23.8% on the incidence of temporal workers. These figures are in a very high level among OECD countries, where the average is 16.3%, 3.38 and 12.0%, respectively. Also, the poverty escape rates in Korea (31.8%) is lower than the OECD average (39.0%)

and the rate for non-regular workers transferring to regular jobs is the lowest among OECD countries, transfer rate being 11.1% after 1 year and 22.4% after 3 years (Kang, 2015). Since the labor market shock was majorly affecting the lower class, the livelihood of these people were put to risk. This in turn led to the rapid destruction of the social reproduction system which could also lead to dissolution of families (Chang, 2011). Since family policy in Korea is too fragile to act as a social safety net, causes for dissolution of family such as divorce, runaway child, domestic violence and suicide were aggravated to the extent where such indexes were reported highest in the world. Further, it became difficult for families to rely on male breadwinner's income only, calling to rise employment for married women and family-run businesses. The social reproduction system where women do not work but stay in charge of housework and childrearing became no longer possible.

In case of Japan, the state has suffered "the lost two decades" caused by the economic recession, massive financial loss and neoliberal restructuring after the bursting of the bubble economy. During this period, unemployment rate gradually increased and the youth underwent a time called an "employment ice age." Also, due to the long-term recession, re-employment was hard, not to mention the hardships existing in regular employment. Notably, the 2008 financial crisis led to massive layoff of temporary workers and dispatched laborers, which led to social issues like NEET (Not in Education, Employment, or Training), *Free-ter* (word combining "free" and "arbiter"), *Hikikomori* (abnormal avoidance of social contact), and parasite single. Also, neoliberal economic and social policies of Koizumi regime have triggered a "gap society" where every relationship of individuals was changed to be mediated with money (Fukushima, 2015).

Particularly in Japan, individualism combined with a unique cultural norm of rejecting helping hands resulted in serious isolation of people. The underlying logic of the norm rests in the series of thoughts: "I don't want to be a trouble to anybody. I don't share anything with anybody. I don't need support from anyone. I make my own money and pay for commodities I need in the market." (Uchida, 2008) Naturally, individuals concentrate on making money in an efficient way. If they are no longer able to live such a lifestyle or are in danger of falling lower in class, they will resort to thinking that it is their fault and responsibilities lie on them.

Meanwhile, China, a state that embodies socialism, has achieved a "*danwei* system" from the mid-1950s).[2] Members of danwei or work unit system are affiliated with the social party organization where each unit are connected with governmental power. A unit was a "lifetime workplace" and the only channel where necessities such as food were distributed. Therefore, the unit offers both the welfare system and communal living, providing everything needed for labor reproduction, such as medical services, housing and culture. However, due to the spread of market mechanism from the state's open door policies, the danwei system was dissolved. Individuals became able to buy necessities in the market, which used to be acquired only through the distribution from the unit. The system was weakened further as public companies got privatized and laborers were switched from being controlled by the company owners to becoming part of the labor-contract system. In response to these changes, from the mid-1980s, a construction of "community" was initiated by the state to provide administrative and welfare system. Also the state began to search for a right mechanism to maintain and control urban cities (Park, 2015).

Another type of individualization is the "avoidant individualization," where individuals reinforce their private life areas in order to reduce uncertainty and to pursue their ego. As mentioned above, economic rationalization has brought flexibility in the labor market and has weakened the opportunity to have a lifetime workplace. An individual's career was destabilized as they fluctuated between employment and unemployment, or regular and non-regular work. In this situation, individuals cannot help but internalize the values of competition, efficiency and self-development required by neoliberalism in order to survive. As they put forth effort to make visible achievements, they tend to be evasive of exhaustive relationships which require time, money, energy or emotions. (Seoul Economic Daily, 2016) We can usually observe this pattern in youth. As youth are forced with competition and continued failure, their self-esteem is lowered and anxiety is increased. In this situation, youth tend to have difficulty communicating with others and over time isolate themselves from the society.

The mechanism of "avoidant individualization" can be described by the notion of "individualization without individualism" (Chang and Song, 2010). In the West where individualism has settled considerably, people can lean on their own philosophy and values to fill their loneliness. They care less about others and are independent from others' responses and opinions. As they respect each other's individuality, they do not place unnecessary interest towards each other and do not interfere nor evaluate others. Rather, they keep an adequate distance from each other, acknowledging difference of life and values. By establishing social norms and orders which overcome each other's difference, people can gain their liberty and freedom. However, when individualism has not taken root in society it can cause an "avoidant" individualization in two ways: first, individuals can interfere with others overtly and second, individuals remain sensitive to others' evaluations and responses (Kim, 2014). Where traditional community has dissolved and intimate relationship is weakened but individualism is not yet firmly established, people tend to get sensitive and anxious regarding external opinions. Therefore, people do not wish to exhaust themselves with feelings by communicating with others. Individuals choose to be indifferent to others except for a select few.

It is usually said that focusing on efficiency and cost-effectiveness is the trend of these days. Since people are having a hard time allocating their schedule to meet with others using their time, energy, and money, they tend to get easily disappointed in others. If there is something that is not compatible with others, people do not think about how to adjust but consider keeping a distance ... They say that even really close friends get in fight sometimes, and they do not really want to get stressed with those who are not that close to them. I think people say "alone, the better" in this kind of context. I understand that people can get exhausted from meetings and relationships and reach conclusions that "you have to live your life alone." (In-depth interview response from a graduate student in his 20s)

3. WEAKENING OF SOCIAL TIES AND ISOLATION OF INDIVIDUALS

(1) The Tragedy of Non-connected Society: Lonely Deaths[1]

As an individual lifestyle changes and social, technological basis that shapes human relationships are changing, previous strength of traditional communities are weakening. It seems that social ties are weakening by day, resulting in the dissolution of family and the increase of single person households. The most tragic byproduct of this change would be the increased solitary or lonely deaths. These kinds of deaths are commonly observed in Japan characterized as a "non-connected society." (NHK, 2010) Usually, lonely deaths refer to "dying alone without recognition by others" and deaths that "do not gain social attention for dying individuals are disconnected from family and neighbors" (Chung et al., 2010: 21).[3] In Japan, where the state was declared as a super-aged society in 2005, the elderly population and elderly single person households are increasing. As is often the case with the elderly living alone, they are isolated from other people and society, often leading to lonely deaths. They are usually tied to a lower income class or have a higher likelihood to be in poverty, have chronic diseases, have a harder time living independently and malnourished. Problems like lonely deaths are tied to increased number of nuclear families, older parents living separately from their married children, weakened family bonds or lack of attention paid to older senior family members.

People commonly assume lonely deaths happen to older people and those who do not have a family. However, recently there have been increased cases of deaths among people with family who have cut off ties back home, those who are homeless and those who have never married but living by themselves. Those who have never married in their lives were often envied and termed the "glorious single" in the past. More recently, they are receiving social attention and labeled "candidates of lonely deaths." (Memorial News, 2011) In Japan, four social factors are understood to have supported the increase of the unmarried: a single-friendly social infrastructure, increase of economically unstable non-regular workers, weakened norms that coerced marriage in the past and the increase of economic competency of women. Among these, the increase of non-regular work is regarded as the highest contributing factor. (NHK, 2010)

To add, the Japanese are quite likely to face death without even applying for welfare. They are skilled at internalizing problems and putting blame and responsibility on themselves in order to "not disturb others." (Fukushima, 2015) In fact, a NHK Non-Connected Society Project Team interviewing for lonely deaths commonly heard this phrase from single person households interviewed: "I don't want to be a burden." The team also witnessed many individuals stressing the true meaning of "responsibility for oneself." (NHK, 2010). To them, not faring for oneself was an unfathomable concept going as far as to say that "there are many elderly believing that it is better to die than become someone else's burden." (NHK, 2015).

Japan had already been using the term "lonely deaths" in 1970s. With the increased number of solitary deaths as a result of the 1995 Kobe Earthquake, many Japanese came to accept this new type of deaths. The problem was pinned as a social issue when an increase of lonely deaths occurred in the old rental apartment complex occupied by the elderly from the late 2000s. It is not easy to grasp the exact status of death in Japan, but number of deaths found in UR rental apartment has increased three-fold within a decade, from 207 deaths in 1999 to 613 deaths in 2008 (Lee, 2014). In 2011, it was reported that 15,603 elderly deaths were found four days after passing (Lee, 2013). NHK Non-Connected Society Project Team has also revealed that according to the survey administered by every local government in Japan, there are around 32,000 recorded lonely deaths (NHK, 2010) .

Korea doesn't seem to be very different from Japan as it experiences aging and increase of single person households, but there is no exact data on lonely deaths. According to a journalist's report, the number of lonely deaths recorded is constantly increasing: 587 in 2009, 636 in 2010, 727 in 2011 and 1,245 in 2015. Among the deaths in 2011, those over age 60 accounted for 47.7% and those below 60 accounted for 48.6%. (The Financial News, 2013) In 2015, those over 65 accounted for 31% totaling 385 deaths. Since Korea's birth rate is even lower than Japan, a state recognized as a super-aged country, and since there are increasing cases of non-marriage and late marriage, lonely deaths is expected to increase. Seoul statistics in 2013 reported 162 actual cases and 2,181 suspected cases of lonely deaths. A group recognized to be in potential danger of a lonely death is male single person households aged 40 to 64 who are disconnected from others and have chronic diseases. (Seoul Welfare Foundation, 2016)

(2) Social Network and Support Network

Figures 7-1 and 7-2 show the results of how people in three countries and three cities live their daily lives creating network and making interactions. Figure 7-1 shows the number of family or relatives people usually interact with. The response "0 person," which is closely related with lonely deaths, in country level, is high in order from Japan (29.6%), China (20.1%) and Korea (14.0%). In city level, from highest in order is 30.9% for Tokyo, 28.4% in Shanghai and 10.7% for Seoul. We can assume that in Japan, where lonely deaths occur the

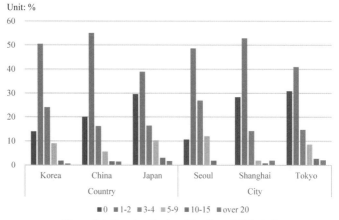

Figure 7-1: Regular Contact (Family and Relative)
Source: East Asia Social Survey Data Archive (2012)

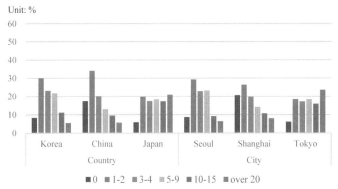

Figure 7-2: Regular Contact (Friend and Neighbor)
Source: East Asia Social Survey Data Archive(2012)

most, disconnectedness between people are most prevalent. Figure 7-2 shows the respondent's answers to number of people other than family or relatives that they label as friends or neighbors. The response "0" is the lowest in Japan (5.9%) and in Tokyo (6.1%). Also, there seems to be an equal distribution for narrow network and wide network. Response "0" is the highest in China (17.7%) and in Shanghai (20.7%), where there is much more narrow network than wide network.

Meanwhile, in OECD's "Better Life Index," looking into social support sector which refers to community, Korea is ranked the lowest and Japan is ranked in the middle-tier. For the question "are there any relatives, friends, or neighbors who you can reach out for help when you are in crisis?" the OECD average for "yes" was 88% in 2015. Meanwhile, Korean response was recorded to be lowest at 72% and Japan ranked around 20th at 89%. This pattern didn't change much in the consecutive year. In 2016, there has been an increase in the positive answer for Korea with the percentage at 76% but this did not affect the ranking. For Japan, there was a steep percentage increase to 91% accompanied by a rank change. It is interesting to note that in Western countries scoring high on individualism and number of single person households, social support ranking was much higher.

Table 7-2: Social Support Among OECD Countries

Unit: %

year	Korea	Japan	USA	Finland	Sweden	German	France	OECD Mean
2013	77	90	90	92	92	92	93	90
2014	77	90	90	93	91	93	91	89
2015	72	89	90	95	92	94	87	88
2016	76	91	90	94	92	92	89	88

Source: http://www.oecdbetterlifeindex.org

4. THE TRANSITION IN SOCIAL TIES AS SEEN BY THOSE EATING ALONE

(1) Eating Alone: The Symbol of Individualization

Putnam, in his book *Bowling Alone* (2000) demonstrates community decline with this example: bowling population is increasing but bowling league is decreasing. He contends that social capital has generally decreased with the decline of American communities. Here, social capital means "the reciprocity and trust that occurs through connections between individuals, or social network." He outlines four factors that contributed to the decline: first, the pressure of time and money from overworking; second, the expansion of residence to suburban areas and the expansion of cities; third, digitalized entertainment medium especially television that made leisure time available for people who are alone, and fourth, the change in generation. The reason why *Bowling Alone* has gained so much attention is because people acknowledge that it is social capital that enables social participation as a citizen and social capital that can affect all life areas and quality living.

Bowling Alone illustrates an aspect of how contemporary people spend their leisure time—drinking alone, watching movies alone or traveling alone. As Putnam pointed out, those who live alone in the United States are called "cocoons," staying at home to not interact with others and also engaging in activities like shopping and culture alone and at home. Those who live alone in Korea are a little bit different. They are individuals looking for relaxation and stability, enjoying their time alone but also participating in social activities (Segye Ilbo, 2009). These individuals see the advantage of being alone as "getting away from others' control and interference," "to enjoy freedom to achieve according to their own choices" and "effectively manage time by not interfering with others' time as well as not getting interfered with their time (Kim, 2014)."

It is worthwhile to see what kind of meaning "eating alone" entails, for eating is not a leisurely activity like bowling per se but it is related to survival. In Japan, eating alone doesn't receive much attention since it has already become a common practice. However, in Korea, it is gaining attention as a new social phenomenon, due to the rapid exposure of this phenomenon in news articles and TV programs. A TV show that follows daily lives of single person households emerged in Korea. Then, a scene in a popular drama demonstrated younger generation's relationships and highlighted how they were drinking alone. A TV program that airs live someone eating alone is also gaining popularity. For a long time, being alone was regarded as out of the norm or an "incomplete status," tied to maladjustment to society. However, more recently, it is regarded and labeled as "freedom," "convenience" and as "power rooted in an individual." For instance, Saito Takashi (2005) claims that "time alone makes individuals strong like a diamond," emphasizing that "those who are swayed like a reed by relationships will be swayed by others' standards for their lifetime."

(2) Eating Alone Versus Eating Together

The Korean definition of family (食口) originates from family practice of eating, grouped around a table. In the national institute of the Korean language dictionary, family is defined as "people living and eating together." Family members would return home before dinner in order to eat together and if a member was late, other members would wait. However, the traditional term has decreased in use with the increase of single person households and increased cases of eating alone (Han, 2016). Korea's greetings unlike other countries, gives importance to the act of eating. "Did you eat?" "Let's eat together sometimes" are common ways to greet each other. These greetings are understood as expressions of interest and in different contexts be interpreted as sympathy or celebration. There is also a common expression "I have no appetite" used to describe a person who one does not wish to meet again. Like this, a meal means more than just a meal in Korea. This context seems to have originated from the past when people suffered from malnourishment and poverty. However, as people come out of poverty, the importance of meals can change; meals can become merely a daily routine, sometimes even an annoying one.

I think eating is one of annoyances in daily living. It is something to be finished quick. When I encounter situations where I have to have a meal while being alone, I just wish for a pill that can give me complete nutrition and satiety at the same time, or wish that the menu I want to be available right away. It is really annoying to find a restaurant to go eat at... (In-

depth interview response from a college student in her 20s)

The reason why we are focusing on the phenomenon of eating alone is that eating has traditionally been regarded as a way to build social connection and as a channel to build intimacy with people, more than just an act of survival. As an individual, if you belong to a certain social group, you experience a lot of "eating together" to be intimate with others. Unlike some foreign companies where parties are occasional events, Korean companies make frequent gatherings just to eat together and hold celebration parties for new members and leaving members. Eating together gives special connection in Korean society. Dining occasions are regarded to be places to update life news and share information. (Prime NEWS, 2016) Therefore, those who eat alone are considered as loners who are not part of any group or who have no close friends. However, people from a younger generation who practice eating alone believe that eating together is not the sole method to interact with others and emphasize that "there are other chances to get close with others".

> *Of course, you can build ties with others by eating together. However, these days, there are a lot of methods or opportunities to interact with others, so the choice to build ties by eating together has been decreasing, I think so. We can still connect with each other by Kakaotalk or Facebook although we do not directly meet with each other, and there are various places people can culturally communicate with each other ...* (Survey response from a graduate student in her 20s)
>
> *(Q: What is the meaning of eating together in making social ties?) Not much meaning. For example, I have two friends who are really close to me. But I haven't eaten any meal with them. Maybe we are too busy. However, I do not believe that our intimacy has decreased whatsoever. Of course, if we do not eat together for a long time, we can get a little bit disconnected ... but if we manage to meet, we can recover our relationships quickly. Also, we contact each other via social media.* (In-depth interview response from a college student in his 20s)

In Japan, there are many people eating alone, both students and workers. For most, they are unconcerned about what others are thinking. The Bento culture is well developed, and there are various types of single customer-friendly restaurants, counter-seats and split-the-bill culture, making it easy for individuals to enjoy their meals comfortably. Also, it is understood in Japanese culture that people do not give much meaning to a meal except for special anniversaries or conferences and there exists no common understanding that people should eat together like in Korea.

As far as solitude eating goes, Chinese culture is more similar to Korea than Japan. In China, the act of eating together is at the center of culture so it is considered a social taboo to eat alone (The Wall Street Journal, 2014). When people in China are in a situation where they cannot help but eat alone, they would take it home or to a dormitory to eat in private. This is because people consider the situation as something to feel sad about (SK Telecom Campus Report, 2014). Also, if people are out and about alone, bypassers would consider them to be loners without friends and consider them to be problematic. However, if we look at the large amount of people moving to cities and the rapid increase of single person households, there are already a lot of people dining alone and their numbers are expected to rise in China.

5. EATING ALONE: ORIGIN AND TYPES

(1) The State of Eating Alone: Why Do People Eat Alone?

In Japan, the culture of eating alone has already existed for some time becoming more visible by single customer seatings and areas installed in public places . Infrastructure that reinforce this culture include restaurants and cafes with single seats, restaurant dishes available for single serving, rich bento culture and DVD customized for people eating alone. In Japan, the culture of eating alone seems to have become widespread from the 1990s with the crash of the bubble economy. As aggressive competition deteriorated life quality and traditional communities, more people started to eat alone. From 2000, the limitations and side effects of Japanese economy have become visible and created gaps in social areas. One of these visible gaps was between social classes: the weakened economy increased social isolation of non-regular workers, the youth and the elderly. At work, opportunities to eat together to connect with colleagues sharply decreased, as colleagues felt pressured by the increased competition.

If we look at the numbers of those eating alone in Japan, half of adults have reported they are eating alone, and among them, 60% of men below 40 were found to eat alone (HanKyung Business Magazine, 2011). 68.8% of single person households responded that they are accustomed to the culture of eating alone. Also, 28.6% of undergraduate students in Japan reported that they eat lunch alone. Notably, 84% of female students eat alone and among them, 21%

eat alone one to three times a week. For reasons on eating alone, possible responses and percentage of responses were as following: "I can eat comfortably" (62%), "I can eat whenever I want" (46.7%), "it is stable" (37.4%), "I can eat whatever I want" (37.1%) and "I can slowly enjoy the meal" (35.8%). In a survey comparing the culture of eating alone between Japan and Korea (Cho et al., 2015), it was found that people assigned eating alone in Japan with various meanings including "freedom" (34.9%), "busy" (22.4%) and "lonely" (21.4%). However, people in Korea majorly associated eating alone with the word "lonely" (55.5%). Further, in Korea, people prefer eating together to eating alone, and they eat more heartily with more variety in food when they eat together, which is not often the case in Japan. Overall, the Japanese are already accustomed to eating alone and they are able to freely choose to dine alone or with people according to their situations.

The analytic interest in eating alone in Korea is mainly focused on youth. On reasons to eating alone, college students have chosen both reasons that they have or don't have control over including— "it is convenient" (23.9%), "I can cut down on dining budget" (13.9%), "I can cut down on dining time" (12.3%), "I cannot match my schedules to others"(21.7%) and "I live alone" (21.6%) (News Wire, 2014). Another survey on college students show "hard to control schedule" (47.8%), "saving time" (16.8%) and "to eat freely" (14.7%) as main reasons for eating alone. Meanwhile, the reasons for eating alone selected by the working population differs according to age groups: the highest response among the twenties was to "want to eat in comfort" (24.2%); among the thirties the response "due to a hard time in finding someone to eat together" (38.7%); among the forties, "having no time to spare" (29.2%); and among the fifties, "due to a hard time in finding someone to eat together" (37.9%) (Kyunhyang Shinmum, 2016).

There are some claims that eating alone is inconvenient due to other people's gazes. However, people do not care about the social pressure depending on specific contexts. The context includes the rising trend of people eating alone and enjoying it. Often when people eat alone, they tend to hold their smartphones. People find it boring if they are not watching their screen while eating. Smartphones and internet messenger applications have made eating alone much easier. While eating, people would watch movies on computers, stream YouTube on smartphones, chat with friends or family and upload their food pictures on social media to exchange comments with others. People do not feel that they are alone being connected together with someone online. The loneliness and boredom they may feel caused by the lack of a physical companion can be offset with online interactions.

(2) Types of Eating Alone: Same on the Surface but Different Inside

We can now look into in what kind of situations people eat alone and how people feel in such situations. According to an internet survey looking into people's experience and perception of eating alone, we can categorize the act of eating alone into three types. First is the act of eating alone due to lack of choice, which can be expressed with the term "lonely eating." (Jun, 2014) People in this category are usually single person households, notably the elderly population living alone. Middle-aged men living alone due to dissolved families or due to other circumstances are also included in this category. Also, as people started embracing the recent trend of valuing the present over the future and delaying marriage due to socioeconomic hardships, single person households have sharply increased even among the youth. To add, living alone has become a part of city-living unlike in the past when it used to be a transient way of living before marriage. Single person households, namely those who practice eating alone due to structural reasons, have learned to accept the act of eating alone. Convenience stores become the best place these individuals can eat by themselves without getting attention. The considerate indifference shown in convenience stores get reinforced into social norms. Due to this anonymity, individuals can enjoy a meal by themselves (Jun, 2014: 135).

Within this context, people in Korea are eating a lot of meals alone. According to the Statistics Korea (KOSTAT), the population of single person households account for 27.2% of the population or 5.2 million in 2015, about a 3.3% increase from 23.9% in 2010. Moreover, the ratio of SPHs is spread out among all age groups: 17% among 20s, 18.3% among 30s, 16.3% among 40s, 16.9% among 50s, 12.8% among 60s and 17.5% among ages 70 and above. An analysis on Korea's future population projected SPH population to increase up to 34.3% by 2035. One third of the state's population is already eating alone and the proportion will continue to climb.

After my military service, I lived alone. The living expenses were more expensive than I thought, and people I used to eat together have all dispersed so I began to refrain from eating outside. When I first started to live alone, I made food in my home or ordered delivery; gradually, I began to buy simple meals, or just ate alone at restaurants. I began to find simple ready-to-eat products which were both cheap and well made. Paris Baguette, the school cafeteria, Salady's salad, or packaged food in conve-

nience stores became my main source of food. All those food are quite good in value and nutrition. (In-depth interview response from a college student B in his 20s)

In Japan, where practice of eating alone has existed for some time, a "social structure of eating alone" has been deeply engrained in Japanese lives. In 2000s, a Japanese exchange student living in Korea has remarked on how hard it was for her to live in Korea since most of the restaurants and cafes were designed to serve more than one person (Fukushima, 2015). What she experienced in Korea was different from the houses, restaurants and even karaokes in Japan that was convenient for single person use. China has also reported a high increase in single person households: it was 16.1% of the total population in 2014, a steep increase from the 6.3% in the 1990s and projected to increase up to 100 million in 2025. With the increase of SPHs, the number of people eating alone will also increase exponentially.

The second type of eating alone is those who happened to eat alone: it includes those who happened to be alone when meal time came or those who missed the proper time to eat. They eat alone when they attend school courses alone, work alone, on a business trip, working overtime or working during holidays or weekends. This could also be termed "contingent eating alone." It happens when people are unable to match their schedule to eat with others. When you are alone, it is sometimes a lot of work to call others to eat. If there were no prior lunch or dinner engagement and meal time approaches, it becomes hard to reach out to others. This behavior reflects the flexible and irregular lifestyles of contemporary human beings. In this society, time management is considered as a practice that leads to economic profit. People are encouraged to work busy hours. Therefore, people often eat at irregular times and it is hard to match eating schedule with others.

I began to eat alone much more this semester. Last semester, I often rested together with my friends but our time tables are quite different this semester. Of course I have some friends in the same class but I am not that close to them and it is awkward to eat together with them. So after class, I just walk out of the classroom alone and my close friends might still be in another classroom. it just became natural to eat alone. (In-depth interview response from a college student A in his 20s)

The pattern of eating alone gets repeated in daily life and people get accus-

A dining area in one of Korea's restaurants where diners can enjoy a meal in private after the server brings out food.

tomed to eating alone. Many begin to think that the purpose of eating is to do work and no longer consider the gaze of other people by thinking, 'why do I need to care when I am paying to eat a good meal.' They no longer feel the stigma of eating alone. Rather, it is more of the inconvenience when they have to use a four-person table to eat alone or they feel like the restaurant owner is not welcoming.

The third type of eating alone is "eating alone to avoid others." This type of eating alone should not be associated with bad social relationships. It often happens among youth for instance. They would say, "I prefer eating alone to eating with others" or "I don't like to eat with people I don't especially like." This type of people gain the interest and concern from the media. However, the reason for their preference for eating alone is very straightforward. The idea behind it is to avoid sharing details of lives with people who they don't feel comfortable or close with. It can also be seen as a defense mechanism against the backdrop of a flexible labor market and unstable employment where individuals internalize competition, efficiency, results over process and self-development. The modern version of fierce competition is detailed as something that "persists, from the time morning alarms sounds to when people return to bed, and from birth to death (Kohn, 1986)." People living in such an atmosphere often question meaning of their existence and live with constant anxiety and stress.

Students who are pressured to earn academic credits and build their resumes and workers suffering from stress and fatigue eventually experience what is called an "emotional hunger" (Park and Cheon, 2012). As a method to appease themselves from this emotional hunger, people choose to be alone. This context is well expressed by the lines of a female actor in a popular Korean TV drama. A scene of the drama shows a woman drinking beer alone under the parasol of a convenience store. She speaks to herself, "there's so little who can truly empathize with me. Drinking beer alone is better consolation." As the scene portrays, modern people eat alone to enjoy their free moments, to not be bothered by people and to eat what they want at their own pace.

> *I ate lunch and dinner alone today. At lunch, I was too busy to call someone to eat together and talk. For dinner, I wanted to eat something special but the location was outside the campus… so it was inconvenient for me to find someone to go outside the campus with. I think about nothing when I eat alone. When I'm eating with someone and talking, I feel my brain working…sometimes I have too much things going on in my head and I just want to dive deeper into work…* (In-depth interview response from a graduate student in her 20s)

We can also find people eating alone to evade stress and fatigue caused by human relationships. These people would remark: "my work often requires me to talk with people, so I just want to have alone time" (Herald Business, 2016) or "I am sick and tired of relationships, so I just want to stay alone." (Anonymous Theqoo, 2016) They have memories of being tired by caring for close ones or just by sharing relationships. They also do not want the negative effects from the relationships, deciding to minimize human interactions and spend more time by themselves. In that sense, the drive to be alone seems to be an instinct to survive in a competitive and complex society. Low self-esteem and damaged relationships encourage people to isolate themselves (Seoul Economic Daily, 2016).

> *We are often demanded to be a "sensible new employee," or a "sensible younger member of the group." For example, we are expected to think of good restaurants to suggest to the group beforehand, set spoons and chopsticks, ask for refills of side dishes […] Beyond the level of being polite, we have to be aware of what's going on in this world, have to entertain, and have to complement older workers. If we do not, seniors at work will com-*

plain or scold us. My friends who eat alone are willing to eat together with close friends but they tend to refrain from eating with seniors. For those eating alone, they especially do not want to go to the drinking party where there is strict hierarchy. (In-depth interview response from a graduate student in his 20s)

We have to think about what "relationship" means to each generation. For people, even relationship is "something to put on paper or a beneficial tool to survive the competitive society. Namely, people tend to find efficiency even in relationships. Efficiency here means, how we can be more effective in pursuing success. That can be everything. Examples include students with high credits, people with parents who are doctors or professors, those who studied abroad, or those who live in Gangnam [...] (In-depth interview response from a graduate student B in her 20s)

6. SOCIAL REACTION AND POLICY CONSIDERATION IN REGARDS TO INDIVIDUALISM

(1) Reinforcing Social Ties by Revitalizing Neighborhood Community

Among social ties, neighborhood relationships can provide similar levels of social support as provided by family and friends. It is different from other social ties in that interactions include ties to residential area. Interaction with neighbors is different in that people share a common residence space and interactions are not always intentional. Historically, a neighborhood network used to be limited and narrow but in modern society, people can run into new people much easily. However, today's reality shows people distancing from each other in their own neighborhood, reluctant to reach out a helping hand or getting into frequent arguments regarding noise levels or parking space.

The "neighborhood effect" associating neighborhood proximity with academic performance, deviant behaviors, crime, health, and social and political participation, has been noted in many studies. Notably, with mass migration of people to cities and increased construction of apartment complexes from the 1970s, neighborhoods has served to provide social resources. Shared communication and resources among residents serve as an important axis of a personal community (Lim, 2015). The importance of neighborhood community has persisted in daily lives and is not expected to vanish during the digital age (Jo and Kang, 2015).

Recently, the neighborhood community is considered to serve as an important mechanism to solve various social issues in cities and to help foster qualify lives. There have been many policy efforts to utilize such social ties (Byun, 2011; Chae, 2014). For example, "Village Making" is a project in Korea where residents are encouraged to point out and solve community problems. The goal of "Village Corporation" is to create workplace and income by using the special resources within the community. There is an emphasis placed on community redevelopment beyond the previous methods in focusing development efforts on places showing physical deterioration. Community, as a place where people interact with neighbors, social spaces and social systems, is regaining in importance. If improving physical conditions of buildings and city structures is considered to be urban redevelopment, then urban regeneration would be enhancing social, environmental and economical conditions of shared places so people would start to gather together and experience enhanced quality in their lives.

Meanwhile, in Japan, where society has already been experiencing social disconnectedness, policies to target and reduce lonely deaths have been in place since the 1970s. The state placed priority in reinforcing the role of the regional society. This was because in the past, when regional communities had maintained their social function, some of the lonely deaths were effectively prevented. The "Lonely Death Prevention Project" launched by the Ministry of Health, Labor and Welfare in 2007 focused on the reasons behind lonely deaths. Some of the reasons that were associated with the deaths were having no relatives, being unemployed and having no interactions with others especially with neighbors. The next project called the "Zero Lonely Death Project" suggested building of communities that can prevent future lonely deaths. The project restored the social network of regional communities. It also created a system where one volunteer and five nearby single person households created an accountability group. This social support network made sure to prevent social isolation of single person households (Lee, 2013). Lastly, the project "Prevention and Early Discovery of Lonely Deaths" in Aichi-ken Aisai-si emphasized the relationship between close neighbors, as well as the importance of an administrative system. In major cities, under the guidance of Ikeda, Osaka and Nakano, Tokyo, plans to restore communities were executed. Steps included regional government restructuring, placement of professional experts and goals to regain social connectedness.

In China, as the welfare unit system weakened, communities were utilized to be a resident administrative system. The community encompasses social organization of the region belonging to an administrative area as well as the members who live in a specific area or region. Inside the community, residents enjoy a comparatively stable life and build lives with strong social ties, receiving social support from family, friends and neighbors. In China, the need for community first emerged with the demand for child and elderly care. Communities also provide basic social integration support for people with disabilities or immigrants. As the neighborhood provides positive effects through providing public order, social activities, and child and elderly care, as well as providing the members with a sense of belonging and identity, it is used as an important index for city development. With the recent rise of people moving to cities, not only is there importance placed on physical redevelopment of buildings and streets but emphasis placed on neighborhood building to combat social gaps, weakened relationships and problems tied to anonymity.

(2) Reorganization of Social Ties Through Flexible Networking

In modern days, unemployment is embedded structurally and unstable employment is expanding. The social ties have weakened compared to the past and people can only turn to themselves to receive care or support. In a society where goal planning for the future becomes impractical through prolonged instability, individuals live with continued risks and anxiety that follows. The youth are especially at risk living at the peak of anxiety and social pressure tied to harsh competition and unstable employment in society. Within this context, it seems that social relationships and group gathering amongst youth is deteriorating. However, we find that they are forming relationships in a new way. We can better observe this new relationship forming through examples of social dining and loose networking.

Unlike the worries of the older generation associating dining alone to unstable lifestyles, eating alone does not always isolate individuals or deteriorate social relationships. Frequently dining alone can indeed increase loneliness for people. People feeling lonely or due to various reasons miss out on regular meals with friends and families make effort to participate in social meal gatherings. The initiative of social dining is for people to voluntarily gather with people they find through smartphone applications and dine together with strangers. It is a new form of relationship-making in that people with similar interests who are strangers eat together and form new connections. Although it may be initially awkward to eat together with strangers most people share their stories and maintain the initial relationship by meeting up with the same people later.

For us, social dining is a platform for consolation, a haven we turn to where we temporarily deviate from the fixed way of life. The fragmented individuals isolated with their own problems can empathize with each other by dining together. (Bait, 2015)

Another form of relationship-making can be seen through gatherings based on common interests. Generally, these gatherings only focus on serving the original purpose of sharing common interests without considering the background of individuals such as what kind of jobs or educational degrees people have. Members do not ask private questions to each other but rather empathize with each other according to the purpose of the gathering. These gatherings do not require people to participate in a small, unofficial party after gathering either. Even if there was a party, it will be light conversations with some snacking or drinking of tea. The border between joining and exiting these social gatherings is blurred. It is a form of loose networking where people participate and break off voluntarily. These gatherings share the value of this generation: it is the value of privacy and not interfering with other people's lives.

Ironically, the stress I receive from these gatherings are much less than what I receive when I meet my family. I don't have to rebrand myself as a "good person." It is actually easy to show my weak side to those who I don't know well. During gatherings with relatives, my exam results were compared with my cousins. They were also asking me when I was going to marry. This is not pleasant. However, here, nobody asks me or pushes me to do anything. (The Chosun Daily News, 2016)

The loose networking based on shared interests is also found in social media relationships. Individuals connected through social media are not organized into a physical gathering in reality. These people prefer to build ties as Facebook friends rather than becoming friends in real life. When people view potential friends through such platforms, although they have limited background knowledge of the person, they choose to connect with certain individuals based on their values and common interest shown though posts, pictures and comments. Although there are some drawbacks to this relationship—the relationship can be weakened or broken if the person isn't active on social media or one person decides to block the other person—most people do not think these limitations are problematic.

Somebody told me that I have no real friends but just a lot of Facebook friends. If "friend" means someone who I will miss when I can't meet up with that person and someone who I have fun with when we are together, then I guess I don't have many friends.. Facebook friends can be called friends too since they are people I have similar interests and values… I don't really have private friends, and I don't actually feel the need to have them. In the real world, I still like to be alone. Maybe I am living a life that would not be possible without the Internet. (Quoted from a Facebook from a male user in his 40s)

7. CONCLUSION

Many social issues have come up in the three East Asian mostly due to the rapid economic development and urbanization. In the major cities where population were rising, building infrastructures such as housing, streets, and public facilities were needed to provide quality living to the residents. These urbanization processes have impacted the lifestyle and social ties of people significantly. One of the core axis of this change was individualization. Individuals started to deviate from intermediary groups like family and class that had connected them to society to voluntarily choose and weigh the risks and opportunities in their lives. Individuals experienced a transition from a previous collective or group relationship to an individualized relationship.

The problem with this transition is the separation or atomization of individual. Individuals are forced to take responsibility and risk that accompanies unstable urban life that is not supported by social safety nets or support. The increase in lonely deaths in Japan and Korea, both countries where family life and community life mattered to a greater degree than the West, illustrates how individuals can be fragmented and isolated from society. The lonely deaths in this disconnected society is concentrated among the elderly who live by themselves. The elderly population is also associated with poverty and lack of social safety. Unlike the West where public welfare is already well developed and acts as a social safety net, the East Asian social safety net is no longer functioning at the same level as the past. This is because historically, family and companies have acted as a safety net to individuals. This calls for the need to develop an official state structure to help these individuals. But with the widespread individualization discourse on "each for oneself," public opinion on welfare spending is not measuring up.

If we approach this matter as individuals choosing their life courses, it can be seen as the spread of individualism from the previous hierarchy and control rooted in family and class. Due to the digital revolution, now anyone can enjoy privacy with individualized mediums including computers, mobile phones and other online devices. What matters here is that the unit of privacy is not based on male heads of households alone but now includes women and the youth. Through virtual spaces created by the information media, cultural autonomy of women and youth was made possible. Because male heads of households were historically more authoritarian and patriarchal, individualization of women and youth emerge as core individuals within the trend of individualism (Hong, 2015: 153-154) .

From such perspective, contemporary individualization is the process where individuals deviate from the old social system to find freedom and regulate and reconvene with each other as new individuals. Here, individualism is connected to the diversification of values. The different value sets settle in: they are the diverse opinions of different individuals, groups and places. Therefore, to conclude the act of eating meals alone as a bypass of a competitive society or a display of egoism by the youth is showing only a limited side. It is only reflective of the concerns of the people from the older generation who are traditional and believe collective relationship to be the standard. The behavior of being alone should be considered as an act of coming to self-realization as the new subject responds to the change of society. Also, in a network society based on a myriad of connections, people are ceaselessly communicating with virtual friends. These people question the conventional belief that one should have many friends and be social—they rather believe that what truly matters is the quality of connection shared. People with such values praise Japanese culture where people do not interfere with other people's lives.

> *Some people think being alone is negative. They are concerned about getting lonely, and view people who are alone as lacking skills to maintain social relationships. However, the most important thing for me is to control my loneliness inside and to cope with my time alone. You can have a good relationship with others only if you can have a good relationship with yourself.* (Kyunghyang Weekly Magazine, 2016)

Those who live alone, especially the youth, are not evading all relationships. They are rather evading hierarchical and socially burdening relationships. They are adept at eating alone, drinking alone and now playing alone. This doesn't mean they do not want to meet up with anyone. Also, in order to live together with others, it is important to have experienced being alone. Everyone needs to learn to lead their own lives before living in a group (Hong and Kim, 2016: 68). It is important that an individual learn to be fully independent before joining a community.

On the other hand, for all people are social animals, they endeavor to keep relationships with each other despite the spread of individualism. There have been efforts to combat lonely deaths by reinforcing the function of neighborhood relationships and regional communities. People have also started forming new relationships through non-traditional methods to share common interests. Traditional types of gathering and relationship may have decreased but new types of "loose relationships" are increasing. As mentioned previously, those who are used to eating alone will make initiative to gather and have social dining when they feel lonely. The loose network based on common interest has been spreading through social media and other online platforms. These types of loose organization based on weak social ties may go beyond the collective society and create "bridging social capital" (Putnam, 2000).

There have been cases where social dining meet-ups have turned into a long-term relationship like sharing of houses. A shared house is a form of living arrangement chosen by mostly the young who do not like living alone but wish to find someone other than family to live with. The shared house which is already a popular trend in Japan is now starting to take root in Korea. Unlike renting out one of the rooms in your house, a shared house way of living is reflective of the individualized lifestyles of today's era. Considering the fact that living in a shared house is not the most affordable option, we can understand this trend as a statement made by the individuals in opposing the old ways of living and embracing new ways of forming relationships. Some Japanese youth choose to live in a shared house as an alternative to living with family. Some choose to voluntarily live in a shared space with strangers. We can envision a future where communities can be rebuilt based on such new ideals and trends (Fukushima, 2015).

NOTE

1   There are other terms like "no-relationship death," "solitary death," and "isolated death" in addition to "lonely death." Since there is no commonly agreed term for this social phenomenon, we are using the more commonly used term "lonely death."

REFERENCES

Anonymous Theqoo. *Enjoying "Solo Culture" in Style..Dining Alone, Watching Movies Alone, Drinking Alone, Singing Alone.* March 8, 2016. Available at: http://theqoo.net/

Bait. *Social Dining Generation: Shall We Dine Together?.* April 28, 2015.

Beck, Ulrich. (1986). *Risk Society: Towards a New Modernity (Risikogesellschaft: Auf dem Weg in eine andere Moderne).* Frankfurt am Main: Suhrkamp Verlag. Translated in Korean by Hong, Seong-Tae, 1997. Seoul: Saemulgyul.

Byun, Miree. (2011). *Community Empowerment for Social Integration.* The Seoul Institute.

Caldera Sánchez, Aida and Andrews, Dan. (2011). To Move or Not to Move: What Drives Residential Mobility Rates in the OECD?. *OECD Economics Department Working Papers*, No. 846. Available at: http://www.oecd- ilibrary.org/economics/to-move-or-not-to-move-what-drives-residential-mobility-rates-in-the-oecd_5kghtc7kzx21-en

Chae, Jongheon et al. (2014). *A Promotional Plan for Social Cohesion Through Community Revitalization.* Korea Institute of Public Administration.

Chang, Kyung Sup. (2011). Developmental State, Welfare State, Risk Family: Developmental Liberalism and Social Reproduction Crisis in South Korea. *Korean Association of Social Policy*, 18(3), 63-90.

Chang, Kyung-Sup and Min-Young Song. (2010). The Stranded Individualizer under Compressed Modernity: South Korean Women in Individualization without Individualism. *British Journal of Sociology*, 61(3), 539-564.

Cho, Wookyoun et al., (2015). Perceptions and Practices of Commensality and Solo-eating among Korean and Japanese University Students: A Crosscultural Analysis. *Nutrition Research and Practice*, Vol.9, No.5, 523-529.

Chung, Soondool and Lim, Hyo-Yeon. (2010). Lonely Deaths Among the Elderly: Comparison Between Japan and Korea. *Lonely Death Forum Archives*, 21-44.

Chung, Jae Eun. (2007). Accumulative Process of Social Capital at the Upper Class' Apartment Complex in a Korean Metropolitan City. Master's Thesis, The Graduate School of Yonsei University.

East Asia Social Survey Data Archive. (2012). *Social Capital Module.* Available at: http://www.eassda.org/modules/doc/index.php?doc=intro

Fischer, Claude S. (1982). *To Dwell Among Friends: Personal Networks in Town and City.* Chicago and London: University of Chicago Press.

14th SK Telecom Campus Reporter. *How People Look at Those Alone.* September 24, 2014.

Fukushima, Minori. (2015). *Quiet Transition: Space of possibilities opened by 3.11.* Seoul: Communebut.

Goffman, Erving. (1971). *Relations in Public: Microstudies of the public order.* London: Allen Lane.

Hankyung Business Magazine. *Japan: Increasing Solitude Dining- Captivate Solo Tribes..A New Business Model.* November, 2011.

Han Sung-woo. (2016). *The Language of Our Food.* Seoul: Across Books.

Herald Business. *What's Wrong With Being Alone 2: I Want To Be Alone. Please Get Out, Everyone.* Setember 1, 2016.

Hong, Chan-Sook. (2015). *The Two Sides of Individualization: Liberation and danger.* Seoul: SNU Press.

Hong, Hyun Jin and Kang, Minsu. (2016). *Village Manual for SPH.* Seoul: OhmyBook.

Jin, Phil-Soo. (2012). The Landscape of Korean Apartment Complex and "Nomadic" Culture in the City. *Journal of Modern Social Science*, 16, 1-26.

Jo, Yeonjeong and Kang, Jeonghan. (2015). *How did KakaoTalk Become a Community?.* Seoul: Dasan Books.

Jun, Sang-in. (2009). *Crazy for Apartments: Sociology of housing in modern Korea.* Seoul: Esoope Publishing

_____. (2014). *The Sociology on Convenience Store.* Seoul: Moonji Publishing.

Kang, Mina, et al. (2014). *Korea Housing Survey.* Ministry of Land, Transport and Maritime Affairs.

Kang, Se Wook. (2015). *Assessment Report on Employment Program for the Marginalized.* National Assembly Budget Office.

Kim, Chan-ho. (2014). *Humiliation: Emotional Sociology of Indignity and Dignity.* Seoul: Moonji Publishing.

Kim, Junghoon. (2015). Symptoms of New Politics Emerged from Ambivalent Individualization of South Korea. *Journal of Korean Social Trend and Perspective*, 94, 9-41.

Kim, Ju-Yeon. (2014). *Leisure Alone: Benefits of Solitude.* Master's Thesis, Konkuk University.

Kim, Myung Hwan. (2016). Dae-chi Dong, A Whirlwind of Winner-Take-All and Surviving Alone. In *Seoul Humanities*, Ryu, Bo Sun et al. Seoul: Changbi Publishers.

Kim, Seungwook. (2009). The Distortion of Urban Space and Memory in Modern Shanghai. *Korean Association for Studies of Modern Chinese History*, 41, 115-140.

Kohn, Alfie. (1986). *No Contest: The Case Against Competition.* Houghton: Mifflin and Company. Translated in Korean by Lee, Young Noh, 2009. Goyang: Sannun.

Kyunghyang Shinmun. *Sociology of Housing, Ambition Inside Us, 9 Out of 10 Remark That Real Estate Agencies Are Increasing the Gap Between the Wealthy and the Poor.* April 13, 2010.

_____. *The 20s Dining Alone..They Select "To Relax" as Main Reason.* May 29, 2016.

Lee, Eungchel. (2012). Memory, Oblivion, Identity and Placeness: Cultural Meanings of Huaihai Road, Shanghai, China. *Journal of Asia-Pacific Studies*, 19(2), 41-68.

Lee, Jin Ah. (2013). An Exploratory Study on Prevention and Countermeasure Against Dying Alone Based on Japan's Experience. *The Research Institute of Social Sciences*, 37(1), 63-86.

Lee, Miae. (2014). *Problem of Japan's Aging Society and Funeral Procedures: how community problems are becoming individual problems.* Seoul: Inmunsa.

Lee, Soon-Mi. (2014). Complex Process of Post-Modernity of Life Course and Dual Process Individualization and Familization: Focused on the Sequence Analysis of transition to Adulthood of 1944-1974 Birth Cohort. *Korean Journal of Sociology*, 48(2), 67-106.

Lee, Young Mee et al. (2015). Differences in Solo Eating Perceptions and Dietary Behaviors of University Students by Gender. *Journal of The Korean Dietetic Association*, 21(1), 57-71.

Lim, Chaeyoon. (2015). Changes in Community Participation and Distribution of Socioeconomic Statuses During Urbanization. Chang Dukjin et al. 2015. *Archeology of Compressed Development.* Seoul: Hanul Books.

Memorial News Korea. Facing an Era Where We Die Alone. *June 23, 2011.*

News Wire. *72% of College Students Say Dining Alone At Least One Meal A Day Saves Trouble.* March 27, 2014.

NHK Old-age Bankruptcy Production Team. (2015). *Old-age Bankruptcy: Nightmare of living a long life (Rōgo hasan: chōju to iu akumu).* Tokyo: Shinchosha. Translated in Korean by Kim, Jung Hwan, 2016. Seoul: Dasan Books.

NHK Non-Connected Society Production Team. (2010). *Non-Connected Society: A society where you live and die* alone (Muen Shakai: "Muenshi" sanman-nisennin no shōgeki). Tokyo: Bungei Shunjū. Translated in Korean by Kim, Bum Soo, 2012. Seoul: Yong5reum.

Nho, Myung Woo and Yun, Myong-Hee. (2008). *The Change of Relationships Among Individuals and Communities in Post-modernized Society.* Korea Information Strategy Development Institute.

Park, Chul-Hyun. (2015). Building Social Governance and Changing the Role of Regional Government in the Reform Era China: The Production of Space and the Knowledge in Developing

Pudong, Shanghai in the 1990s. *The Korean Association of Space and Environment Research*, 25(2), 115-152.

Park, In-Suk. (2013). *Apartment Korean Society.* Seoul: Hyeonamsa.

Park, Ji Nam and Cheon, Hyejung. (2012). Leisure-Alone Folks: Their Experiences and Meaning. *Journal of Leisure*, 10(2), 87-105.

Prime NEWS. *Grief of "Single Servings".* June 8, 2016.

Putnam, Robert D. (2000). *Bowling Alone: The collapse and revival of American community.* New York: Simon & Schuster.

Saito, Takashi. (2005). *The Strength of Time Spent Alone (Kodoku no Chikara).* Tokyo: PARCO Syuppan. Translated in Korean by Jang, Eun Joo, 2015. Seoul: Wisdom House.

Sampson, Robert. J. (2012). *Great American City: Chicago and the Enduring Neighborhood Effect.* Chicago and London: University of Chicago Press.

Segye Ilbo. *Solo Tribes are "Valued Individuals" for Performance Arts Market.* Setember 1, 2009.

Seoul Economic Daily. *Solo Youths Seek Consolation From Closed Spaces, Lowered Self-esteem from Continued Failure.* June 17, 2016.

_____. Increasing Number of Solo Youths Struggling to Find Work. June 5, 2016.

Seoul Welfare Foundation. (2016). *Welfare Issue Today,* Vol. 42.

Shim, Young-Hee. (2011). In Search of Community Family Model of the 21st Century: From the Perspective of the Second Modernity and Individualization Theory. *Research Institute of Asian Women*, 50(2), 7-44.

_____. (2013). Two Types of Individualization: Focusing on "Family-centered Survival Type" and "Twilight and Domestic Divorce Type". *Korean Society for Social Theory*, 23, 277-312.

Shim, Young-Hee and Han, Sang-Jin. (2010). "Family-Oriented Individualization" and Second Modernity: An Analysis of Transnational Marriages in Korea. *Sozialie Welt*, 61(4), 237-255.

Suzuki, Munenori, et al., (2010). Individualizing Japan: Searching for its Origin in First Modernity. *British Journal of Sociology*, 61(3), 513-538.

The Chosun Ilbo. *It is Easier to Not Know People's Age or Work. A "Loose Meet-up" for People Who Are Tired of People: Share Activities and Part Ways.* July 2, 2016.

The Financial News. October 13, 2013.

The Kyunghwang Shinmun. *Is 'Alone' and "Loneliness' a Trend?.* March 1, 2016.

The Wall Street Journal. *Breaking Taboos: Chinese Diners Learn, Slowly, to Eat Alone.* October 17, 2014.

Uchida, Tatsuru. (2008). *Talent of Not Being Able to Live Alone: How the weak survive in a risk society (Hitori Dewa Ikirarenai no mo Gei no Uchi).* Tokyo: Bungei Shunjū. Tranlsated in Korean by Kim, Kyoungwon, 2014. Seoul: BookBang.

Yan, Yunxiang. (2010). The Chinese Path to Individualization. *British Journal of Sociology*, 61(3), 489-512.

Zhang, Dunfu. (2014). The Commodification and Marketization of Housing and its Social Consequences in Urban China. *Korea Sociology Research*, 45-62.

8

Urban Policies That Challenge Urban Changes

Miree Byun
Daishiro Nomiya
Dunfu Zhang

1. EAST ASIAN METROPOLIS GROWTH AND CRISIS

Large cities of the twenty-first century expand into metropolises. East Asian cities, notably, are experiencing changes superseding that of just expansion; they are experiencing a "compressed development," a sped-up version of what happened over many decades in Western cities. These same patterns have emerged in Seoul, Tokyo and Shanghai—the capital cities of Korea, Japan and China.

To observe the trends in the tree cities, we can first look into the past development and transition of Tokyo metropolis and how they have led to the city's current state. Global companies and transnational businesses had already piled into Tokyo by the end of the twentieth-century. With the added rapid development of communication technology, Tokyo was already deep in the center of globalization. These developments have influenced the city structure of Tokyo. The expansion of global business in Tokyo have garnered new groups of people in the city. One might say in describing the city, "If you walk through the streets of Roppongi in Tokyo, you will run into people dressed in white collars and different colored suits called *Hiruzuzoku.*" The population of these groups of people increased in the city due to the escalating number of companies in broadcasting, media, finance and other businesses. These globetrotters do not limit their activities to Japan but move between cities flexibly (Shibata, 2007). All in all, Tokyo's identity and reputation have been cemented as one of rising global cities and the city continues to grow as a megalopolis.

In the mid-1990s, however, Tokyo received a huge impact from the bursting of its bubble economy. Due to bankruptcy of major companies, unemployment rates skyrocketed and even affected industries of the peripheral cities. The weakened economy of Japan eventually led to a national economic recession. The city was characterized by a continued low growth economy and an aging society where 20.4% of society were 65 and older in 2010. It has been projected that in 2025, one out of four Japanese will be older than 65, which is 25% of the society, and the young population 15 years and under would be less than 10% of the total population. To add, over 40% of those residing in Tokyo live alone and many choose to remain single. Tokyo's unmarried rate between the ages 25 and 34 have continuously climbed from 1975 and remains around 10% higher than the national average (Tokyo Metropolitan Government, 2015). This ratio represents the large amount of young workers who have moved to the city during the economic boom who have remained and aged with the city. With the declining rate of young people coming into the city and more elderly residing alone, the city has lost its past vitality.

Korea's capital city Seoul reveals yet another angle to global city problems. Seoul has been in the center of urbanization and economic development from the 1960s. The result was a booming growth over half the century and gaining of international recognition as a global city. Income levels increased many times over, a "my car" era was introduced and apartments became the main residential type for city dwellers. Lastly, with the growth of a strong middle class, "the miracle of the Han river" seemed to have come true for Seoul. However, in the mid-1990s, the economy that seemed infallible took a heavy blow and fell into the managing hands of the IMF. Seoul's economy was weakened considerably and the capital lost its past vigor and role in driving national economy. Seoul began to face new obstacles as it entered a low growth period. The compressed growth has revealed its many dark sides that had been hidden. Negative impacts have continued to weaken past and modern heritage of the city. The city has also moved away from its past lifestyle centered people and nature. People began to notice that economic development was not paired with an increased quality in life. Today, more people are starting to leave Seoul due to its lack of residential options apart from living in standardized apartments and increasing conflicts in urban renewal.

Starting off as a small town supported by an industry in fishing, Shanghai is recognized today as one of the most influential global cities. Shanghai's growth was mainly fed by the influx of migration of people coming from other cities in China and immigrants. Historically, modern Shanghai was formed from centuries of transformations that started from the 1842 Treaty of Nanjing. The developmental stages of Shanghai can be categorized into three stages: the period from mid-90s to mid-twentieth century, the "Mao era" and finally, the "Deng

Xiaoping era." Through these stages, Shanghai experienced a planned or controlled economy and an expansion of economy through reforms.

The city infrastructure between years 1842 and 1949 was heavily influenced
by the industrialization of the West and provided Shanghai residents with services necessary for modern lifestyles. The social structures also influenced pattern formation of activities and attitudes between the native-born and immigrants in the city. Relative to other cities, Shanghai's civil society developed in
the direction of promoting individual rights, freedom and equality over group
commonality. Therefore, the residents of the city were open to new ideas and
diversity in culture and alert to business opportunities. Those from other parts
of China, especially people from the north saw Shanghai residents as rational,
mild in nature and precise. Over time, people living in Shanghai continued to
value individual rights and roles through high individualistic agency and became highly practical. Within the city, the rich Chinese and foreigners resided
in upper quarters while lower quarters were inhabited by low-skilled laborers
and the unemployed. However, excluding the war times, people of different
nationalities from diverse backgrounds lived in harmony (Bickers and Wasserstrom, 1995).

During the Mao Zedong era, Shanghai developed into China's economic
center. The era pursued a planned economy under a unit system where each
detail of society was controlled. Under this system, every single step of life was
broken down into "units." Activities within national factories, schools and hospitals could also be interpreted as individual units. Since most activities were
understood as units, people within the same community became common members of the same unit. Both at work and outside of work, these members shared
time, space, tools and other commodities. This included sharing of passage-
ways, the restroom or the kitchen and even the faucet for water usage. As the
members of the unit became closer with time, they were more willing to cooperate with each other. Although this system reduced individual privacy, most
people were willing to sacrifice their privacy by choosing to embrace close relationships with members of the unit.

Economic reforms and expansion started in China with the opening of the
Deng Xiaoping era in 1978. Until the 1990s, national factories were either shut
down or near bankruptcy. With the start of the twenty-first century, development plans for Pudong and other cities were released by the central government
and within this planned economy, Shanghai held a pivotal position in its transition as a center for international economy, finance and trade. Following this
transition was a wave of people coming in from local Chinese provinces includ-

ing Anhui, Zhejiang, Jiangsu, Shandong, Jiangxi and Heilongjiang as well as immigrants from South Korea (hereinafter "Korea"), Japan, the United States, Germany and France among others. Most people migrated for the same reasons prior to 1949: they were looking for economic, work and even romantic opportunities in the city that will bring new prospects. The changed economic structure birthed millionaires and billionaires overnight. However, the structure also increased many times more those who are poor. The newly developed gated community started categorizing people into either high class or "regular" class. Unlike the Mao Zedong era, the gated community increased foreign neighbors and reduced the importance of apartments and lodgings designated and managed as units. People were distinguished by the ability or lack of ability to purchase these apartments and the solidarity that had once existed during the Mao Zedong era became no longer. What continues to exist in Shanghai is the widening segregation of social classes.

At slightly different times, the three Asian cities have faced transitions rooted in similar socioeconomic changes. A report by an international organization has contended that for the past half century the world has gone through a tremendous development but people's happiness levels have not increased nor their levels of trust in their states (Helliwell, Layard, and Sachs, 2012). This calls to question the act of basing social development on a nation's GDP. It also calls to question what goals global, state and city developments should target and what human-centered development entails.

Today's policies of Tokyo, Seoul and Shanghai rest on the reflections on the meaning of social development and "better life." Tokyo's social problems are mainly rooted in the weakened community caused by long-term economic slowdown in Tokyo. Seoul is also facing problems that have now surfaced and once shadowed by a compressed economic development. Seoul records the highest suicide rate and the lowest birth rate among OECD countries. Seoul residents also report low social trust. As a result, Seoul has transformed into a low trust society demanding high costs in maintaining social communities. These problems faced by the three cities pose as both a threat and a challenge to city planning. In order to recover economically as a coexisting and sustainable metropolises of East Asia, the governing bodies of the cities need to heavily invest themselves in policy formation and advocate for a new municipal paradigm. This chapter analyzes the three cities within this context; it will detail the various efforts and solutions recruited by the three cities as they face urban growth and accompanying complications.

2. RESPONDING TO COMMUNITY PROBLEMS: URBAN POLICIES

(1) Evolution of Japan's Policies for Community

Changes within local community took place in Japan ahead of Seoul. In Japan, neighborhood associations called *cho-naikai* founded on citizen participation, have existed regionally for decades. These associations were made up of members within the same neighborhoods and interactively fostered relationships and communication. During the war times, these associations protected communities from sudden attacks and acted as regional governing bodies within the state governance to take part in activities like collecting metals for production of war equipment. However, after the war, the general headquarters in charge of Japan's occupation policy discontinued the association from having a role as a local government (Yokomichi, 2009). As a result, it took another twenty years for Japan to introduce a new concept of a regional community geared toward enhancing the life quality of community residents.

In 1969, the National Lifestyle Council of Japan published a report titled, "Community- Revival of Humanity in Regional Life." This was a time when Japan was riding the wave of economic and population growth but also experiencing the breakdown of traditional local communities. Since this was a time when debates surrounding the concept of "community" was still ongoing, there was not yet an agreed community concept in Japan. The government was involved in this affair by supporting the reconstruction of community lifestyles. In time, the local community embraced conceptual units of family, former neighborhood associations and urban citizens to give provision for an enhanced life (Yokomichi, 2009). With the concept of a community well-established, the government spent the next years laying the foundation for policy building. A policy proposal was announced in 1971 describing government plans to build a "model community." Following the proposal, relevant policies were continuously introduced. Through various cultural events and environmental projects, the idea of a model community became a goal for local communities. Utilizing the new community centers, local residents contributed to local community development. In 1983, with the initiation of a state policy, 147 neighborhoods were selected for model community building. In 1990, 141 additional neighborhoods were selected. During the process, the traditional concept and importance of *cho-naikai* acting as role in restoring local communities was restored by the government. (Yamazaki, 2007: 83-86).

After the 1995 Hanshin-Awaji earthquake, efforts toward community restoration expanded further. This disastrous event reporting 50,000 casualties found that a greater survivability was recorded within communities with stronger ties. People started to acknowledge close-knit communities as a survival unit that can reduce damage coming from disasters. Strong communities took up important roles for *cho-naikai* and NGO activities (Yamamoto and Yuuta, 2013). The natural disaster provided an incentive to reevaluate *cho-naikai* as an important contributor to local communities as a non-government entity. Japan's first decade of the twenty-first century can be characterized by the coexistence of traditional *cho-naikai,* NGO and newly formed groups of the later twentieth-century, all under the umbrella of so-called local community (Yamamoto and Yuuta, 2013: 88-106).

(2) Local Community Development Projects in Tokyo

Relative to Japan in its entirety, Tokyo's local community efforts to strengthen local community ties have been lacking. Communities including the traditional *cho-naikai* set in the urban setting struggled to survive. The breakdown of Tokyo communities was especially escalated in late 1990s as urban residents migrated out and global white collar business workers took their spots in the 2000s. The foundation of the local communities was especially weakened in urban and business-centered neighborhoods. Tokyo residents were well aware of the negative effects of community breakdown including rise in crimes and reduced community-building and tried to turn back the negative effects. Efforts from community members continued until the end of the 1990s with little success.[1]

Tokyo needed a new way to rebuild their community effectively. In 2005, a research team in ministry of internal affairs and communications suggested including a new concept termed "new public" in community policies. This was an important attempt to introduce a new angle to problems related to local welfare policies. The "new public" highlighted the need for support from the local government, central government and other organizations to provide public services in response to Tokyo's social problems rooted in low birth rate and aging population. For it to be successful, the "new public" would need to build a working relationship between *cho-naikai* and a three-legged social structure consisting of private, civic and state support. As support from state and local governing bodies fell short of achieving community restoration, state administration department reached out to private organizations, private companies and NGOs. As a result, many businesses targeting community revamping have been introduced to Tokyo and other large cities of Japan.

We must take note that despite policy efforts to restore local communities in the late twentieth century, the results fell short of the expectations. In 1999, when the state executed a policy to merge cities and villages as a larger administrative unit, the communities were further damaged. Due to this policy, 3,229 local administrative regions in 1999 became 1,820 in 2006. The administration of larger units did not help with building closer ties with your own community or community members.

In order to strengthen local community foundation, Japan introduced a policy on "urban regeneration" as well as baking up businesses targeting economic revitalization for large cities like Tokyo. The urban restoration efforts deemed effective in Tokyo. Population started to increase in Tokyo's central locations including Chuo Ward, Chiyoda Ward and Minato Ward just like the times before the economic bubble burst. Tokyo's skyline took on new shapes with new skyscrapers and apartment buildings. Roppongi and Marunouchi building, both good places to people watch are reviving. New high-rise buildings are gaining in number within Tokyo including in neighborhoods of Harumi, Toyosu and Shibaura. In response to the economic resurgence and growing business opportunities in the city, these apartments are now receiving new residents from satellite cities (Miyake and Keiji (Eds.), 2007: 62-65).

(3) Community in Seoul: Inequality as the Dark Side of Development

Seoul has gone through the process of development from being in war ruins to becoming a global city, alongside the Korean society. As mentioned previously, the rich fruits from the sudden growth did not come free of cost to Seoul residents. Since the fruits were not distributed among the population equally, some people's lives were inevitably burdened. The metropolis housing 10 million population previously known by the name "our city" to the residents is now on its way of becoming a "city of inequality." Residential inequality is perhaps the most salient feature of Seoul's inequality. Within the 25 administrative districts of Seoul, socioeconomic difference is most prevalent between the three districts in Gangnam area (Gangnam, Seocho and Songpa) and Gangbuk area. The ratio of high-income earners who earn more than 5 million Korean won monthly range from 37 to 40% in Gangnam and Seocho, but stay less than 10% in Geumcheon and Gangbuk (see figure 8-1). The inequality in income is also reflected in educational inequality. Comparison of household head income reveals the ratio of four-year college graduates ranging from 45 to 52% in Gangnam and Seocho while ratio in Geumcheon and Gangbuk is known to be 12 to 20% (Seoul Institute, 2014).

Unit: %

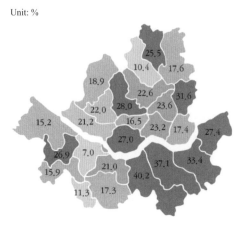

Figure 8-1: Ratio of High-income Earners (5 million KRW) by district
Source: Seoul Institute (2014)

Inequality in Seoul as shown by residential inequality can also be found in the city's hierarchical structure. Seoul's middle class ratio is being maintained within 65% but a closer look reveals that the structure is actually supporting the increase of a marginal middle class. This means that the heterogeneity within the middle class is increasing. The marginal middle class is a class that rests at the possibility of falling lower in class when economy is weakened. The reason

Unit: %

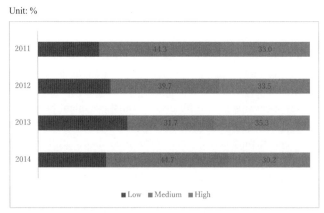

Figure 8-2: Level of Optimism on Social Mobility for Seoul Residents (2011-2014)
Source: Seoul Institute (2011-2014)

why a society needs a strong middle class is because this class can respond with great flexibility to social changes. However, the increase of marginal middle class weakens this supporting middle class buffer and only deepens social inequality. Social inequality has already affected the mindset of Seoul residents who believe that "rags to riches" is no longer achievable in the city. In other words, there are not many remaining optimists who believe that social class is something one can overcome with personal effort (Seoul Institute, 2014).

(4) Urban Policy to Restore Seoul Communities: Village Making Project

Is it possible to live together under the label "community" in a local society characterized by polarization and segregation? It has been a long time since the disappearance of "villages" that have once clustered near alleys in the 1970s. And now, in a city like Seoul, filled with same-looking rows of apartments where multi-generations reside, we wonder if the sentiment of "our neighborhood" can be recreated. To everyone's surprise, Park Won-soon, the mayor of Seoul, has proclaimed the initiative of "Village Restoration" in a city nearing 10 million in population. A social activist and social entrepreneur, Park called himself a social designer and was elected as Seoul mayor through continued political engagement. During his career, Park actively communicated and actualized his beliefs and values for the city. The city he envisioned for Seoul was not defined by growth and development but rather by integration and inclusiveness. He believed restoration of communities was absolutely necessary for Seoul.

The village making project to restore communities was initiated in 2012 in Seoul based on citizen participation. This policy was founded on a vision of achieving cooperative and shared living between people. Grassroots movement and grassroots activities were supported to create sustainable communities where members of such communities were able to raise their children together, raise food, share labor and keep communication alive between village units. The project envisioned a slow but steady expansion of these communities in the long-term (Seoul City, 2012). Various policies were enacted to help support programs that engaged village projects that pulled together activists and projects that addressed social issues with economical and service-minded solutions. The core of village making project's policy was to lay the foundation for village restoration through cooperative citizen governance. Policies were formed to support businesses and projects suggested by community members. Specific examples of these projects included: community archive building, seeking for best practice cases for village education, running community expansion businesses and opening of book cafes. The policy was characterized by a triangulation system supported three ways by the Seoul city, community residents and an intermediate support system. It was supported and funded by the Seoul Innovation Bureau, an administrative organization of Seoul. The Seoul Community Support Center, primarily run by community activists, filled the role of the intermediate support system by gathering, selecting and supporting business ideas from residents and mediating the relationship between residents and government officers (Seoul City 2012; 2013). All of these policy details and execution were new attempts in Seoul.

(5) Gentrification and Disintegration of Community Spaces

Seoul's spaces are filled with personal ambitions. In Seoul, the capital city of Korea, development of spaces are closely tied to proliferation of wealth. For this reason, when people think of space, they don't relate to it as physical locations imbued with memory of living but as a commodity that can increase their wealth. City development is a process of increasing the value of urban spaces by revitalizing old spaces. Theoretically, those who participate in spatial planning or development should be able to share the results of value increase. However, development of Seoul spaces do not follow such processes. It is important to remember this fact in order to understand the processes of gentrification in Seoul.

Gentrification refers to a phenomenon of new middle class residents moving into newly developed spaces that are left behind by former resident who can no longer afford to pay rent, leading to spatial segregation and change to social structure (Glass, 1964). This concept has been utilized to understand commercial and cultural value changes in the process of recreating commercial-cultural locations into "hot spots" in the cities (Smith, 2002). It can also be used to interpret urban neighborhoods as a "cultural constitution" from the perspective of "market and place" (Zukin, 1987) to emphasize widespread spatial segregation during urban redevelopment stages (Atkinson and Bridge, 2005).

For a specific place to become a "hot spot" it needs to be recognized as a "trending spot" by the public due to its attractive lure. Gentrification happens during this process. An urban neighborhood that is relatively deprived and characterized by cheap rent and affordable housing can be gentrified to upgrade in value. For instance, addition of a trendy cafe, restaurant, gallery and concert house to these neighborhoods with time will draw more people through social media postings and through word of mouth. In the case the neighborhood is a commercial region, cafes with commercial characteristics will increase rapidly, guaranteeing positive revenue up to some time. As the neighborhood becomes a "hot spot," a once-quite place will be characterized by increase in rent. The former residents that have contributed to making their place a "trendy spot" are no longer able to afford living in the new space and move out involuntarily. And as the former residents are pushed out, new residents who are able to afford newly developed places move in. In such a way, urban spaces can be seen to be controlled by capital.

(6) Seoul's Gentrification and Policy Responses (or Initiatives)

In Seoul, areas near Hongdae in Gangbuk district and Sinsa-dong Garosu-gil in Gangnam are main areas that have already been gentrified or in the process of being gentrified. Recently, gentrification processes can be seen in Hapjeong-dong, Sangsu-dong and Mullae-dong near Hongdae, Serosu-gil next to Garosu-gil, Gyeongridan-gil in Itaewon and Seochon in Jongno district.

Before mid-2000s, neighborhoods like Seochon and Gyeongridan-gil of Itaewon were older urban residential areas for the working class. However, as stores in these areas became rejuvenated with the development of the alley culture, more people gathered and neighborhood value went up with increased regional investment. Samcheong-dong in Jongno district is also a result of Seoul's urban regeneration. It was also a relatively deprived area, but in the early 1990s, many artists that used to be based in Insa-dong moved to Samcheong-dong, changing this neighborhood into a distinct and artsy area. Even Hongdae, perhaps Korea's most well known gentrified neighborhood, used to be a residential area before underground musicians started to gather in the neighborhood. The gathering of musicians and artists paired with Seoul's support policies for cultural districts gifted the streets of Hongdaea with a distinct residential identity. The irony lies in the fact that the more attractive Hongdae became, it became harder for musicians and artists—who have mainly contributed to creating Hongdae's identity—to reside in the neighborhood.

People gather in the streets of Hongdae to listen to music and dance. Shop owners then raise rents for these shops forcing struggling artists who can't pay rent to move to cheaper neighborhoods like Mullae-dong and Sangsu-dong. The artist groups who move to Hapjeong-dong, Sangsu-dong and Mullae-dong again draw cultural activities and people interested in such culture. The cycle repeats itself where more neighborhoods are revived and artists are pushed out. Like this, gentrification processes spread through the urban areas in diverse forms.

Additionally, Gyeongridan-gil in Itaewon used to be a residential area but increasing rent eventually drove out lower income residents to be replaced by trendy artists and young chefs who have studied abroad. Media described the changes met by Seochon and Gyeongridan-gil with a quote "as people and money flooded Seochon [...] Mrs. Song who owned the flower shop and Mr. Kim who ran the laundromat disappeared" or with a title "paradox of the rising neighborhood" (The Hankyoreh, 2014; The Asia Business Daily, 2015).

Seoul has recognized that gentrification has both its positive side of developing older and deprived neighborhoods and negative effect of weakening communities by creating over dependence on capital with the rise of value that follows regional development. Thereby, the city has attempted various policy initiatives to address these problems. The city attempted to obtain general consensus on problems related to gentrification by publicizing the issue through governance. The city also encouraged partnership of residents and governing bodies to coexist under a drafted agreement. Laws to protect commercial building tenants were established in addition to provision of legal support. Policies regarding gentrification also include management of safe long-term commercial buildings and support for soft loans (Seoul City, 2015). These Seoul policies are hitting a brake on urban regeneration and development advancements driven by market logic. The policies actively reflect the city's motivation to realize a "virtuous city."

(7) Shanghai's Regional Governance

Shanghai is made up of three local bodies including the local autonomous government, street office and residents committee. Since 1995, street office and residents committee have transitioned from being in positions of low influence to becoming main offices that oversee government duties. Residents committee are placed in each neighborhood to inspect residents. By the end of 2015, Shanghai's local governing body excluding Chongming district included 16 autonomous districts, 104 street offices and 4,154 residents committees. This new structure shows that government authorities are attempting to intervene in grassroots public life.

(8) Activity in a Shanghai Local Community

In one residential community in Shanghai, residents have persisted their collective effort for 9 years in order to protect the community greenbelt owned by enterprises and local governments to achieve positive outcomes in 2001 (Shi and Cai, 2006: 314). The experience of this community shows how important interconnectivity is for the core leader of the collective, public officers of local governing bodies, decision-makers and media. In the collective effort against real estate agencies, the local community formed connections with politicians and social networks to maintain their community. From time to time, the community leader obtained information from a friend in the local office. This information led to better strategic planning. Also, since the leader was elected to the garden and forestry bureau, he was able to justify the case for collective resistance (Shi and Cai, 2006: 331).

The residential district mentioned above is a representative case of attempting a new vision for a local community backed by the hope in grassroots democracy and autonomous communities. However, most communities experience despair during the process. The influence of social network and personal connections are widespread in groups seeking for capital gain and in important civil decisions. Taking into consideration the added control of an authoritarian government, we can understand that these connections are often used to profit individuals that own or manage buildings. It is rare for government officers to provide important information on building ownership risking their job positions. In most cases, local community residents are unable to form helpful social ties with government or media insiders.

The government wishes to apply reconstruction policy and community building to solve problems related to social order and social stabilization. However, community situations can be complex where we see different types of communities made up of internally heterogenous characteristics. If the housing association had ample amount of resources to make decisions in a complex urban environment, a balance may be reached between core individuals looking to improve resident life and pursue grassroots activities.

3. URBAN POLICIES IN RESPONSE TO THE INCREASE OF SINGLE PERSON HOUSEHOLDS

(1) Increase of Single Person Households and Accompanying Social Problems in Tokyo

The ratio of single person households in Japan exceeds 30% and is even more higher in Tokyo. The increase of single person households is a direct result of the decline in traditional multigenerational households. Such social change paired with a community breakdown can lead to increase in social problems such as lonely deaths and social isolation. Japan has the world's greatest ratio of elderly population made up of people 65 years and older.[2] The reason why modern Tokyo is termed a "single city" is due to the high ratio of single person households (Shibata, 2007: 50). As seen from the statistics, single person households are increasing in Tokyo. Also, there has been a concentration of the elderly population in cities and areas hit by declining population rates, which can be problematic. In an area with population decline, the young and midd-age workers leave to the city to find work, leaving the elderly population behind. Breakup of families create more single person households for the ones left behind and ones who left reside alone, as evidenced by many datasets of Japan. The cities with the highest single person household ratio are Kagoshima and Tokyo. Both cities are undergoing major population declines. In 2005, the ratio of single person households hit 33.7% for Kagoshima and 30.9% in Tokyo. In Tokyo, the ratio has continually climbed: the single person household ratio increased from 25.5% in 1995, 28.4% in 2005 to 30.9% in 2005 (Kawai, 2009: 3).

In Tokyo, elderly single person households are concentrated in areas with more city functions. The ratios for each cities are 42.4% in Minato, 42% in Toshima, 41.1% in Shinjuku and 40.4% in Shibuya. In an apartment in Shinjuku first constructed in 1949 and renovated to be a high-rise apartment building in 1970s, about half of the residents reside alone (Kawai, 2009: 63). A rise in households living alone is closely tied to rise in solitary deaths and death by starvation. According to the report published by Tokyo Inspection Medical Institute in 2006, 1,460 men and 1,150 women were found to have experienced isolated deaths. Increasing number of the elderly population is reported to die alone. In 1999, 45% of solitary deaths or lonely deaths were caused by elderly aged 65 and older, to increase up to 65% in 2006 (Kawai, 2009: 56). Experiencing deaths in isolation has become one of the characteristics of a large city.

Like other larger cities, Tokyo has been called a "paradise for the singles." In the city, the younger generation could carry on their free lifestyles away from families. However, the makeup of single person households reveals another interesting side to this phenomenon. Out of the total single person household population, those under 34 make up 34% of the total population. 35% of the single person households consist of people in ages between 35 and 64. These people live alone even after end of marital relationships. The high ratio of single person households in this age group has revealed that rise in single person households is not limited to younger and the elderly population (Diamond IT& Business, September 25, 2016). Today, Tokyo stands on the front line of this new trend.

(2) Increase of Single Person Households in Seoul and Its Causes

By 2015, single person household ratio in Korea was 27.1%, meaning close to one-third of all households in Korea were non-family households. Ratio for Seoul is slightly higher at 29.1% (Census Bureau, 2015). Just two decades ago, the ratio was lower than 9%. Three decades ago in 1980, when the term single person household was unfamiliar to many, only 4.5% of households were composed of single individuals. This means that during the past three decades, single person household population increased more than ten-fold. What is the underlying cause behind this sudden change? It would be hard to pinpoint a single explanation. Analyzing this phenomenon through a demographic and socioeconomic perspective, we can say layers of complicated factors are behind this change. They include: the rise in women's economic activity; increase of late-marriage and never-married individuals; increase of "wild geese" families spurred by Korea's competitive education; increase of involuntary singles through divorce, separate living and economic hardships; and increase of the elderly single person households with the advancement of the aging society.

The increasing women's economic participation rate has accompanied attitudinal changes. More people believe that marriage is not essential or and there are more people who delay marriage to reside alone during the time they stay single. This trend is seen for both women and men. Terms like spinster or old bachelor is used less often to be replaced by terms like "gold miss" and "gold mister," implying a certain level of coolness to living alone. Seoul statistics showing median age for first marriage to be 29.8 to 32.2 for men and 29.8 for women reflect these social changes. Another explanation for the increase of single person households has to do with the aging society. The ratio of the elderly population has surpassed 10% in Korea and many of the elderly reside alone without a partner. To add, increase of divorce rates and wild geese families as a sociocultural phenomenon have added to the rise in single person households. In the case of Seoul, total divorce rate lies at 7 to 8% but for those in their 40s and 50s it is 12 to 13%. All of these complicated factors have become compressed together to result in an increase of single person households.

(3) Seoul's Four Types of Single Person Households and Policy Responses

As underlying causes for the increase of single person households are complex and many, single person households are also not to be understood as a homogenous group. Four different types of single person households with distinct characteristics reside in Seoul. They are: the "industrial reserve of young single person households" in their 20s and early 30s who face hardships in getting married due to not having secured job security; "the anxious single group" in their 40s and 50s; elderly single person households; and finally, the "trend-setting gold tribe" who are usually professionals and enjoy their single lives. The common problem faced by those who reside alone involuntarily— which are the anxious singles, young single person households and elderly single person households—are "isolation" and "social poverty." The anxious singles are byproducts of family dissolution caused by the high number of divorces in Seoul for those in their 40s and 50s.

The city of Seoul and its National Assembly enacted a support legislation for single person households and are in the process of advancing various policy initiates in support of young single person households and baby boomers who reside alone. Most older to elderly single person households reside alone involuntarily. The social isolation they feel can become a more complicated social problem with time. Seoul as a city is recognizing the need for care services for single person households such as services for restoration of social networks, medical check-ups by community units and therapy. For young single person households, immediate solution lies in creating quality jobs which still remains as a challenge. For younger women who reside alone, there is a high demand for housing stability. These women rate highly the security and stability of their communities. In response to these concerns, the city continues to develop policies related to housing and employment support for youth.

There have been survey results that show the hardest daily struggle for young single person households has to do with eating.[3] Young individuals often skip breakfast and even dinner or think of eating dinner as "checking off a meal." Recent trends like "social family" and "social dining" are new attempts made by the young singles to try to tackle their problems of dining alone.

For elderly who live alone, financial assistance should be prioritized but social exclusion is also one of the bigger problems they face. The suicide rate for the elderly in Korea is 64.9 persons out of 100,000, which is double the cases in Japan. The primary cause for suicide is economical but we cannot ignore the emotional well-being of the elderly who suffer social isolation. Support system for "silver single minorities" need to be expanded and solutions need to be sought to increase social connection for the excluded. For example, a program run by the city called "intergenerational empathy under one roof" connect elderly people who have spare rooms with college students needing to board. The students are able to provide some daily assistance while saving on rent. This program, modeled after Japan's co-housing program, attempts to connect and spread awareness between different types of single person households.

The rise in single person households in East Asian countries may be a natural result of capitalist development. In Western societies we see a similar pattern: ratio of single person households is nearing 40% for northern European countries and is around 30% for the United States. The increase of single person households in Tokyo and Seoul are similar to what is observed in the west. However, the problem that exists for Seoul is how rapid the increase is. Most people in Seoul still think of a family to be made up of four members but are realizing it has quickly come down to two or one for modern households. The mosaicked diversity found in a society can only become integrated when people are able to: accept with open attitudes the diverse family types and coexist in society together despite the increasing trend of people living alone. Also, there needs to be continued attempts to maintain social values and healthy communities.

4. GLOBAL URBAN POLICIES FOR SOCIAL INNOVATION

(1) Policies for Social Innovation and Urban Development

Since the 21st century, capitalism has gone through various internal changes and created various social issues. In facing these issues, societies have come up with solutions of their own. During this process, the world "innovation" has often used. Innovation refers to "a new idea, thought or system that are different from previous ones." After the 1980s, the term became widespread with the expansion of "technology innovation." Social innovation combines innovation with society. Social innovation was selected as an international agenda during the topic discussion on "The Great Transformation: Shaping New Models" presented in 2012 The World Economic Forum. A contention was made that social innovation could enhance the current limitations faced by capitalistic countries spurred on by long-term global economic crises. In other words, social innovation gained momentum due to the problem-conscious attitudes people maintained to address the inherent problems surfacing with capitalistic growth.

Social innovation as a concept can be very broad. It can describe a process of changing the value system or lifestyle of a society but the term could also be used to describe a new idea or a system created to solve a specific social problem. The core of social innovation lies in creating a new idea, product, service or model that can satisfy social needs and make new social ties and partnerships. Also, in the process, social capital will be accumulated for solving problems. The "social" from social innovation stands for social demands, social problems, and creation of new social values. Social innovation can enhance society by tackling social needs and problems with creative and useful solutions that are more efficient and effective than previous solutions, as well as creating new social value. According to Geoff Mulgan, a leader of Young Foundation—which is a non-governmental think tank specializing in social innovation—social innovation is a process of confirming the theory of "connected difference." He goes on to say that "social innovation is a combination of things that have existed previously and not a completely new innovation—barriers between disciplines, groups and sectors need to be let down in order for the separated individuals and groups to form new social relationships. These new relationships can foster more innovation" (Mulgun. 2007).

(2) Policies for Social Innovation in Tokyo

In Tokyo, policies for social innovation can be understood as an effort produced by the community where the community is made up of new actors seeking new goals and values. Historically, social ties between neighbors have been considered to be a driving source behind community formation. In the 20th century, however, these traditional ties have been weakened. Recently, a neighborhood called Kanda in Chiyoda, Tokyo, has attempted to rebuild communities. The project called Chiyoda platform square aspired to establish a new Soho community. The platform square was located in the old building owned by Chiyoda city which used to be operated as a school. The project was carried out by a company that did not seek for revenue profit. The company provided a space where many artists including painters, craftsmen, potters and musicians could gather to share information and bounce ideas. Other residents were provided with opportunities to freely approach and participate in artist workspaces and exhibitions. The artists were encouraged to participate in community fairs and local events to continue to maintain and build up traditional local communities. Another project in this neighborhood was founded on a cooperative partnership between a conglomerate and local government with a goal to reconstruct the underground square connecting JR Tokyo station and other regions. Through these efforts, Marunouchi Cafe and Marunouchi shuttle started their operations again, helping traditional local communities function further (Okuno and Kurita, 2012: 77).

Community reconstruction projects as a policy for social innovation share certain characteristics. First, rather than limiting the project to the local community only, the project focuses on including the perspective of individuals outside of community who are willing to partake in the program. Social innovation for community is open to anyone interested. Second, community is no longer a comprehensive concept but founded on a specific goal. In other words, social innovation projects are executed with specific goals for the communities. Lastly, in addition to the government and community residents, private companies partake in the community reconstruction projects (Inoue, 1992: 72-73). The concept of creative city is rooted in community innovation. The creative city creates a new movement and rejuvenates the urban space, ultimately giving birth to a new industry. New movements include innovation in fields of information technology and arts including architectural design, film, illustration, handicraft, arts performance, game, computer, broadcast and communication. A traditional concept like a local community may not have a place in a creative city project. The project will rather create an environment where individuals with shared interests can come together to share ideas and create innovation (Shiozawa and Kazuyuki, 2008: 32). In the near future, Tokyo will become a city founded on social ties and networking.

(3) Youth Policies as Social Innovation Policies in Seoul

In Seoul, among the policies for social innovation, policies for youth have shown big growth. Seoul has been drafting a "2020 Seoul Youth Action Plan" to confront the challenges faced by youth. This plan seeks to provide to the youth: a place to stand, a place to work, a place to play and a place to live. To provide youth with a "place to stand," the Seoul Youth Guarantee Center helps youth obtain a minimum condition to start on their own feet. The program especially targets NEET youth that have not received job or education training to encourage them to engage in job experiences and therefore, build up their capacity for social participation. Seoul Youth Guarantee Center selects 3,000 Seoul-based youth with below 60% of median income to provide them with a stipend of 500,000 Korean won every month for six months (Seoul City, 2015). These policies supporting youth is considered innovative considering the political paradigm that has existed in Korea historically. It is innovative in a way the youth are given a chance to increase their personal competitiveness rather than being pushed into a re-training program or introduced to new jobs. The program recognizes that today's youth face more challenges in the process of graduating and seeking work compared to the previous generations. Instead of coming up with policies that give youth "time, space and opportunity," the current policy supports the youth value of "I decide what I want to do." The city of Seoul has made an effort to move away from making decisions that give immediate results to invest in longer-term goals.

5. CLOSING THOUGHTS: CAN URBAN POLICIES SOLVE CITY PROBLEMS?

Until now, we have observed the social problems faced by metropolises Tokyo, Seoul and Shanghai and political decisions the three cities have made to solve these problems. In order to restore communities, Tokyo has carried out programs related to urban restoration and Seoul has launched the village making project and gentrification policies. The success of these policy and project decisions are too early to measure. Seoul and Tokyo are both characterized by shrinking households. In Seoul, single person households and two-person households have become the norm. In Tokyo, the elderly population ratio is the highest in the world. The cities are aging fast and one day in the future, those in their 50s might become the new youth. What hope can we find for these cities? Can we say with confidence that urban policies have contributed in enhancing the society by alleviating social problems and increasing hope for the community?

Tokyo seems to have partly achieved the restoration of communities through the urban restoration processes. For Seoul, it is too early to judge whether the community restoration projects have spread widely in Seoul or have taken root in everyday lives of the people. However, the city of Seoul has raised public awareness of the social issues and have attempted new urban policies. The policies and the way these policies were executed were innovative in nature. The policy directions for urban development as shown by the keywords "village communities," "social innovation," and "sharing city" are results of innovation mayor Park has pushed for.

The global East Asian cities of Tokyo, Seoul and Shanghai are facing new chapters. Continued growth is no longer guaranteed and segregation within the cities are becoming more salient. There is weakened opportunity for social mobility, which means personal efforts could be deemed less valuable. Within this context, the cities are coming up with comprehensive and innovative urban policies to reduce inequality and control social disintegration. A continued effort needs to be made to make sure social inequality is not strengthened in the cities.

One of those efforts must involve strengthening of social capital rather than economic resources. There needs to be strengthening of trust, value and connection, for these are the building blocks that hold communities together. A society's structure of trust, notably, is an important frame necessary for social integration and social inclusion while reducing structural inequality. There has been contention that in order to increase life quality, people need to feel higher trust in their neighbors. Level of trust Seoul residents feels toward their neighbor was recorded to be 5.54 points out of a 10-point scale, evidencing a lower level of trust. Surveyed levels of trust measured for a statement: "I trust my neighbor" revealed that only 39.9% respondents in Seoul said "yes" while 42.1% responded "somewhat" and 18.9% responded "no" (Seoul City and The Seoul Institute, 2015). This statistics show that it is too early to say that there is general trust between neighbors in Seoul. It is not an easy feat to establish trust and build a community in a city where anonymity and individualization have taken root. Despite the challenge, our society's future depends on laying down the groundwork for communities while fighting against social inequality.

City is an invented space made by humans. Human prosperity is held by the modern cities and the cities will continue to evolve to gain more prosperity. A mature urban space of global cities become future goals for other cities. Seoul, Tokyo and Shanghai, as global cities, share each other's past and the future. A glimpse of modern Seoul may have existed in Tokyo a decade ago and the increasing number of people who reside alone in Tokyo may be Seoul's future story.

NOTES

1   We must take note that despite policy efforts to restore local communities in the late twentieth century, the results fell short of the expectations. In 1999, when the state executed a policy to merge cities and villages as a larger administrative unit, the communities were further damaged. Due to this policy, 3,229 local administrative regions in 1999 became 1,820 in 2006. The administration of larger units did not help with building close ties with the community or community members.

2   The ratio is 11% for Korea and 23% for Japan (Ministry of Internal Affairs and Communications, 2009).

3   According to the survey carried out by The Seoul Institute in 2014 on single person households, 31% (multiple responses possible) of respondents have answered it is hard to "eat a meal" in daily life and 62.2% have responded "yes" to the statement "I eat lightly for both breakfast and dinner" (The Seoul Institute, 2014).

REFERENCES

Atkinson, Rowland and Bridge, Gary. (2005). *Gentrification in a Global Context: The new urban colonialism.* London: Routledge.

Bickers, Robert. A and Jeffrey N. Wasserstrom, 1995, "Shanghai's 'Dogs and Chinese Not Admitted' Sign: Legend, History and Contemporary Symbol", *The China Quarterly*, No. 142, pp444-466.

Brown-Saracino, Japonica. (2013). *The Gentrification Debates: A Reader.* Routledge.

Byun, Miree. (2014). *Study on Single Person Household Policies.* Seoul: The Seoul Institute.

Byun, Miree et al. (2012). *Study on the Asia's Social Innovation Ecosystem.* Seoul: The Seoul Insti-

202

tute.

Census Bureau. 2015. *Census Report 2015, Statistics Korea.*

Diamond IT& Business. *One out of Two Households is Single-Person Occupied, Tokyo's 23 Wards.* September 25, 2016.

European Union. (2010). *This is European Social Innovation.* Available at: http://europa.eu

Florida, R. *No One's Very Good at Correctly Identifying Gentrification.* City Lab. December, 2014.

Helliwell, John F., Richard Layard, and Jeffrey Sachs, eds. 2012. *World Happiness Report 2012.* New York: UN Sustainable Development Solutions Network.

Mulgan, Geoff, Tucker, Simon, Ali, Rushanara and Sanders, Ben. (2007). *Social Innovation: What it is, Why it Matters and How it can be accelerated.* Working paper, SAID Business School.

Glass, Ruth. (1964). *London: Aspects of Change.* Centre for Urban Studies, London.

Hertz, Daniel. *There's Basically No Way Not to be a Gentrifier.* City Lab. April, 2014.

Inoue, Shigeru. (1992). *Japanese City in Transition: Software of city management (Hen'yōsuru Nihon no Toshi: Toshi keiei sofuto ron).* Tokyo: Douyuu-kann.

Kawai, Katsuyoshi. (2009). *Elderly Living Alone and Social Isolation in Big Cities (Daitoshi no hitorigurashi kōreisha to shakaiteki koritsu).* Kyoto: Houritsu Bunka Press.

Ministry of Internal Affairs and Communications. (2009). *Japan National Census 2008.*

Miyake, Hiroshi and Goishi, Keiji (Eds.). (2007). *Expanding Cities in East Asia: The growth and control.* Tokyo: Kokusai Shoin.

Nikkei Newspaper. (2014). *Elderly Population in Tokyo: 44% Will Live Alone. 20 Years Later.* April 12, 2014.

Okuno, Nobuhiro and Kurita, Takuya. (2012). *New Public in Cities (Toshi ni Ikiru Koukyou).* Tokyo: Iwanami.

Seoul City. (2012, 2013, 2015). *Internal Administrative Documents.*

_____. (2012). *Internal Administrative Documents.*

Seoul City and The Seoul Institute. (2011-2015). *Seoul Survey.*

Shi Fayong and yongshun Cai, 2006, "Disaggregating the State: Networks and Collective Residence in Shanghai", *The China Quarterly*, No. 186, pp314-332.

Shibata, Tokuei. (2007). *Tokyo Problem (Toukyou Monndai).* Kyoto: Kamogawa Press.

Shiozawa, Yoshinori and Konagaya, Kazuyuki. (2008). *Town Buidling and Creative City 2: City Revitalization (Machizukuri to Sōzō Toshi 2: Chiiki Saiseihen).* Kyoto: Koyo Shobo.

Smith, Neil. (2002). New Globalism, New Urbanism: Gentrification s Global Urban Strategy. *Antipode*, 34, 3, 427-450.

Statistics Korea. (2015)

The Asia Business Daily. *Gentrification-the Paradox of a Rising Neighborhood.* September 15, 2015. Available at: http://view.asiae.co.kr/news/view.htm?idxno=2015080715385469397

The Hankyoreh. *As People and Money Flow into Seochon…Mrs. Song's Flower Shop and Mr. Kim's Laundromat Disappears.* November 24, 2014. Available at: http://hani.co.kr/arti/society/society_general/665778.html

Tokyo Metropolitan Government. (2015). *Tokyo Statistical Yearbook 2015.* Available at: https://www.toukei.metro.tokyo.lg.jp/homepage/ENGLISH.htm.

Wada, Kiyomi (Ed.). (2011). *Urban Policy with Reversed Ideas.* Tokyo: Gyousei.

Wards, *"Towns with Those Living Alone," A Stark Difference Across Life Stages and Gender, How to Select Living Alone Areas.* Available at: http://diamond.jp/articles/-/18105 (Data taken in September 25, 2016)

Yamamoto, Kazuoki and Hiramatsu, Yuuta. (2013). Alienated Society and Regeneration of Local Community: Examination Current Status and Tasks of the Big City Tokyo. *Journal of Urban Policy Study*, 7, 79-112.

Yamazaki, Takeo. (2007). Examining Model Community Issued by the Ministry of Home Affairs: Achievements and Remaining Tasks of Community Policy. *Community Policy*, 5, 26-97.

Yokomichi, Kiyotaka. (2009). *Recent Community Policy in Japan.* Association of Municipal Internationalization (Jichi-tai kokusai-ka kyoukai). Comparative Local Municipality Research Center, Graduate School of Seisaku Kennkyu University.

Zukin, Sharon. (1987). Gentrification: Culture and Capital in the Urban Core. *Annual Review of Sociology*, 13.

9

General Trust[1] among Megacities:
The Case of Shanghai, Seoul and Tokyo[2] **

Masamichi Sasaki

Trust has become a major issue in social science as globalization has become widespread. This means that people and nations are more connected than ever before. But, with this phenomenon seems to be an apparent growing level of uncertainty about the trustfulness of strangers. Hence the study of generalized social trust has become essential in terms of the need to understand and cope with the serious impacts of globalization, especially as expressed through inter-personal communication.

This is especially the case for contemporary globalized "megacities," where major economic activities are conducted and exert an exceptional influence upon nations' economies and where great numbers of people flow both into and out of countries, such as newcomers coming to live in a new country or visitors conducting business or touring for leisure. While these people would certainly like to have the expectation that they will be safe, events in recent decades make that expectation less tenable. That is, for the most part, the security and interpersonal trustworthiness of life in the village has been supplanted by some-thing much different, where people move about and are now an amalgam from a variety of cultures and social systems. The former social structure, the village (or smaller city), involves particularized (personal) trust, whereas the latter, i.e. mega-scale society, involves generalized trust as the personal element fades in the face of industrialization, urbanization, and globalization. Putnam states "As mobility, divorce, and smaller families have reduced the relative importance of kinship ties, especially among the more educated, friendship may actually have gained importance in the modern metropolis" (2000: 96).

Trust, as addressed by sociologists such as Ferdinand Tönnies, Georg Sim-mel, Emile Durkheim, and Talcott Parsons, was deemed essential to social re-lationships. Simmel (1950: 326) stated that "trust is one of the most important synthetic forces in the society." Today, many scholars are taking yet another closer look at trust. For instance, Blau (1964: 99) stated that trust is "essential for stable social relationships." Many other scholars emphasize that trust plays a critical role in interpersonal and group relationships (e.g., Golembiewski and McConkie 1975; Lewis and Weigart 1985; Zucker 1986). Our economic system is in many ways entirely dependent upon trust because if there were no trust there could be no economic transactions (cf. Hirsch 1978). Thus trust has profound implications for interpersonal and social cooperation. Indeed, without trust, societies really could not exist (Bok 1978: 26). Niklas Luhmann comes to mind as perhaps one of the most important scholars to have considered the role of trust in social systems, or in sociology for that matter. To Luhmann (1979: 8) trust "reduces [social system] complexity." Unquestionably, social systems are becoming increasingly complex and confounded, and for Luhmann this means that trust plays an ever-increasingly critical role.

Today, it has been observed that trust levels are declining among many industrialized nations (e.g., Dalton 2004; Hardin 2006; Putnam 1993), thus calling for greater attention and concern. Social isolation brought about by modernization is frequently cited as one of many reasons to reexamine social trust. Other reasons include dramatic changes in demographics, politics, cultures, institutional structures and all that these influence.

As a consequence of trust's ostensibly unique position, there is often a temptation to leave it undefined. Of course, there is a considerable degree of complexity, and controversy, when it comes to defining trust. Should one merely attempt to define trust, or should one focus on its contextual implications and roles? For instance, is trust perceptual or attitudinal at the individual level, or is it an essential component of the social structure itself? If the latter is true, then social trust must be looked upon with reference to social norms and expectations. Hence, trust must then be "understood sociologically, just as social institutions, social stratification, and social change must be" (Wuthnow 2004: 151-152). Wuthnow (2004: 146) further stated that "Any investigation of trust must, therefore, pay attention not only to the behavior of individual actors but also to the norms and expectations embedded in the social settings in which these actors behave. The link between individual behavior and these embedded norms and expectations suggests that trust must be conceived of as an element of social structure."

There is a contextual element to trust as well. What is the context in which trust must be expressed? This gets at the importance of the underlying social structural context which plays an essential role in interpersonal and social relationships. And it must not be overlooked that quite often an important part of the underlying social structural context is the accompanying cultural context. In this regard, Barber (1983: 5) states "Luhmann and I regard trust primarily as a phenomenon of social structure and cultural variables."

Numerous trust scholars have pointed out that what is considered trust in one culture may not be so in another, and by the same token, what is considered trustworthy in one culture may be considered untrustworthy in another (cf. Dietz, Gillespie, and Chao 2010). Since then, a number of cross-national studies of trust have been conducted (e.g., Delhey and Newton 2003, 2005; Paxton 2007; Gheorghiu, Vignoles, and Smith 2009; Wasti and Tan 2010; Hosking 2012; Sasaki 2012; Uslaner 2012; Yoshino 2012; Delhey et al. 2018; Sasaki 2019). Sounders et al. (2010) state that trust's cultural dimension is especially important and should be seen as central to trust research. Dietz, Gillespie, and Chao (2010: 23) emphasize that empirical work and consequent theoretical models are sorely needed to attempt to bridge cross-cultural gaps in understanding the dynamics of social trust (also cf. Barber 1983 and Luhmann 1979).

There are two approaches to the study of trust. The first is the micro-societal approach and the second is the macro-societal approach, which is the top-down approach to the properties of social systems (Delhey and Newton 2003). The present study targets the micro-societal approach to trust, which has two elements. The first element takes the view that trust is an individual property (Misztal 1996) and that "it is associated with individual characteristics, either core personality traits, or individual social and demographic features such as class, education, income, age, and gender" (Delhey and Newton 2003: 94).[3] This approach has been developed by Uslaner (1999, 2000). To reinforce the point about the social psychological origins of trust, Uslaner argues that it is based on two other core personality characteristics: optimism and the capacity to control the world, or at least one's own life. Optimism, he writes, "leads to generalised trust" (Uslaner 1999: 138). Finally, Uslaner argues that "subjective measures of well-being are more closely associated with trust than objective ones related to economic circumstances. In other words, trust is more closely associated with the individual features of personality types and subjective feelings, than with the external circumstances of economic life" (Delhey and Newton 2003: 95). Also, regarding well-being, Inglehart (1999) and Putnam (2000) emphasize the association between social trust, health, and well-being.

The other element of the micro-societal approach is the personal network.[4] Today we are seeing phenomenal growth in personal social networks with an attendant fall of traditional structures. Cook, Levi & Hardin (2009: 71) have stated: "…understanding the way in which an actor is embedded in a social network or networks is crucial to understanding the ways in which an actor's greater social world influences their capacity to trust and be trustworthy." Field (2008: 3) also put it succinctly: "People's networks should be seen, then, as part of the wider set of relationships and norms that allow people to pursue their goals and needs, and also serve to bind society together." Field also mentioned that "researchers have uncovered an extraordinary range of ways in which people's networks can help make their lives better" (2008: 48).

The present study focuses on the comparative analysis of general trust among three "megacities" (Shanghai, Seoul, and Tokyo), where involvement of particularized (personal) trust and kinship ties have reduced relative importance, where great numbers of people flow both into and out of these cities, as well as where major economic activities are conducted in the face of urbanization and globalization.

The followings four objectives are addressed: (a) What kinds of trust structures can be identified among them? (b) Can optimism (as one of the personality characteristics) and individual properties such as age, gender, education and well-being be associated with trust? (c) Are personal networks associated with trust? And if so, what kinds of networks are associated with it? (d) As megacities have and do play a major role in economic activities, how does trust relate to determinants of success in successful people?

Studies on trust from comparative perspectives can no doubt illuminate what is really happening with regard to trust in large-scale urban-industrial megacities such as Shanghai, Seoul and Tokyo in the era of globalization. The present study will use available survey data to pursue the above mentioned four objectives.

1. METHODOLOGY

There have been many general attitudinal surveys conducted throughout the world which include one-, two- or three-item questions regarding the assessment of levels of trust. These questions were first formulated by Rosenberg (1956) and developed by the Institute for Social Research at the University of Michigan and are known as the "Three-Item Rosenberg Scale" or "Misanthropy Measures." They are "widely viewed as being essential for both individual and societal well-being" (Wilkes 2011: 1596) and focus intensively on trust from various perspectives. Paxton (1999: 105) also points out that "Although only one of the variables uses the word 'trust,' all three reflect the trustworthiness or integrity of others." This measurement of trust is regarded as a "quite good measure of the underlying theoretical concept" (Bjornskov 2006: 3).

Also, several studies have stated that the General Social Survey's one-item question ("In general, do you think that most people can be trusted, or that you can't be too careful in dealing with people?"), which has a long history of use,[5] is a rather imprecise, ambiguous, and possibly invalid or unreliable measure of trust (cf. Yamagishi, Kikuchi, and Kosugi 1999; Schwarz, 1999; Glaeser et al. 2000; Miller and Mitamura 2003; Reeskens and Hooghe 2008; Yoshino and Osaki 2013; Yoshino 2015). Reeskens, and Hooghe (2008: 530) claim that:

> ...one cannot recommend measuring generalized trust with just a single item, as is often done in comparative research.... We can be quite confident that a single item does not provide us with a reliable measurement of generalized trust. The two-item solution included in the General Social Survey[6] solves this problem to some extent, but self-evidently a three-item scale allows for a more precise measurement.

In analyzing European Social Survey data, Reeskens and Hooghe (2008: 515) stated that a three-item scale on general trust can be considered as a reliable and cross-culturally valid concept. According to Reeskens and Hooghe (2008: 519) "It is not advisable to measure basic attitudes with just one item." And Smith (1988)[7] stated: "Especially in cross-national research it is suggested that at least three items are necessary to measure a construct in a valid manner."

The present study uses a three-item general trust scale (i.e., the "Three-Item Rosenberg Scale"), which has been used quite often, mainly in general attitudinal surveys in the west. These questions ask respondents for judgments about the trustworthiness of others and their estimates of the trustworthiness of the society around them (Putnam 2000: 138; Newton 2001: 203-4).

For the analysis, correspondence analysis, utilized in the present study, is a statistical technique especially useful for those who collect categorical data; for example, data collected in social surveys. "It is commonplace to speak of correspondence analysis as 'Bourdieu's statistical method.'" In sociology, multiple correspondence analysis has figured prominently in the work of Pierre Bourdieu (Le Roux and Rouanet, 2010: viii and 4). The method is particularly useful in analyzing cross-tabulated data in the form of numerical frequencies, and it results in elegant but simple graphic displays in Cartesian coordinates, thereby facilitating holistic understanding of the data (cf. Greenacre and Blasius 1994). The basic outcomes of these geometric methods show a multidimensional pattern of relative degrees of similarity between items or objects. In the technical sense that they do not depend on the size of the data set (Le Roux and Rouanet 2010: 2).

(1) DATA

The data for the present study were collected based on nationwide attitudinal general social surveys including trust items among nine nations in the Pacific region conducted by three institutions under the leadership of Ryozo Yoshino at the Institute of Statistical Mathematics of Tokyo (financially supported by the Japan Society for the Promotion of Science, JSPS).

The present study uses data from three megacities, samples extracted from nationwide data for South Korea and Japan. Personal (face-to-face) interviews were used for all three surveys. For the Shanghai data, the survey, using a quota sampling method, was conducted among persons 18 years of age and over between November and December of 2011, in collaboration with the East China University of Political Science and Law (ECUPL); 1,000 Shanghai samples were used for the present analysis. For the South Korean data, the survey, using a quota sampling method, was carried out among persons 18 years of age and over between October and November of 2012 by Gallup Korea; 214 Seoul samples were used for the analysis. For the Japanese data, the survey, using a two-stage stratified random sampling of residential or voter lists, was carried out among persons 20 years of age and over in December of 2010 by the Shinjoho Center of Tokyo; 55 Tokyo samples were used for the analysis. Because this sample size was too small to represent the population of Tokyo, nationwide Japanese survey data (with a sample size of 852) were also used (for reference) for all the analyses in the present study, as a means for comparison with the other two megacities.

Did individuals in Shanghai, South Korea and Japan interpret the questions asked in the same way? This of course is a crucial issue. The data set using pretest samples in Shanghai, South Korea and Japan, utilizing the back translation technique, confirmed nearly equivocal interpretation of the questions (see pp. 332-372 of http://ismrepo.ism.ac.jp/dspace/bitstream/10787/974/4/kenripo 105.pdf for the Chinese questionnaire; pp. 359-394 of http://ismrepo.ism.ac.jp/dspace/bitstream/10787/2927/4/kenripo110.pdf for the Korean questionnaire; and pp. 172-186 of http://ismrepo.ism.ac.jp/dspace/bitstream/10787/902/4/kenripo103.pdf for the Japanese questionnaire).

2. RESEARCH FINDINGS

(1) The trust structure among three megacities

For the present study, cross-tabulations and correspondence analyses were conducted. The three questions and their response categories, i.e., the Three-Item Rosenberg Scale used for the present study, appear in Table 9-1. The cross-tabulations of the responses to the three questions by the three megacities and Japan (for reference) are shown in the Appendix, Table A.

Table 9-1. Survey Questions and Response Categories Used for the Analysis

Question 1. Would you say that most of the time people try to be helpful, or that they are mostly just looking out for themselves?

1. Try to be helpful
2. Look out for themselves
3. Other
4. Don't know

Question 2. Do you think that most people would try to take advantage of you if they got the chance, or would they try to be fair?

1. Take advantage
2. Try to be fair
3. Other
4. Don't know

Question 3. Generally speaking, would you say that most people can be trusted or that you can't be too careful in dealing with people?

1. Most people can be trusted
2. Can't be too careful
3. Other
4. Don't know

As the response categories for the three questions are binary choices (excluding "Other" and "Don't know," categories regarded as "junk"; Le Roux and Rouanet 2010, p. 62), we assign a positive value (1) for Question 1's first response category (i.e., most of the time people try to be helpful), and a negative value (2) for the second category (i.e., they are mostly just looking out for themselves). By the same token, we assign a positive value (1) for Question 2's first response category (i.e., they would try to be fair), and a negative value (2) for the second response category (i.e., most people would try to take advantage of you if they got the chance), and we assign a positive value (1) for Question 3's first response category (i.e., most people can be trusted) and a negative value (2) for the second response category (i.e., you can't be too careful in dealing with people).

The correspondence analysis was conducted to determine response patterns for the three questions for the three megacities and Japan. From Figure 9-1, we can see that the X-axis partitions the response categories of the first three questions (Questions 1, 2 and 3). Inertia (i.e., chi-square/total N) for the X-axis is 0.517 for Shanghai, 0.469 for Seoul, 0.486 for Tokyo, and 0.499 for Japan (simply for reference), indicating that the contribution of the X axis is significant for this partition.

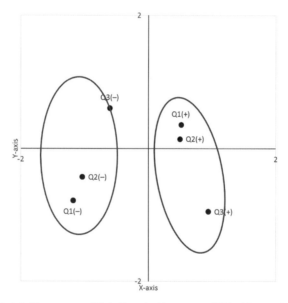

Q1(+) = Try to be helpful   Q2(+) = Try to be fair   Q3(+) = Most people can be trusted
Q1(−) = Look out for themselves   Q2(−) = Take advantage   Q3(−) = Can't be too careful

Question 1: Would you say that most of the time people try to be helpful, or that they are mostly just looking out for themselves?

Question 2: Do you think that most people would try to take advantage of you if they got the chance; or would they try to be fair?

Question 3: Generally speaking, would you say that most people can be trusted or that you can't be too careful in dealing with people?

Figure 9-1-1. Trust Structure: Three-Item-Rosenberg Scales for Shanghai

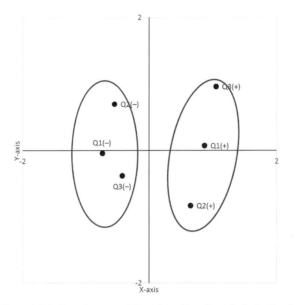

Figure 9-1-2. Trust Structure: Three-Item-Rosenberg Scale for Seoul

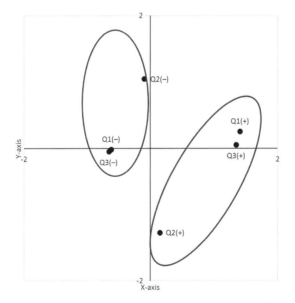

Figure 9-1-3. Trust Structure: Three-Item-Rosenberg Scale for Tokyo

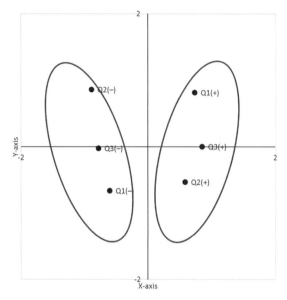

Figure 9-1-4. Trust Structure: Three-Item-Rosenberg Scale for Japan

The results indicate that in Figures 9-1-1 through 9-1-4, the positive (right) half of the X-axis reveals scatter plots of the three positive responses for trust in the three megacities and Japan (for reference). The negative (left) half of the X-axis reveals scatter plots of the three negative responses for trust in the three megacities and Japan (for reference).

In these figures we can see that for the three megacities, responses with positive values and those with negative values are partitioned and gathered on the first principal axis. As the inertia of the first dimension is close to 0.5 for the three megacities, we can display the trust and distrust clusters in the first dimension for all three megacities and Japan (for reference) (see Greenacre and Blasius 1994). Accordingly, the trust structures analyzed using the Three-Item-Rosenberg Scale are similar among the three megacities and Japan (for reference).

(2) Individual circumstances

(a) Age, gender, and education

The trust scale and the three status characteristics of age, gender, and education were utilized for the analysis because all three status characteristics seem to have bearing on trust (Delhey and Newton 2003). Cross-tabulations of the three status characteristics by the three megacities and Japan are shown in the Appendix, Table B.

Figures 9-2-1, 9-2-2, and 9-2-4 show the results of the correspondence analysis for Shanghai, Seoul, and Japan. For the case of Tokyo, education was excluded from the analysis as its sample size was too small to carry out reliable correspondence analysis in combination with the trust scale; therefore, only age and gender are shown in Figure 9-2-3 which is the result of rotating both axes 90 degrees in a clockwise direction.

From the figures we can see that Shanghai, Seoul and Tokyo, as well as Japan, have homogeneity for females and for those over the age of 50 as they locate on the trust side, whereas males and those under 34 locate on the distrust side. Those 35-49 years old locate on the side of distrust for Shanghai, Tokyo, and Japan. For Seoul, those aged 35-49 locate quite closely to the origin of the X and Y axes, meaning that this Seoul age group is neutral (i.e., it is between trust and distrust).[8]

For education, university graduates (showing as tertiary in Figures 9-2-1 and

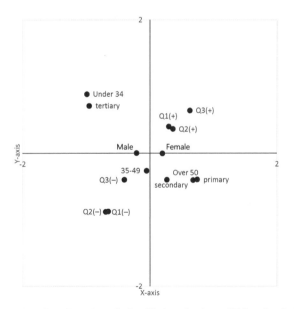

Figure 9-2-1. Three-Item Rosenberg Scale with Age, Gender and Education for Shanghai
In the figure, primary means elementary (including less than one year) or junior high school; secondary means high school; and tertiary means junior college, professional school, 4-year college, or graduate school.

216

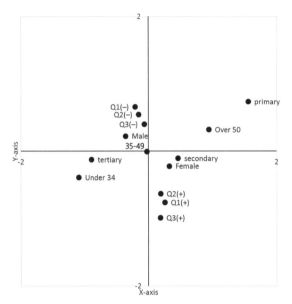

Figure 9-2-2. Three-Item Rosenberg Scale with Age, Gender and Education for Seoul
In the figure, primary means elementary or junior high school; secondary
means high school; and tertiary means junior college, professional school, 4-year college, or
graduate school.

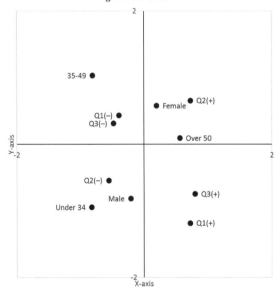

Figure 9-2-3. Three-Item Rosenberg Scale with Age and Gender for Tokyo

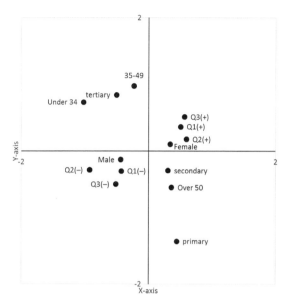

Figure 9-2-4. Three-Item Rosenberg Scale with Age, Gender and Education for Japan
In the figure, primary means elementary or junior high school; secondary means high school;
and tertiary means junior college, professional school, 4-year college, or graduate school.

9-2-2) for Shanghai and Seoul, and junior college graduates (showing as terti-ary in Figure 9-2-4) for Japan are located on the side of distrust. High school graduates and non-high school graduates (showing as primary and secondary in Figures 9-2-1, 9-2-2, and 9-2-4, respectively) for Shanghai, Seoul and Japan are located on the side of trust.

From Figures 9-2-1 through 9-2-4, the results of the analysis are summarized in Table 9-2.

(b) Optimism as one of the personality characteristics, and well-being

To examine whether trust and optimism and well-being are associated, four questions and their response categories were used for the analysis, as shown in Table 9-3. For optimism (Q4, i.e., one's living conditions will be better or worse over the next five years) and for well-being (Q5 through Q7, i.e., satisfaction with one's health, satisfaction with one's family life, and satisfaction with one's life) were used.

**Table 9-2. Summary of Three-Item Rosenberg Scale
with Gender, Age, and Education for Three Megacities and Japan**

	Shanghai	Seoul	Tokyo	Japan
Gender				
Male	Distrust	Distrust	Distrust	Distrust
Female	Trust	Trust	Trust	Trust
Age				
Under 34	Distrust	Distrust	Distrust	Distrust
35-49	Distrust	Neutral	Distrust	Distrust
Over 50	Trust	Trust	Trust	Trust
Education				
Primary	Trust	Trust	--	Trust
Secondary	Trust	Trust	--	Trust
Tertiary*	Distrust	Distrust	--	Distrust

*For Shanghai and Seoul, tertiary means beyond university graduation; for Japan tertiary means beyond junior high school graduation.

Cross-tabulations of the response categories to the four questions by the three megacities and Japan are shown in the Appendix, Table C-1 through C-4. For the case of Tokyo, Q7 (How satisfied are you with your life as a whole these days?) was excluded from the analysis as its sample size was too small to carry out reliable correspondence analysis when putting it together with the trust scale.

For the correspondence analysis for Question 4 (Over the next five years do you think your living conditions will be better or worse?"), we combined[9] "much better" and "slightly better" into "better," and "much worse" and "slightly worse" into "worse." For Question 5 ("For your age, how satisfied are you with your health?), "very satisfied" and "fairly satisfied" were combined into "satisfied," and "very dissatisfied" and "fairly dissatisfied" were combined into "dissatisfied." For Question 6 (All things considered, how satisfied are you with your family life – the time you spend and the things you do with members of your family?), "very satisfied" and "somewhat satisfied" were combined into "satisfied," and "very dissatisfied" and "somewhat dissatisfied" were combined" into "dissatisfied." For Question 7 (How satisfied are you with your life as a whole these days?), the responses were combined as for Question 6. Figures 9-3-1 through 9-3-4 show the results of the analyses. Figure 9-3-2 is the result of rotating both axes 56 degrees in a clockwise direction.

Table 9-3. Four Questions and Response Categories for Optimism and Well-Being

Q4. Over the next five years do you think your living conditions will be better or worse?

1. Much better
2. Slightly better
3. About the same
4. Slightly worse
5. Much worse
6. Other
9. DK

Q5. For your age, how satisfied are you with your health? Would you say…?

1. Very satisfied
2. Fairly satisfied
3. Fairly dissatisfied
4. Very dissatisfied
8. Other
9. DK

Q6. All things considered, how satisfied are you with your family life – the time you spend and the things you do with members of your family?

1. Satisfied
2. Somewhat satisfied
3. Neither satisfied nor dissatisfied (neutral)
4. Somewhat dissatisfied
5. Dissatisfied
8. Other
9. DK

Q7. Now I would like to ask about your life as a whole. How satisfied are you with your life as a whole these days?

1. Satisfied
2. Somewhat satisfied
3. Neither satisfied nor dissatisfied (neutral)
4. Somewhat dissatisfied
5. Dissatisfied
8. Other
9. DK

From Figures 9-3-1 through 9-3-4, the results of the analysis are summarized in Table 9-4.

To sum up, the three megacities, as well as Japan (for reference), exhibit homogeneity regarding locations of the response categories for the four questions (one question was not used for Tokyo and "about the same" of Q4 for Japan is located on the trust side) for the trust and distrust sides.

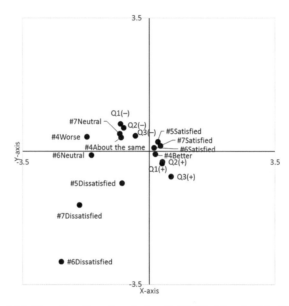

Figure 9-3-1. Three-Item Rosenberg Scale with Q4, Q5, Q6, and Q7 for Shanghai

#4= (Q4. Over the next five years do you think your living conditions will be better or worse?)

#5= (Q5. For your age, how satisfied are you with your health?)

#6= (Q6. All things considered, how satisfied are you with your family life – the time you spend and the things you do with members of your family?)

#7= (Q7. Now I would like to ask about your life as a whole. How satisfied are you with your life as a whole these days?)

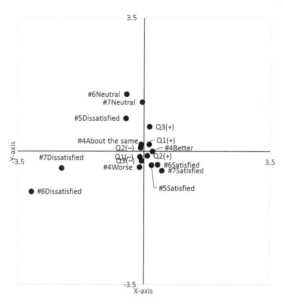

Figure 9-3-2. Three-Item Rosenberg Scale with Q4, Q5, Q6, and Q7 for Seoul

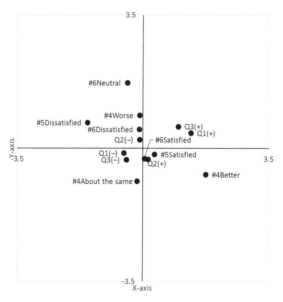

Figure 9-3-3. Three-Item Rosenberg Scale with Q4, Q5, and Q6 for Tokyo

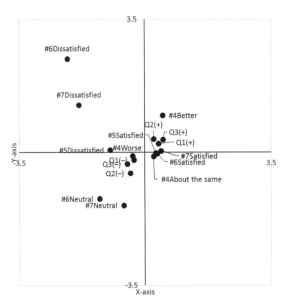

Figure 9-3-4. Three-Item Rosenberg Scale with Q4, Q5, Q6, and Q7 for Japan

Table 9-4. Summary of the Results of Analysis for
Questions, 4, 5, 6, and 7 for Three Megacities and Japan

	Q4		Q5		Q6		Q7	
	Trust	Distrust	Trust	Distrust	Trust	Distrust	Trust	Distrust
Shang-hai	Better	Worse	Satisfied	Dissatis-fied	Satisfied	Dissatis-fied	Satisfied	Dissatis-fied
		About the same				Neutral		Neutral
Seoul	Better	Worse	Satisfied	Dissatis-fied	Satisfied	Dissatis-fied	Satisfied	Dissatis-fied
		About the same				Neutral		Neutral
Tokyo*	Better	Worse	Satisfied	Dissatis-fied	Satisfied	Dissatis-fied		
		About the same				Neutral		
Japan	Better	Worse	Satisfied	Dissatis-fied	Satisfied	Dissatis-fied	Satisfied	Dissatis-fied
	About the same					Neutral		Neutral

＊Q7 was not used for the analysis.

c) Personal networks

To determine whether personal networks were associated with trust, the question and the response categories are shown in Table 9-5.

Table 9-5. Question 8 and Its Response Categories

Q8 Including your family members, about how many people can you count on for each of the following?

Please use a four-point scale, where 1 means a lot, 2 means some, 3 means one, and 4 means none.

1. A lot   2. Some   3. One   4. None   9 D. K.

①=a. Lend you money, a helping hand, or anything you might need
②=b. Understanding your feelings and situation
③=c. Let you call or see them anytime to speak freely or seek advice
④=d. Highly appreciate and respect you

For the correspondence analysis "one" and "none" were combined[10] into "one and none" for the response categories for all four questions. For the analysis of Tokyo, the response categories of "a lot" and "some" were combined into "some and more" due to the small sample size. Cross-tabulations of the responses to Question 8 by the three megacities and Japan are shown in the Appendix, Table D. Figures 9-4-1 through 9-4-4 show results of the analysis. Figure 9-4-2 is the result of rotating both axes 76 degrees in a clockwise direction. Figure 9-4-3 is the result of rotating both axes 130 degrees in a clockwise direction.

From Figures 9-4-1 through 9-4-4, the results of the analyses are summarized in Table 9-6.

From the summary in Table 9-6, we can see that for Shanghai, Seoul and Japan, "a lot" for all four questions is located on the trust side and "one or none" is located on the distrust side. For Tokyo,"more than some" is located on the trust side and "one or none" is located on the distrust side.

224

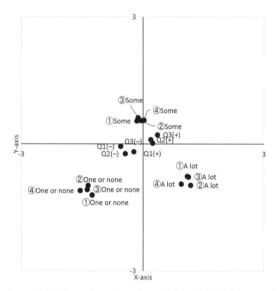

Figure 9-4-1. Three-Item Rosenberg Scale with Q8 for Shanghai

①= Lend you money, a helping hand, or anything you might need

②= Understanding your feelings and situation

③= Let you call or see them anytime to speak freely or seek advice

④= Highly appreciate and respect you

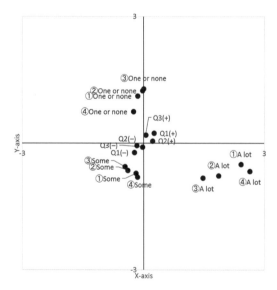

Figure 9-4-2. Three-Item Rosenberg Scale with Q8 for Seoul

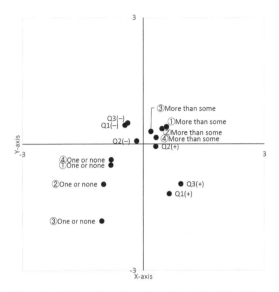

Figure 9-4-3. Three-Item Rosenberg Scale with Q8 for Tokyo

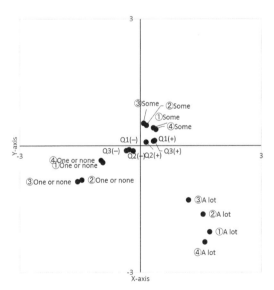

Figure 9-4-4. Three-Item Rosenberg Scale with Q8 for Japan

Table 9-6. Summary of Trust and Personal Networks Among Three Megacities and Japan

Q8	①		②		③		④	
	Trust	Distrust	Trust	Distrust	Trust	Distrust	Trust	Distrust
Shanghai	A lot	Some	A lot	Some	A lot	Some	A lot	
		One or none		One or none		One or none	Some	One or none
Seoul	A lot	Some	A lot	some	A lot	Some	A lot	Some
		One or none		One or none		One or none		One or none
Tokyo*	More than some	One or none	More than some	One or none	More than some	One or none	More than some	One or none
Japan	A lot	One or none	A lot	One or none	A lot	One or none	A lot	One or none
	Some		Some		Some		Some	

* Response category d was not used for the analysis.

d) The antecedent(s) of trust in success among successful people

To determine the antecedent(s) of trust in success among successful people, the question and the response categories are shown in Table 9-7.

Table 9-7. Question 9 and its Response Categories

Q9 If you look at successful people in society today, which do you think has played the largest part in their success: their ability and effort, luck and chance, or personal relationships through kindred, countrymen/countrywomen, and alumni/alumnae?

1. Ability and effort
2. Luck and chance
3. Personal relationships through kindred countrymen/countrywomen, and alumni/alumnae
4. Others
9. D.K.

Cross-tabulations of the responses to Question 9 by the three megacities and Japan (for reference) are shown in the Appendix, Table E. Figures 9-5-1 through 9-5-4 show the results of the analysis.

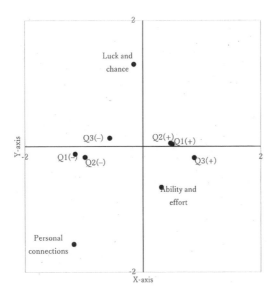

Figure 9-5-1. Three Item Rosenberg Scale with Q 9 for Shanghai

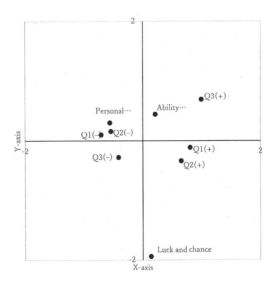

Figure 9-5-2. Three-Item Rosenberg Scale with Q 9 for Seoul

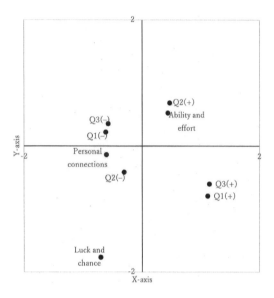

Figure 9-5-3. Three-Item Rosenberg Scale with Q9 for Tokyo

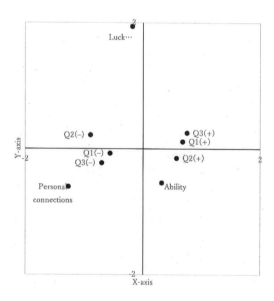

Figure 9-5-4. Three-Item Rosenberg Scale with Q9 for Japan (for reference)

The results indicate the positive (right) half of the X-axis reveals scatter plots of the three positive responses for trust in the three megacities and Japan (for reference). The negative (left) half of the X-axis reveals scatter plots of the three negative responses for trust in the three megacities and Japan (for reference). From these figures we can see that Shanghai, Seoul, Tokyo and Japan have homogeneity as their "Ability and effort" locates on the same trust side, and "Personal relationships through kindred, countrymen/countrywomen, and alumni/alumnae" locate on the same distrust side. For "Luck and chance," it is located on the distrust side for Shanghai, Tokyo and Japan, but it is located on the trust side for Seoul. The reason why "Luck and chance" is located away from the original point among Seoul, Tokyo and Japan is their relatively lower response percentages.

3. DISCUSSION AND CONCLUSION

The literature on trust has many conflicting empirical findings on both within-in-nation and cross-national research. In the present study, we compared and contrasted three megacities in which all three countries have been viewed as having cultures of collectivism and high context. We set out to determine whether or not there are any variations in the relationship between trust and individual circumstances among the three megacities (see Choi and Han 2008; and Han and Choi 2012 who discussed trust in South Korea; and Liu 2008 for trust in China). The following are the findings of the present study.

(1) The trust structures analyzed using the Three-Item-Rosenberg Scale are similar among Shanghai, Seoul, Tokyo, and Japan (for reference).

(2) It was found that trust is associated with the social status characteristics of age, gender, and education. Regarding the association between trust and age (seen as one of the major demographic variables), it was found the young people are distrusting, while the elderly (i.e., over 50 years old) are trusting. This finding supports those of Glaeser et al. (2000) and Alesina and la Ferrara (2000).

With respect to the association between trust and gender (although gender makes little difference in western countries; Whiteley 1999 and Newton 2001), some findings (e.g., Delhey and Newton 2003) have confirmed that women are distrusting. The present study, to the contrary, found that women are trusting and men are distrusting. This contrary finding might be attributed to the fact that some surveys utilize only one question on trust (i.e., Generally speaking, would you say that most people can be trusted or that you can't be too careful in dealing with people?) rather than the Three-Item-Rosenberg Scale. It might be speculated that the reason why women are trusting is due to their particularistic trust developed in close-knit circles as opposed to the large-scale generalized trust of everyday life. Women may perceive trust through or based on their close-knit personal relationships with neighbors, friends, and acquaintances as opposed to men where they have wider access to both official and unofficial contacts with various kinds of people, some of which may involve greater levels of suspicion and distrust. Why women are more trusting suggests considerable opportunities for future research.

With regard to the association between trust and education, positive relationships between them have been found previously (see, e.g., Knack and Keefer 1997; Warren 1999; Putnam 2000; Uslaner 2002). For instance, Yamagishi (2001: 127) states "…a positive relationship between level of formal education and generalized trust or distrust would provide intuitively convincing evidence against the popular belief that high trusters are naïve and gullible…." Moreover, Yamagishi (2001: 127) states "…the proportion of generalized distrusters (operationalized as those who believe they cannot be too careful in dealing with people) declines with formal education."

The present study does not support this claim and, to the contrary, the present study's findings indicate that trusters are less educated people. It is not clear whether or not this is due to naïveté or gullibility. It can be speculated that, like our finding that women are trusting, those who have low education have particularistic and limited personal networks and/or relationships and do not have many opportunities to communicate with unfamiliar people and/or strangers. The reasons for this finding also beg further investigation.

3) The present study supports the claim of Uslaner that optimism (one's living situation will be better or worse over the next five years) is associated with trust among the three megacities and Japan and the findings of Inglehart (1999) and Putnam (2000) that well-being (in the present study, satisfaction with one's health, satisfaction with one's family life, and satisfaction with one's own life) is associated with trust among the three megacities and Japan, although one question item was excluded from the analysis of Tokyo because of its quite small sample size.

4) The present study confirms the findings of Delhey and Newton (2003) that informal social personal networks are associated with trust. For informal social networks, Delhey and Newton (2003) use (a) close friends (response category is yes or no), (b) number of close friends, (c) frequency of contacts, and (d) feeling lonely. For informal social networks, the present study used the broader and more concrete items: (a) lend you money, a helping hand, or anything you

might need, (b) understanding your feelings and situation, (c) let you call or see them any time to speak freely or seek advice, and (d) highly appreciate and respect you.

5) The present study found that for trusters "Ability and effort"[11] and for distrusters "Personal relationships through kindred, countrymen/countrywomen, and alumni/alumnae" play the largest part in the success of successful people among the three megacities in common. In other words, this finding indicates that trusters rely on themselves (i.e., "Ability and effort") and distrusters rely on others ("Personal relationships" and "Luck and chance").

Overall, the findings of the present study are identified as commonalities of the general trust structure among the three megacities and affirm that these are commonly associated with optimism as one of the personality characteristics and individual properties such as age, gender, and education, well-being, and personal network (including such dimensions as help, empathy, availability in need, appreciation and respect, as well as ability and effort being regarded as an antecedent for success). In other words, the present study indicates that general trust is perceptional and attitudinal at the individual level and based on personal social networks among three megacities although national (and presumably cultural) differences in embedded norms and expectations among the three megacities of the three countries might be different.

Hence, the present study empirically supports some of the speculations gleaned from the trust literature. Further studies are needed to determine whether the commonalities stem from characteristics of the megacities (such as being reinforced by and/or converging through urbanization, modernization, and globalization) or other determinants such as commonly embedded traditional cultural norms and expectations, social values, and/or the commonly regarded collectivist and/or high context cultures.

** An earlier version of this chapter was published in *Development and Society* (Vol. 45 No.3, 2016).

ACKNOWLEDGEMENTS
I wish to thank Fumi Hayashi for her helpful advice in carrying out the correspondence analyses, and Ryozo Yoshino for graciously providing his 9-nation data set to make possible the analyses of the present study and for his helpful comments on an earlier version of this paper, and finally to Dan Hatch for his helpful review of this and earlier versions.

NOTES

1 As the concept of trust is quite broad, the present study, like other trust research, uses the terms trust, general trust, social trust, and generalized social trust interchangeably.

2 This chapter is a revision of an article entitled "A Comparative analysis of trust among megacities: The case of Shanghai, Seoul, and Tokyo," Sasaki, Masamichi. (2016), *Development and Society,* 45(3), 503-536.

3 The individual property approach to social trust regarded trust, in the 1950s and 1960s in the United States, as a core personality trait of individuals (Delhey and Newton 2003).

4 The terms "personal networks," "social networks," and "informal social networks" are used interchangeably in the present study.

5 According to Ermisch et al. (2009: 750), "this question (i.e., generally speaking, would you say that most people can be trusted, or that you can't be too careful in dealing with people?) has been used to measure trust in around 500 references that analyze the economic effects of trust" (also according to Sapienza et al. 2013).

6 In the World Values Survey, generalized trust is measured with just one item. The General Social Survey includes two items. The European Social Survey has three generalized trust items.

7 See also the revised article in *IASSIST Quarterly* 12 (4), 18-24, 1988.

8 To determine whether this finding for Seoul was different from that of South Korea, we analyzed the data for South Korea and found that those under 34 years old are located on the distrust side.

9 It is recommended to construct questions having about an equal number of categories, possibly after grouping (Le Roux and Rouanet 2010: 38).

10 It is recommended to construct questions having about an equal number of categories, possibly after grouping (Le Roux and Rouanet 2010: 38).

11 Mayer et al. (1995) posited (besides perceived benevolence and perceived integrity) perceived ability as one of three dimensions of trustworthiness. Wasti and Tan (2010) in their comparative study between China and Turkey found integrity to be the most essential antecedent across both countries, followed by ability.

APPENDIX

Table A. Cross-tabulations of the Response Categories to Questions 1 through 3 by Three Megacities and Japan (for reference)

Q1: Would you say that most of the time people try to be helpful, or that they are mostly just looking out for themselves?

	Try to be helpful	Look out for themselves	Other	D.K.	Total (%)	Total (N)
Shanghai	65.5	29.3	0.8	4.4	100	1,000
Seoul	45.8	53.3	0.0	0.9	100	214
Tokyo	23.6	56.4	5.5	14.5	100	55
Japan	41.0	50.1	1.5	7.4	100	852

Q2: Do you think that most people would try to take advantage of you if they got the chance, or would they try to be fair?

	Try to be fair	Take advantage	Other	D.K.	Total (%)	Total (N)
Shanghai	57.9	24.8	3.5	13.8	100	1,000
Seoul	44.9	52.3	0.0	2.8	100	214
Tokyo	41.8	47.3	1.8	9.1	100	55
Japan	56.8	36.2	0.0	7.0	100	852

Q3: Generally speaking, would you say that most people can be trusted or that you can't be too careful in dealing with people?

	Most people can be trusted	Can't be too careful	Other	D.K.	Total (%)	Total (N)
Shanghai	36.4	59.1	0.4	4.1	100	1,000
Seoul	28.0	71.0	0.5	0.5	100	214
Tokyo	27.3	56.4	7.3	9.1	100	55
Japan	43.9	48.0	2.2	5.9	100	852

Table B. Cross-tabulations of Age, Gender, and Education by Three Megacities and Japan (for reference)

	Shanghai	Seoul	Tokyo	Japan
Age				
Under 34	27.9	30.0	21.8	16.4
34-49	30.0	35.0	16.4	22.3
Over 50	42.1	35.0	61.8	61.3
Total (%)	100	100	100	100
Total (N)	1,000	214	55	852
Gender				
Male	49.6	48.1	40.0	43.5
Female	50.4	51.9	60.0	56.5
Total (%)	100	100	100	100
Total (N)	1,000	214	55	852
Education				
Primary	31.3	12.6	12.7	14.4
Secondary	32.5	43.0	49.1	45.7
Tertiary	34.3	44.4	38.2	39.9
Total (%)	100	100	100	100
Total (N)	981	214	55	846

Table C-1. Cross-tabulations of Response Categories to Q4 (Over the next five years do you think your living conditions will be better or worse?) by Three Megacities and Japan (for reference)

	Shanghai	Seoul	Tokyo	Japan
Much better	35.9	2.3	5.5	0.2
Slightly better	48.1	36.4	43.6	9.3
About the same	8.5	35.0	41.8	43.2
Slightly worse	3.4	22.0	7.3	37.0
Much worse	1.1	0.5	1.8	8.7
Other	0.6	0.5	0.0	0.1
D.K.	2.4	3.3	1.8	1.5
Total (%)	100	100	100	100
Total (N)	1,000	214	55	852

Table C-2. Cross-tabulations of the Response Categories to Q5 (For your age, how satisfied are you with your health?) by Three Megacities and Japan (for reference)

	Shanghai	Seoul	Tokyo	Japan
Very satisfied	17.3	15.9	23.6	17.0
Fairly satisfied	58.8	53.7	58.2	58.8
Fairly dissatisfied	16.8	28.0	16.4	18.5
Very dissatisfied	6.3	2.3	1.8	5.5
Other	0.6	0.0	0.0	0.0
D.K.	0.2	0.0	0.0	0.1
Total (%)	100	100	100	100
Total (N)	1,000	214	55	852

Table C-3. Cross-tabulations of the Response Categories to Q6 (All things considered, how satisfied are you with your family life – the time you spend and the things you do with members of your family?) by Three Megacities and Japan (for reference)

	Shanghai	Seoul	Tokyo	Japan
Satisfied	61.1	18.7	54.5	49.8
Somewhat satisfied	32.2	53.7	29.1	32.3
Neither satisfied nor dissatisfied	3.4	21.0	10.9	10.9
Somewhat dissatisfied	2.6	5.6	3.6	4.5
Dissatisfied	0.3	0.9	1.8	2.1
D.K.	0.4	0.0	0.0	0.5
Total (%)	100	100	100	100
Total (N)	1,000	214	55	852

Table C-4. Cross-tabulations of Response Categories to Q7 (Now I would like to ask about your life as a whole. How satisfied are you with your life as a whole these days?) by Three Megacities and Japan (for reference)

	Shanghai	Seoul	Tokyo	Japan
Satisfied	38.9	9.3	47.3	36.6
Somewhat satisfied	43.6	50.0	20.0	36.0
Neither satisfied nor dissatisfied	6.6	27.6	12.7	13.8
Somewhat dissatisfied	7.5	11.7	16.4	9.2
Dissatisfied	3.1	1.4	3.6	4.3
Other	0.1	0.0	0.0	0.0
D.K.	2.0	0.0	0.0	0.0
Total (%)	100	100	100	100
Total (N)	1,000	214	55	852

Table D. Cross-tabulations of Response Categories to Q8 (Including your family members, about how many people can you count on for each of the following?) by Three Megacities and Japan (for reference)

a. Lend you money, a helping hand, or anything you might need

	Shanghai	Seoul	Tokyo	Japan
A lot	22.3	7.0	7.3	6.3
Some	60.0	53.7	47.3	58.6
One	2.6	15.9	12.7	8.8
None	9.8	22.0	25.5	22.4
D.K.	5.3	1.4	7.3	3.9

b. Understanding your feelings and situation

	Shanghai	Seoul	Tokyo	Japan
A lot	19.6	12.1	9.1	11.4
Some	61.0	51.9	58.2	68.7
One	7.2	26.2	23.6	12.4
None	7.7	8.9	5.5	6.2
D.K.	4.5	0.9	3.6	1.3

c. Let's you call or see them any time to speak freely or seek advice

	Shanghai	Seoul	Tokyo	Japan
A lot	23.7	16.4	10.9	17.1
Some	57.5	50.0	72.7	66.4
One	7.0	20.1	10.9	8.2
None	7.8	12.6	3.6	7.7
D.K.	4.0	0.9	1.8	0.5

d. Highly appreciate and respect you

	Shanghai	Seoul	Tokyo	Japan
A lot	20.1	7.5	5.5	5.4
Some	55.2	40.2	61.8	54.9
One	3.5	22.0	14.5	9.3
None	8.2	25.7	12.7	22.1
D.K.	13.0	4.7	5.5	8.3
Total (%)	100	100	100	100
Total (N)	1,000	214	55	852

Table E. Cross-tabulations of the Response Categories to Q9 (If you look at successful people in society today, which do you think has played the largest part in their success, their ability and effort, luck and chance, or personal relationships through kindred, countrymen/country women, and alumni/alumnae?) by Three Megacities and Japan (for reference)

	Shanghai	Seoul	Tokyo	Japan
Ability and effort	50.7	59.8	60.0	63.1
Luck and chance	37.8	14.5	20.0	21.1
Personal relationships through kindred, countrymen/country women, and alumni/alumnae	9.5	24.3	12.7	12.2
Other	0.7	0.5	1.8	0.6
D.K.	1.3	0.9	5.5	2.9
Total (%)	100	100	100	100
Total (N)	1,000	214	55	852

REFERENCES

Alesina, Alberto and Eliana La Ferrara. (2000). Participation in heterogeneous communities. *Quarterly Journal of Economics*, 115, 847-904.

Barber, Barnard. (1983). *The logic and limits of trust.* New Brunswick, N.J.: Rutgers University Press.

Bjornskov, Christian. (2006). Determinants of generalized trust: A cross-country comparison *Public Choice*, 130,1-21.

Blau, Peter. (1964). *Exchange and power in social Life.* New York: Wiley.

Bok, Sissela. (1978). *Lying: Moral choice in public and private life.* New York: Pantheon.

Choi, Sang-Chin and Gyuseog Han. (2008). Immanent trust in a close relationship: A cultural psychology of trust in South Korea. In Ivana Markova and Alex Gillespie (Eds.), *Trust and distrust: Social cultural perspectives* (pp.79-104). Charlotte, NC: Information Age Publishing.

Cook, Karen S., Margaret Levi, and Russell Hardin (Eds.). (2009). *Whom can we trust?* New York: Russell Sage Foundation.

Dalton, Russell. (2004). *Democratic challenges, democratic choices, the erosion of political support in advanced industrial democracies.* Oxford: Oxford University Press.

Delhey, Jan and Kenneth Newton. (2003). Who trusts: The origins of social trust in seven nations. *European Societies*, 5, 93-137.

Delhey, Jan and Kenneth Newton. (2005). Predicting cross-national levels of social trust: Global pattern or Nordic exceptionalism? *European Sociological Review*, 21, 311-327.

Delhey, Jan, Klaus Boehnke, Georgi Dragolov, Zsofia S.Ignacz, Mandi Larsen, Jan Lorenz, and Michael Koch. (2018). Social cohesion and its correlates: A comparison of Western and Asian societies. *Comparative Sociology*, 17(3-4), 426-455.

Dietz, Graham, Nicole Gillespie and Georgia T. Chao. (2010). Unraveling the complexities of trust and culture. In Mark N. K. Saunders, Denise Skinner, Graham Dietz, Nicole Gillespie, and Roy J. Lewicki (Eds.), *Organizational trust: A cultural perspective* (pp.3-41). Cambridge U.K.: Cambridge University Press.

Ermisch, John, Diego Gambetta, Heather Laurie, Thomas Siedler, and S.C. Noah Uhrig. (2009). Measuring people's trust. *Journal of the Royal Statistical Society Series* A, 172,749-760.

Field, John. (2008). *Social capital.* London and New York: Routledge.

Fischer, Claude. (1992). *America calling: A social history of the telephone.* Berkley, CA: University of California Press.

Gheorghiu, Mirana, Vivian Vignoles, and Peter B. Smith. (2009). Beyond the United States and Japan: Testing Yamagishi's emancipation theory of trust across 32 nations. *Social Psychology Quarterly*, 72,365-383.

Glaeser, Edward L., David I. Laibson, Jose A. Scheinkman, and Christine L. Soutter. (2000). Measuring trust. *The Quarterly Journal of Economics*, 115(3), 811-846.

Golembiewski, Robert T. and Mark McConkie. (1975). The centrality of interpersonal trust in group processes." In Cary. L. Cooper (Ed.), *Theories of group processes* (pp. 131-185). New York: Wiley.

Greenacre, Michael and Gorg Blasius (Eds.). (1994). *Correspondence analysis in the social sciences.* London: Academic Press.

Han, Gyuseog and Sang-Chin Choi. (2012). Trust working in interpersonal relationships: A comparative cultural perspective with a focus on East Asian culture. In Masamichi Sasaki and Robert Marsh (Eds.), *Trust: Comparative perspectives* (pp.237-268). Leiden, The Netherlands: Brill.

Hardin, Russell. (2006). *Trust.* Cambridge, U.K.: Polity.

Hirsch, Fred. (1978). *Social limits to growth.* Cambridge, MA: Harvard University Press.

Hosking, Geoffrey. (2012). Structure of trust: Britain and Russia compared. In Masamichi Sasaki and Robert Marsh (Eds.), *Trust: Comparative perspectives* (pp.31-68). Leiden, The Netherlands: Brill.

Inglehart, Ronald. (1999). Trust, well-being and democracy. In Warren, Mark. E.

(Ed.), *Democracy and trust* (88-120). Cambridge, Cambridge University Press.

Knack, Stephen and Philip Keefer. (1997). Does social capital have an economic payoff? A cross-country investigation. *Quarterly Journal of Economics*, 112, 1251-1288.

Le Roux, Brigitte and Henry Rouanet. (2010). *Multiple correspondence analysis.* Los Angeles: Sage.

Lewis, J. David and Andrew Weigert. (1985). Trust as a social reality. *Social Forces*, 63, 967-985.

Liu, Li. (2008). "Filial piety, guanxi, loyalty, and money: Trust in China. In Ivana Markova and Alex Gillespie (Eds.), *Trust and distrust: Social cultural perspectives* (pp.51-77). Charlotte, NC: Information Age Publishing.

Luhmann, Niklas. (1979). *Trust and power.* New York: John Wiley and Sons.

Mayer, R.C., J.H. Davis, and F.D. Schoorman, (1995). An integrative model of organizational trust. *Academy of Management Review*, 20, 709-734.

Miller, Alan S. and Tomoko Mitamura. (2003). Are surveys on trust trustworthy? *Social Psychological Quarterly*, 66, 62-70.

Misztal, Barbara A. (1996). *Trust in modern societies: The search for the bases of social order.* Cambridge: Polity Press.

Newton, Kenneth. (2001). Trust, social capital, civil society, and democracy. *International Political Science Review*, 22, 201-214.

Paxton, Pamela. (1999). Is social capital declining in the United States? A multiple indicator assessment. *American Journal of Sociology*, 105, 88-127.

Paxton, Pamela. (2007). Association memberships and generalized trust: A multilevel model across 31 countries. *Social Forces*, 86, 47-76.

Putnam, Robert. D. (1993). *Making democracy work: Civic traditions in modern Italy.* Princeton, N.J.: Princeton University Press.

Putnam, Robert. D. (2000). *Bowling alone: The collapse and revival of American community.* New York: Simon and Schuster.

Reeskens, Tim and Marc Hooghe. (2008). Cross-cultural measurement equivalence of generalized trust: Evidence from the European social survey (2002 and 2004). *Social Indicators Research.* 85, 515-532.

Rosenberg, Morris. (1956). Misanthropy and political ideology. *American Sociological Review*, 21: 690-695.

Sapienza, Paola, Anna Toldra-Simats, and Luigi Zingales. (2013). Understanding trust. *The Economic Journal*, 123 (573), 1313-1332.

Sasaki, Masamichi. (2012). Cross-national studies of trust among seven nations. In Sasaki, Masamichi and Robert Marsh (Eds.), *Trust: Comparative perspectives* (pp.347-376). Leiden, The Netherlands and Boston, U.S.A.: Brill.

Sasaki, Masamichi. (2019). A Cross-national study of criteria for judging the trustworthiness of others before a first meeting In Sasaki, Masamichi (Ed.), *Trust in contemporary society* (pp. 177-209). Leiden, The Netherlands and Boston, U.S.A.: Brill.

Schwarz, Norbert. (1999). Self-reports: How the questions shape the answers, *American Psychologist*, 54,93-105.

Simmel, Georg. (1950). *The sociology of Georg Simmel,* translated and edited by Kurt Wolff, Glencoe, Ill: Free Press.

Smith, Tom W. (1988). The ups and downs of cross-national survey research. GSS cross-national report No. 8. Chicago: National Opinion Research Center. University of Chicago.

Saunders, Mark. N. K., Denise Skinner, Graham Dietz, Nicole Gillespie, and Roy J. Lewicki. (Eds.) (2010). *Organizational trust: A cultural perspective.* Cambridge, Cambridge University Press.

Uslaner, Eric. M. (1999). Democracy and social capital. In Mark. E. Warren (Ed.), *Democracy and trust* (pp.121-150). Cambridge, Cambridge University Press.

Uslaner, Eric. M. (2000). Producing and consuming trust. *Political Science Quarterly*, 115, 569-590.

Uslaner, Eric M. (2002). *The moral foundations of trust.* Cambridge: Cambridge University Press.

Uslaner, Eric M. (2012). Trust, diversity, and segregation in the United States and the United Kingdom. In Sasaki, Masamichi and Robert Marsh (eds.), *Trust: Comparative perspectives* (pp.69-97). Leiden, The Netherlands and Boston, U.S.A.: Brill.

Wasti, S. Arzu and Hwee Hoon Tan. (2010). Antecedents of supervisor trust in collectivist cultures: evidence from Turkey and China. In Mark N. K. Saunders, Denice Skinner, Graham Dietz, Nicole Gillespie and Roy J. Lewicki (Eds.), *Organizational trust* (pp. 311-335). Cambridge, Cambridge University Press.

Warren, Mark. E.(Ed.). (1999). *Democracy and trust.* Cambridge, Cambridge University Press.

Whiteley, Paul F. (1999). The origins of social capital. In Jan van Deth, Marco Maraffi, Ken Newoton, and Paul Whiteley (Eds.), *Social capital and European democracy* (pp.25-44). London: Routledge.

Wilkes, Rima. (2011). Re-thinking the decline in trust: A comparison of black and white Americans. *Social Science Research*, 40, 1596-1610.

Wuthnow, Robert. (2004). Trust as an aspect of social structure. In Jeffrey C. Alexander, Gary Marx, and Christine L. Williams (Eds.), *Self, social structure, and beliefs: Explorations in sociology* (pp.145-167). Berkeley, University of California Press.

Yamagishi, Toshio, Kikuchi Masako, and Kosugi Motoko. (1999). Trust, gullibility, and social intelligence. *Asian Journal of Social Psychology*, 2, 145-161.

Yamagishi, Toshio. (2001). Trust as a form of social intelligence. In Karen Cook (Ed.), *Trust in society* (pp.121-147). New York: Russell Sage Foundation.

Yoshino, Ryozo. (2012). Reconstruction of trust on a cultural manifold: Sense of trust in longitudinal and cross-national surveys of national character. In Sasaki, Masamichi and Robert Marsh (Eds.), *Trust: Comparative perspectives* (pp. 297-346). Leiden, The Netherlands and Boston, U.S.A.: Brill.

Yoshino, Ryozo. (2015). Trust of nations. *Behaviormetrika*, 42, 131-166.

Yoshino, Ryozo and Hiroko Osaki. (2013). Subjective social class. *Japanese Journal of Behaviometrics*, 40, 77-114.

Zucker, Lynne. G. (1986). Production of trust: Institutional sources of economic structure, 1840-1920. *Research in Organizational Behavior*, 8, 53-111.

10

Attitude on Immigration and Globalization

Seokho Kim
Haidong Zhang
Hirohisa Takenoshita

1. GLOBAL CITY SCAPES: SHANGHAI, TOKYO, SEOUL

In November 2016, news that would reverberate through soccer fans worldwide came from Shanghai. It was news about an Argentine professional footballer Carlos Alberto Tevez, a former Manchester United player and a close friend of Korean football hero Park Ji-sung, signing a 40-million-dollar contract with a Shanghai club. This career decision of Tevez was surprising for he had previously left the prestigious Italian football club Juventus for an Argentine club Boca Juniors based on reasons of wanting to return home. His decision to leave his home ground again after turning away a prestigious career in spotlight to join a minor East Asian football club was indeed an intriguing turn of events. This was also a moment of realization for the world in recognizing the sheer size of financial resources held by Chinese football clubs. The globalization trends of East Asian football are ongoing; the FIFA Club World Cup is held annually in Tokyo and the FC Seoul football club is recently tasting success by strategically placing experienced players from South America and Europe. With these three cities at the core, globalization of East Asian football has been steadily making advancements.

The reason why this chapter starts out with a football story when addressing the globalization of the three cities characterized by capitalistic advancements is to emphasize that these global cities are not only ahead of the economic game but also excelling in the spheres of sports, culture and lifestyle among others. From the rapid industrialization and urbanization that took place from the mid-20th century, the three cities created numerous jobs as large-sized companies backed by resources crowded the cities. There is a shared commonality between the three cities in migration of people and capital.

Globalization and migration patterns are impacted by immigration policies and industrial structures of receiving countries (Choi, 2013). In the same vein, patterns of globalization and immigrant integration are different between countries. Cities with main job categories in service and non-technical production lines draw immigrants who are low-skilled and non-professional whereas financial hubs will draw global elites as its immigrants. It would seem as globalization is advancing independently within the transnational context apart from individual nation states. However, states modify policies according to transnational migrations and maintain their positions with these regulations (Zolberg, 1999). Therefore, governments of China, Japan and Korea have different positions in regards to immigration and respond to international migration differently. These differences alter reasons for immigration, immigration routes, socioeconomic characteristics of immigrants as well as the relationships formed between the immigrant population and the native-born population.

With globalization, movement of people, goods, resources and information have overcome spatial barriers—migration of people from diverse cultural backgrounds to large cities of East Asia have now become prevalent. Castles and Miller (1993) have pointed out the limitations of forming immigration discourse with nation states as basic units. They emphasized the importance of using a transnational analytic tool to analyze transnational migration within globalization. Understanding immigration by only focusing on distinct characteristics of the three global cities of East Asia will miss the broader immigration patterns in the three cities. In order to analyze the results of immigration within the three cities, it is critical to note the importance of immigration within globalization, as well as the East Asian context and the national contexts of the three cities.

However, it becomes tricky to consider the importance of all three factors. For instance, trying to take to consideration three different contexts can be a futile effort especially within the scope of this chapter. We will thus try to focus on the attitudes and sentiments of the native-born population as an index which can reveal some similarities and differences between the immigrants in the three cities, as well as migration patterns of people and goods in East Asia. The relationships formed between immigrants and native-borns might look very different in Shanghai, where most foreigners are either employees of global companies or their families, and in Seoul, where most people categorized as foreigners are either *joseon-jok* or low-skilled laborers. The difference in the native-born attitude on globalization and immigration are based on but not limited to these factors: the political and economic contexts of immigration flow, demographic characteristics of immigrants, relationship between immigrants and native-born and immigrant integration processes. Analyzing native-born attitudes regarding globalization and immigrants can reveal to us various implications including how relationships are formed between people from different structural, economic and cultural backgrounds. Further, we can try to extrapolate the results to envision whether the three cities will continue to make advancements based on globalization and international migration of human capital, information and other goods and resources.

2. GLOBAL CITY IMMIGRANTS: SHANGHAI, TOKYO AND SEOUL

Are Shanghai, Tokyo and Seoul global cities? How much of an impact are the three cities receiving from globalization driven by neoliberalism? Who are the people recently arriving to these cities? What does the relationship between the immigrants and native-borns in these three cities look like? In this chapter, we try to address such questions.

In order to answer the first question, it is important to understand the characteristics of these cities. Sassen (2001) conceptualizes "global city" as a transnational center of business and finance providing international trade, investment and other services. Sassen puts forth four key functions of the global city which are: command posts of organizations of the global economy; key locations for finance and special services provided by service-centered companies; sites for production especially innovative productions; and key markets for products and innovations in these cities. Global cities are grounded on their duality. The complex duality means spatial separation paired with integrated global economic activities. Sassen (2001) contends that global cities are birthed by economic activities of transnational companies promoted by developments in transportation and communication. Regional dispersion of economic activities gives rise to centralized control and management focused in one region. Under these circumstances, although varying in degree, Shanghai, Tokyo and Seoul seem close to functioning as global cities. All of these cities encompass the four key functions and duality that a global city as defined by Sassen should have.

According to the annually reported global city index by AT Kearney (2016), Shanghai, Tokyo and Seoul are included as one of the top 25 global cities. Figure 10-1 that shows in a table the ranks of the 25 cities places Tokyo at 4th, Seoul at 11th and Shanghai at 20th. Global city indexes base the ranks on the following factors among others: business activity (30%); human capital (30%);

244

information exchange (15%); cultural experience (15%); and political engagement (10%). As global cities are not just major foci of international economy but places where goods and services are produced as well as where transnational culture is created by the influx of people, information and capital, the factors considered for the index ranking seem appropriate. Seoul places high on business activity and information exchange but places low on human capital, cultural experience and political engagement. As for Shanghai, the city upheld a high score for business activity and human capital while receiving relatively low scores on information exchange, cultural experience and political engagement.

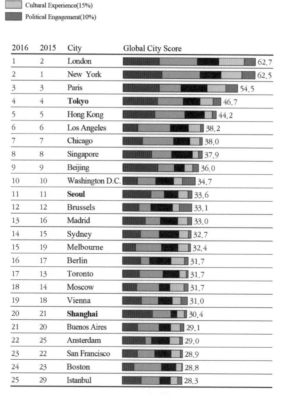

Figure 10-1: Top 25 Global City Rank and Score(2015-2016)
Source: AT Kearney, "Global Cities Index 2016"

Global cities are maintained through networks and it is through these ties migration patterns form. Which groups of people come to the cities then? According to Sassen (2001), most immigrants who come to these cities are global elites who are proficient in transnational activities. The presence of manufacturing companies that provide essential products as well as the service industries that maintain convenience of the cities continue to create new jobs for foreign workers. With globalization, cities experience economic segmentation where global elites are situated on top and low-skilled workers stay on the bottom of the socioeconomic ladder (Sassen, 2001).

When trying to unravel the characteristics of people who migrate to global cities and the relationships they form with the native-born population, it is helpful to look at theories on international migration. Analyzing personal motivations as well as structural background of people who migrate to specific places backed by theoretical underpinning can provide fertile ground to examine relationships between immigrants and native-borns. International theories can be distinguished between those that explain the causes behind migration and those that explain the perpetuation of migration. The former theories include neoclassical economics (micro and macro), new economics of migration, segmented labor market theory and world-systems theory. The latter theories include network theory, institutional theory and accumulative causation theory, emphasizing the importance of network (Massey et al., 1993; Burnley, 2016). The discussion of this chapter focuses on the causes of migration.

Why do people migrate? The neoclassical economics approach can be distinguished between micro and macro approaches. The macro approach emphasizes the differences in the supply and demand for labor between locations. People from places with lack of capital but more labor force will migrate to countries with more capital in demand for labor. Countries with labor shortage will have higher pay for labor while countries with more laborers will experience higher unemployment rates and lower pay. The micro perspective, also known as human capital theory, is closely related to the macro perspective. The macro perspective looks at differences in the supply and demand for labor while the micro perspective conceptualizes migration as driven by the incentive to yield profit by investing in individuals. In other words, people with agency will invest in their human capital and move to a place that will provide them with most economic benefit. The net benefit takes into account the profit gained by difference in labor wage minus the cost of moving and adjusting.

The new economics of migration centers around the agency of individuals. It emphasizes interpersonal ties and collective ties; migration decisions are not just made by a sole individual but is a collective group or a household decision. This theory effectively explains the migration decisions made by household units in developing countries to minimize risk and loss by escaping an unstable labor market. Due to unstable private and public insurance structures in developing countries, many household economies are not protected. In order to insure against financial insecurities, households will make decisions to disperse family members to different locations to diversity income sources. This theory effectively explains emigration of families from rural areas but is not as effective in explaining migration decisions for small-sized families since these families often lack extra labor force to disperse to other regions.

The segmented labor market theory turns to capitalistic labor market characteristics to explain migration. Since developed countries offer high-skilled workers with stable work and wage but cannot do the same for low-skilled workers, the labor market becomes segmented. Since domestic workers of developed countries will evade employment in low-skilled labor market, international migration is driven by state or company initiatives and policies of developed countries that lure low-skilled workers to fill the shortage in labor market.

Lastly, the world-systems theory sees the core reason of international migration rising from core countries of the capitalistic system penetrating the market of peripheral countries. The capitalists from the core countries will penetrate into peripheral countries by exploiting farms, raw materials, labor and consumer markets for profit. In this process, capital from the core countries will move to peripheral countries and labor force from the peripheral countries will migrate to core countries. This theory contends that international migration flows against the flow of capital and goods. Also, this pattern is contended to be more prevalent between core countries that have colonized the peripheral countries in the past. This is due to the prior establishment of culture, language and transportation as well as the previously formed relationship between culture and market.

The four theories of international migration can each provide meaningful explanations for migration patterns in Shanghai, Tokyo and Korea. We can now look at immigrant group characteristics and immigrant patterns of the three cities in detail. The next sections will cover immigrant statistics, socioeconomic characteristics of immigrants, social problems associated with immigration and relationship between immigrants and native-borns in the three cities.

(1) Shanghai: Immigrant or an Outsider?

Shanghai's population has been maintained without any abrupt change for the recent years; it was 24.15 million in 2013, 24.25 million in 2014 and 24.15 million in 2015 (Shanghai Municipal People's Government, 2016). However, the ratio of foreigners within the total population is not that high. According to the 2010 survey, the population of foreigners that have registered in Shanghai was 160,000, where 35,075 were Japanese, 24,358 were American and 21,073 were Koreans. Out of them, 95,623 were either employees of international companies or their families and 16,064 were international students and their families (Country Digest, 2016). According to Shanghai immigration statistics, nationalities and population of foreigners who registered their residence in Shanghai in 2013 are as follows: 37,671 Japanese, 26,279 Americans, 20,578 Koreans, 9,828 French, 8,948 Germans, 6,717 Singaporeans, 7,823 Canadians, 6,917 Australians and 6,547 British among others. Most Shanghai foreign residents are from developed countries and are employed by international companies or are family members of global elites. According to the data secured from the "Survey on the living conditions of foreigners in Shanghai," 83.26% of expats have a job in Shanghai and 89.7% have stable jobs (Shanghai Social Science Research Center, Shanghai University, 2014). They hold jobs in production, wholesale or retail, culture or entertainment, computer service or software. In Shanghai, most workers in production and service sectors come from other Chinese cities; Chinese who have migrated to Shanghai mostly hold jobs in production (41.3%), sales (18.4%) and service (6.8%). Service work includes jobs in hotels or restaurants. In contrast, there is a low concentration of Chinese migrants employed in information and finance industries (Country Digest, 2016). Broadly speaking, migrants to Shanghai include global elites and international workers from overseas, and Chinese workers who have migrated from other cities to find work in the city. To add, we could say that the group of migrants who would better fit the migration theories mentioned earlier are not the foreign expats but the native-born.

The fact that most foreigners in Shanghai are global elites and expatriates working for international companies implies that not many foreigners are in the city to settle permanently. This is due to the characteristic of global elites—they are known to have an attribute similar to migratory birds, never staying in one place for more than three to five years. They migrate between global cities depending on where work calls. Global elites are like professional freelancers who work for a company based on projects they partake in only to upgrade and hop to a better job offer (Beaverstock, 2012). Therefore, most expats in Shanghai are likely to think of themselves as outsiders rather than permanent residents. There are foreigner-concentrated areas like Xintiandi and ethnic enclaves like Korea Town in Shanghai but it would be rare for foreigners to share living spaces with the native Chinese population. Due to this context, Shanghai residents' attitude and values regarding globalization and immigration are highly likely to be abstract and overly general rather than based on personal experience. Taking to consideration the living and working conditions of the foreign expats as well as their distinct subculture, most Shanghai residents are likely to consider foreigners as different people set apart from them.

(2) Tokyo: Migrant Laborers in the City

Unlike Shanghai, most foreigners in Tokyo are migrant laborers who are in a lower economic standing. Tokyo's population makes up 11% of the state's population with 13.491 million people, the largest out of the 47 prefectures of Japan (Tokyo Metropolitan Government, 2016). According to 2016 data, number of foreigners residing in Japan was around 2.33 million, which was 5.2% higher than the previous year. The top nationalities and population of foreigners in Tokyo are: 665,847 Chinese, 457,772 Koreans and 229,595 Filipinos (Immigration Bureau of Japan, 2016). There is also a population of Brazilian immigrants of Japanese descent but they are small in number and often have a hard time adjusting to Japanese culture. Most Chinese and Filipino immigrants in Japan are either students in their 20s and 30s or unskilled laborers. Immigrants with Korean nationalities consist of those who have lived in Japan generationally since the period of Japanese imperialism and those who have recently arrived from South Korea for various reasons.

It was in the 1990s when Japan started to welcome more foreigners to the country. The period was characterized by a large influx of foreigners or "newcomers" to the country. Through increased number of marriage migrants arriving to rural areas, inflow of migrant laborers in response to economic globalization, and state projects like "100,000 International Students Goal," more foreigners entered the country. With modification to immigrant laws, new resident statuses like "permanent resident" and "study or train abroad" categories were added. Through permanent resident status, Brazilian immigrants of Japanese descent were allowed to work in any occupation. Chinese and Southeast Asians came to Japan under the "study or train abroad" visa qualification. The central government of Japan made effort to bring in more professional and skilled laborers but most foreigners who arrived were unskilled laborers.

Since 2000, the Japanese government has made effort to promote policies on multiculturalism and population control but has refrained from executing policies on expanding options on long-term residency for foreigners. This careful attitude toward immigration policies seem to be rooted in Japan's history as an ethnically homogenous nation as well as the public sentiment regarding immigrants. Japan has been often criticized to have approached immigration policies with a view to provide quick remedies for labor shortage or population decline (Lee, 2015).

The problems of reduced birth rate and aging society Japan is facing have gained worldwide attention. In order to tackle the shortage of labor, the Japanese government had opened doors to migrant laborers from late-1980s. Laborers from Asia, Middle East and the United States were among the various regions' migrants came from to enter Japan. Most of the arriving laborers were unskilled or low-skilled laborers. The number of these laborers stayed constant even during the economic recession in Japan. This fact demonstrates that Japan's labor market is highly dependent on overseas laborers (Tsuda, 2008). From 2014, the Japanese government was considering immigration law reforms to combat the problems caused by low birth rate and aging society. In 2015, the state made limited efforts to draw in more international students and professional workers with no lasting results. For instance, only a small group of 1,500 skilled laborers entered Japan through this system in 2015 (East Asia Forum, 2016).

Although having passed the 5% foreigner's ratio mark, Japan still remains as an unfamiliar place for many to consider settling down permanently. This is closely tied to the Japanese state's exclusive immigration policies. In order to block off unskilled laborers, Japan launched the Immigration Control and Refugee Recognition Act in the 1990s. However, this Act eventually led to the coming of more unskilled laborers as companies experiencing labor shortage utilized training programs to draft more workers (Tsuda, 2008). As made obvious by the introduction of the term "3D," working conditions are not the most ideal for migrant laborers in Japan (Wickramasekera, 2002). Even the technology internship program that has been promoted and expanded by the state has been misused to recruit more laborers within major industries, private businesses and agricultural work. These laborers are not protected by the employment contracts and receive below minimum wage (Kodama, 2016). Recently, number of illegal immigrants have been on the rise: they are either people who have come with tourist visa or come through the industrial training program and have overstayed (The Japan Times, 2016).

Japanese are found to carry a double-sided attitude regarding globalization and immigration. According to the 2003 and 2013 International Social Survey (ISSP) data carried out under the theme "national identity," Japanese citizens were found to have contrasting views on immigrants. Most are aware that immigrants will help the economy and bring in new worldview and culture but they are also under the impression that immigrants will raise crime rates and take jobs from domestic workers. Recently, the negative opinions have been strengthened (Yoon, 2016). Also, discrimination levels toward immigrants are tied to immigrant nationalities: Japanese hold positive opinions regarding increase of immigrants from Europe or North America but think otherwise toward immigrants from China. Notably, older Japanese women were found to hold negative perspectives on Chinese immigrants (Zhang, 2015).

(3) Seoul: At the Crossroads Between Historical Suffering and Economic Prosperity

Seoul's population is recorded to be 10.236 million in 2016. Overall, 9.996 million Koreans and 272,117 registered foreigners make up Seoul's population. Foreign population of Seoul has increased 5.4-fold within the last 15 years. Among them, 130,335 are male, 141,781 are female and 130,006 are Korean Chinese or *joseon-jok*. Excluding the *Joseon-jok* population, there are 62,293 Chinese, 9,365 Americans, 8,738 Taiwanese, 8,458 Japanese, 9,729 Vietnamese, 5,139 Mongolians and 3,614 Filipinos in Seoul (Seoul Statistics, 2017). Most Chinese including Korean Chinese live in Yeongdeungpo district, while most Americans and Japanese cluster in Yongsan district and most Taiwanese settle in Seodaemun district.

Figure 10-2 shows the distribution of foreign population within Seoul. The top two districts with most foreign population are Yeongdeungpo with 39,307 and Guro with 32,512 registered foreigners. The next two districts are Geumcheon and Gwanak. The major foreign group residing in these four districts is *joseon-jok (Korean Chinese) and han-jok (Chinese)*. According to the third quarter of 2016 statistics, top visa categories of Korean Chinese were employment, permanent residence and marriage migration. For Chinese, top visa category was student visa. In other words, next to employment and permanent residency, the largest group of Korean Chinese residing in Seoul is marriage migrants while majority of the Chinese are students (Seoul Statistics, 2017).

Next to migrant laborers and the *joseon-jok* population, other immigrant groups have started to settle in Korea. The majority of them are Asian women coming to Korea through international marriages. These marriages have given rise to the number of multicultural children. The number of marriage migrant women has steadily increased starting from early 1990s due to social reactions to sex ratio imbalance and migration to cities among others. 40,000 internation-

Unit: person

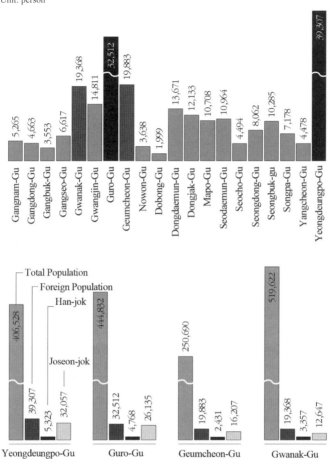

Figure 10-2: Foreign Population in Seoul by District (2015)
Source: Seoul City, "Seoul Statistics"

al marriages were recorded up to 2015, taking up more than 10% of national marriages in Korea.

Based on the immigration history and demographic characteristics of immigrants in Korea, most Koreans think of marriage migrant women, migrant laborers or *joseon-jok* when they hear the word "immigrant." These major immigrant groups also come into contact with the native-born as they participate in economic activities or build their living spaces. Koreans have initially expressed hope in immigrants, believing they would help build up Korea's economy and future. However, with more frequent contact, Koreans have expressed more complaint toward immigrants who have separated themselves in enclaves away from responsibilities of being a member of the Korean society (Kim, 2016; Kim et al., 2015). Discrimination depending on immigrant's nationality is increasing with surfacing social problems such as job competition, sham marriage or divorce, culture clash, crime and ghettoization. The problem lies in the fact that most foreign groups in Korea are from developing or underdeveloped countries. To add, media representation of the groups has not been positive. We can say that Koreans are open-minded and liberal regarding immigrants within a normative perspective but in reality become more exclusive and strict, resulting in harnessing a double-sided sentiment.

3. DATA AND METHODS

(1) Data

This study utilizes the 2008 East Asian Social Survey (EASS) to look into attitudes on immigration in Shanghai, Tokyo and Seoul. EASS provides a cross-national network of surveys including the Chinese General Social Survey (CGSS), Japanese General Social Surveys (JGSS), Korean General Social Survey (KGSS) and Taiwan Social Change Survey (TSCS). EASS was found in 2003 by the organization administering the General Social Survey (GSS) in four East Asian countries including China, Japan, Korea and Taiwan. From 2006, EASS has been delivering diverse data on these East Asian countries under specific themes such as family (2006), culture and globalization (2008), health (2010), social capital and politics (2012) and occupation and economy (2014). The 2008 EASS module used for this study includes East Asian data on attitude regarding globalization and immigration. Indexes that can help assess the impact received by the citizens due to mobility of people, capital and information related to globalization and immigration trends are also included. Notably, data related to native-born's attitude on globalization and immigration closely matches the objective of this study. However, data included in EASS are sampled within the sampling frame of each country resulting in different size samples for countries and cities. The sample size of China, Japan and Korean are 3,010, 2,160 and 1,508, respectively. The sample size of Shanghai, Tokyo and Seoul are 120, 598 and 277, respectively. The sample sizes of the cities could be considered small to look into the effects of socio-demographic and socioeconomic characteristics on attitudes toward globalization and immigration through a multivariate analysis. However, there are no other existing data that includes the variables of interest and sample groups from the three cities. Therefore, this study utilizes both country and city samples for descriptive characteristics and country sample for multivariate analysis.

(2) Variables

1) Dependent Variables

Five dependent variables are utilized for analysis including three variables tied to globalization attitude and two variables tied to immigration attitude. All questions linked to these variables are rated on a seven-point Likert scale where response of 1 is "extremely negative" and response of 7 is "extremely positive." The higher the rating on the scale for response items, more positive the attitudes tied to globalization and immigration. The response items are worded as below.

<Attitude on Globalization>
- "Import of foreign products should be limited to protect the national economy."

- "Frequent exposure to foreign film, music and literature will diminish national culture."

- "National interest should be prioritized even when it can cause conflict with another nation."

<Attitude on Immigration>
- National interest should be prioritized even when it can cause conflict with another nation."

- "The effect on labor market caused by the migration of people, goods and capital between cities and countries."

2) Independent Variable

This chapter observes the mobility of people and capital within the immigration frame in three East Asian cities Shanghai, Seoul and Tokyo as well as how these changing trends have affected the native-born population. Through the observations, we are able to pinpoint similarities and differences between globalization and immigration trends as well as relationships between immigrants and native-born in the three cities. To add, we will look at how attitudes and values regarding immigration and globalization are distinguished according to socioeconomic characteristics. The socioeconomic variables included in the analysis are education (number of years), income (family income in third quarter), occupational rank (high, middle or low), subjective SES level (10-point scale) among others. Control variables for multivariate analysis include age, sex (male or female), marital status (married, separated or single), family size and size of residence.

(3) Methods

This study compares attitudes on immigration and globalization according to demographic characteristics of the native-born citizens in the three cities. Next, an ordered logit model is presented including the five dependent variables.

Table 10-1: Demographic Characteristic of Three Cities: Shanghai, Tokyo, Seoul

	Nationwide	City	Age Group				
China	Nationwide	Shanghai	20s	30s	40s	50s	60s
	3,008	120	582	739	692	553	354
Japan	Nationwide	Tokyo	20s	30s	40s	50s	60s
	2,136	598	243	346	327	402	441
Korea	Nationwide	Seoul	20s	30s	40s	50s	60s
	1,462	277	289	353	338	195	146

Source: EASS (2008)

4. RESULTS

(1) Attitudes on Globalization and Immigration: Comparisons Between Three Countries and Their Cities

Table 10-1 shows the demographic characteristics of the samples from 2008 EASS. Out of 3008 survey respondents in China, 120 are Shanghai residents. The age groups that has the most respondents are the "30s" and "40s" with 739 and 692 samples, respectively. The age group with 354 and least amount of respondents is the "60s" group. For Japan, out of the 2,136 nationwide respondents, 598 are Tokyo responders. With 402 respondents in their 50s, 441 respondents in their 60s and 243 respondents in their 20s, top age groups of the sample are from their 50s or 60s while the least represented age group are the 20s. For Korea, out of the 1,462 respondents, 277 respondents are residents of Seoul. Top two represented samples are in their 30s and 40s with 353 and 338 respondents respectively, while the smallest group with 146 respondents are in their 60s. Among the three cities of interest, the order of cities with the highest ratio of respondents are Japan, Korea and China. Japan is characterized by a high ratio of the elderly population whereas the ratio of those over 60 in China and Korea are comparatively lower than other age groups.

Figure 10-3 shows the distribution of responses from the three countries and three cities for globalization attitude item: "Import of foreign products should be limited to protect the national economy." China (62.9%) has the highest percentage of respondents who answered "agree" for this item followed by Korea (45.7%) and Japan (35.8%). This ranking is also reflected in cities: 45% of Shanghai respondents, 40.9% of Seoul respondents and 34.9% of Tokyo re-spondents answered positively for this response item. By comparing country to city, we can see that nationwide openness to globalization is higher in cities and attitude differences are more drastic nationwide. In other words, those who re-side in cities have a more positive attitude on globalization in all three coun-tries. Also, age is positively related to thinking import of foreign products should be limited in all three countries and three cities.

In comparison to Korea and Japan, citizens of China held a more nationalis-tic stance, believing the national economy must be protected. We can now look at responses for import of foreign culture due to globalization. Figure 10-4 shows the distribution of respondents that believe exposure to foreign culture

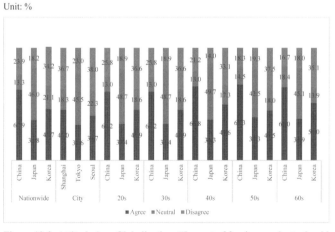

**Figure 10-3: Attitude 1 on Globalization: "Impact of foreign products should
be limited to protect the national economy"**

Source: EASS (2008)

Unit: %

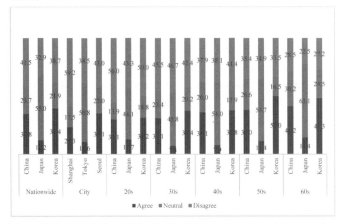

Figure 10-4: Attitude 2 on Globalization: "Frequent exposure to foreign film, music and literature will diminish national culture"
Source: EASS (2008)

due to globalization will damage national culture. Showing a contrast from the economic response, Koreans were most likely to endorse the protection of Korean culture with 39.4% nationwide and 35.4% of Seoul residents agreeing to the response item. According to this response item, we can conjecture that Seoul residents are less open-minded in regards to globalization of culture compared to residents in Shanghai and Tokyo. At the opposite end, most Tokyo residents do not believe import of foreign culture will diminish national culture. Put differently, Japanese may be more confident about their culture compared to Koreans. Age breakdown reveals that with older age, both Chinese and Koreans agree more strongly to the invasive nature of foreign culture while there was no relevant difference found among age groups in Japan.

We have now looked at differences between the attitudes of city residents regarding the effect of globalization on economy and culture. Figure 10-5 shows the response distribution for response item: "National interest should be prioritized even when it can cause conflict with another nation." The order of countries with the most to least nationalistic response is China, Korea and Japan. This pattern is also reflected in the cities. 80% of Shanghai residents believe that despite conflicts that may rise with other nations, national interest should be protected. On the other hand, the percentage of respondents who agreed to this response item was 59.8% for Seoul and 41.1% for Tokyo.

Unit: %

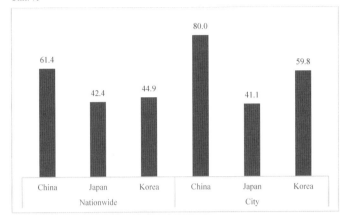

Figure 10-5: Attitude 3 on Globalization: "Nationwide interest should be prioritized even when it can cause conflict with another nation"
Source: EASS (2008)

The most salient observation we see by comparing countries and cities is the strong nationalistic characteristic of respondents from China and Shanghai. The notably strong nationalistic stance on economy is historically rooted in China's neo-nationalism and government intervention after the Tiananmen Square protests (Gries, 2004). There are many interpretations for the strong nationalism that exists in China but perhaps the most convincing explanation is this. It is interpreting the Chinese nationalism as a newly constructed value and culture formed within the context of potential conflicts that could have risen between China's civilization and other civilization during the time of fast-paced modernization. During the Mao Zedong era based on egalitarianism, "us and others" were not one of the pursued national values but as China experienced reforms in the 1980s, the importance of national boundaries became factored into Chinese identities (Kim et al., 2016). This value change was also fueled by the state's continued interpretation of Western capital and technology as tools for Chinese development. The state also continued to emphasize the value of "Chineseness" and communicated to the public a clear distinction between the Chinese and Western civilization. Within this context, citizens prioritizing national interest even when it may cause conflict with other nations is a representation of the nation's core neo-nationalistic values.

We can now observe the different survey responses among the three coun-

258

Unit: %

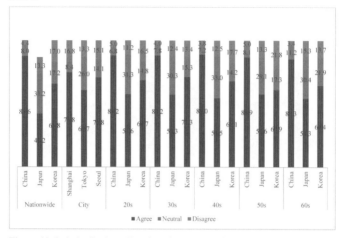

Figure 10-6: Attitude 1 on Immigration: "The effect on national economy caused by the migration of people, goods and capital between cities and countries"

Source: EASS (2008)

tries and cities regarding the effect of immigration on economy and labor market. Figure 10-6 shows the results of how respondents rated the item on effect of migration of people, goods and capital between cities and countries on the national economy. 87.6% of Chinese and 65.8% of Koreans were found to positively connect such mobility to an economic boost to one's nation. On the other hand, 55.5% or just slightly more than half of Japanese respondents agreed to this positive effect. City results are similar to nationwide percentages. 74.8% of Shanghai residents, 70.8% of Seoul residents and 60.7% of Tokyo residents responded migration of goods and people across borders will benefit the economy. Among all three countries, positive attitudes tied to immigration were higher among the younger generation.

Chinese citizens hold an attitude that for national gain—especially if it is an economic gain—conflict with other nations can be justified. However, most Chinese also believe that migration of people, goods and capital are beneficial for the Chinese economy. How can we interpret this? As conductors of this study, we interpret this positivity toward immigration to an internalization of the "Chinese dream" for the citizens—the dream emphasizing global dominance of China through economic and military power. Chinese believe that immigration will ultimately support the "great revival of the Chinese nation" as stressed by Xi Jinping during his speech at the 12th National People's Congress.

By contrast, Japanese hold an open attitude toward globalization of culture while having a more cautious stance toward the economic effect of immigration. This cautious attitude is more prevalent in the city of Tokyo compared to the nation as a whole. Koreans believe that immigration is necessary to economic development. However, we find that opposite opinions also exist at a relatively high number.

Figure 10-7 shows the distribution of responses on the item: whether migration of people, goods and capital between national and regional borders is beneficial to the labor market. 78.7% of Chinese, 41.6% of Koreans and 36.1% of Japanese have answered positively to this item. When looking at cities, the order of highest to lowest responses to the item is Shanghai, Seoul and Tokyo but the order of negative responses from lowest to highest is Seoul, Tokyo and Shanghai. It is interesting to note that those who reside in Seoul and Tokyo are cautious about the effect of immigration on the labor market. By contrast, this concern seems to be less for Shanghai residents. This difference seems to be rooted in dissimilar socioeconomic status of foreigners residing in each city. Foreigners residing in Shanghai have generally high SES levels, often em-

Unit: %

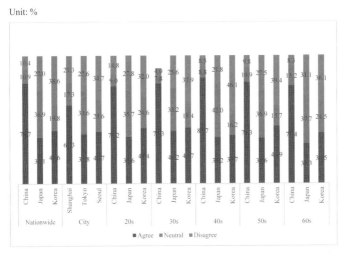

Figure 10-7: Attitude 2 on Immigration: "The effect on labor market caused by the migration of people, goods and capital between cities and countries"

Source: EASS (2008)

ployed in finance or at international companies. Most foreign population in Seoul are migrant laborers from Southeast Asia or Korean Chinese where both groups are generally concentrated in the lower SES. Foreigners in Shanghai do not have much relevance to the labor market of Chinese workers but foreigners in Seoul may pose some competition for jobs sought by Korean workers. Therefore, more Koreans compared to Chinese have developed an attitude that foreign workers may heighten competition in the labor market. Another thing to note is the more cautious attitude toward foreign workers for Shanghai residents compared to the nationwide attitude. This may be due to the more frequent contact Shanghai residents have with foreign workers in the city. The responses on the effect of foreigners on the labor market do not show differences between age groups.

(2) Socioeconomic Characteristics & Attitudes on Globalization and Immigration

We have taken time to observe some similarities and differences between the attitudes on globalization and immigration from the three countries and three cities. We expand our analysis to see how these attitudes differ according to socioeconomic characteristics. Although not shown in the table, the ordered logit model includes other control variables in addition to socioeconomic variables. In other words, a statistically relevant association between attitudes on globalization and immigration and socioeconomic characteristics means that relevance exits even with the effects of other variables. In the table, a positive bolded coefficient means a positive effect and a negative bolded coefficient means a negative effect.

Table 10-2 shows which socioeconomic factors are related to the attitude on globalization especially regarding import of foreign goods in China, Japan and Korea. In China, positive attitude on globalization is associated with more education and higher income. People with higher SES levels believe that foreign goods should not be controlled to protect the national economy. In Japan, only the years of education has statistically significant relationship to the globalization attitude where more education is related to a negative attitude towards limiting foreign goods. In Seoul, there is a statistically significant relationship between income and occupation types: people have negative views on limiting foreign products to protect national economy with higher family income and higher occupational prestige.

Table 10-3 shows the influence of socioeconomic characteristics on the attitude toward exposure to foreign culture in China, Japan and Korea. In China,

Table 10-2: Relationship between Socioeconomic Characteristics and Attitude on Globalization: "Import of foreign products should be limited to protect the national economy. (Ordered Logit Model)

	China		Japan		Korea	
	N	Standard Error	N	Standard Error	N	Standard Error
Education	.030	(.010)**	.110	(.021)***	N.S	
Income (34-67%)	N.S		N.S		N.S	
Income (top 33%)	.318	(.108)**	N.S		.324	(.149)*
Clerical work, Sales, etc. (ISCO 3, 4, 5)	N.S		N.S		.511	(.121)***
Executive, Professionals, etc. (ISCO 1, 2)	N.S		N.S		.639	(.214)**
Unemployed	N.S		N.S		N.S	
Subjective SES	N.S		N.S		N.S	

Source: EASS (2008)

※1: very negative on globalization, 7: very positive on globalization

※Control variables age, sex, marital status, family size, size of residence are not shown.

※N.S – statistically not significant

Table 10-3: Relationship between Socioeconomic Characteristics and Attitude on Globalization: "Frequent exposure to foreign film, music and literature will diminish national culture."(Ordered Logit Model)

	China		Japan		Korea	
	N	Standard Error	N	Standard Error	N	Standard Error
Education	.033	(.010)**	.161	(.021)***	N.S	
Income (34-67%)	N.S		N.S		.467	(.133)***
Income (top 33%)	.343	(.106)**	N.S		.595	(.150)***
Clerical work, Sales, etc. (ISCO 3, 4, 5)	N.S		N.S		N.S	
Executive, Professionals, etc. (ISCO 1, 2)	N.S		N.S		.393	(.120)**
Unemployed	N.S		N.S		.571	(.211)**
Subjective SES	N.S		N.S		N.S	

Source: EASS (2008)

※1: very negative on globalization, 7: very positive on globalization

※Control variables age, sex, marital status, family size, size of residence are not shown.

※N.S – statistically not significant

people who have higher level of education and in highest income tier have a more positive attitude on foreign culture and believe frequent exposure to foreign film, music and literature will not diminish national culture. In Japan, education level is the only statistically significant factor. In Korea, all socioeconomic characteristics have relevance except education. In other words, Korea has the highest influence of socioeconomic characteristics on globalization attitude.

Table 10-4 breaks down the factors that affect nationalistic attitudes by country. In the case of China, only those who hold executive positions or are working professionals believe that it would be wrong to prioritize national interest despite potential conflicts with other nations. Other factors are not statistically significant. As mentioned previously, most Chinese believe that it is permissible to be in conflict with other nations to protect national interests. The fact that only high job positions were found to be influential in turning around this attitude can support the idea that except for a select few most Chinese citizens pursue national interests as characterized by neo-nationalism. In Japan, people with more education believe that it is unnecessary to prioritize national interest if it means to be in conflict with other nations. However, those with higher occupational positions responded otherwise. Those in higher level positions or in

Table 10-4: **Relationship between Socioeconomic Characteristics and Attitude on Globalization: "National interest should be prioritized even when it causes conflict with another nation."(Ordered Logit Model)**

	China		Japan		Korea	
	N	Standard Error	N	Standard Error	N	Standard Error
Education	N.S		.055	(.021)**	N.S	
Income (34-67%)	N.S		N.S		N.S	
Income (top 33%)	N.S		N.S		N.S	
Clerical work, Sales, etc. (ISCO 3, 4, 5)	N.S		-.247	(.122)*	N.S	
Executive, Professionals, etc.(ISCO 1, 2)	.375	(.132)**	-.511	(.176)**	N.S	
Unemployed	N.S		N.S		N.S	
Subjective SES	N.S		N.S		N.S	

Source: EASS (2008)

※1: very negative on globalization, 7: very positive on globalization

※Control variables age, sex, marital status, family size, size of residence are not shown.

※N.S – statistically not significant

professional jobs were found to strongly support national interests. In contrast from the two countries, no statistically significant socioeconomic characteristics were observed in the Korean sample.

We can now look at sociodemographic characteristics that influence attitudes on immigration. For China, statistically significant characteristics were not found (see Table 10-5). In Japan and Korea, people with higher education level and higher family income have more positive attitude toward the effect of immigration on economy. In other words, people with higher SES are found to have more positive attitude toward immigration and its effect on national economy.

Table 10-6 shows the relationship between socioeconomic characteristics and attitude on the effect of immigration on the labor market. In China, those in higher-level or professional positions hold more negative attitude toward immigration's effect on labor market compared to those who have lower-paying jobs. This may be due to the high number of global elites residing in Shanghai who have jobs in high-paying positions. The Chinese elites may feel threatened by the foreign presence and may believe immigrants cause more competition within the labor market. In Japan, higher education, higher family income, higher occupational status and higher subjective SES are associated with positive atti-

Table 10-5: Relationship between Socioeconomic Characteristics and Attitude on Globalization: "The effect on national economy caused by the migration of people, goods and capital between cities and countries."(Ordered Logit Model)

	China		Japan		Korea	
	N	Standard Error	N	Standard Error	N	Standard Error
Education	N.S		.107	(.021)***	.072	(.019)***
Income (34-67%)	N.S		.265	(.128)*	.427	(.139)**
Income (top 33%)	N.S		.392	(.142)**	.441	(.157)**
Clerical work, Sales, etc. (ISCO 3, 4, 5)	N.S		N.S		N.S	
Executive, Professionals, etc.(ISCO 1, 2)	N.S		N.S		N.S	
Unemployed	N.S		N.S		N.S	
Subjective SES	N.S		N.S		N.S	

Source: EASS (2008)

※1: very negative on globalization, 7: very positive on globalization

※Control variables age, sex, marital status, family size, size of residence are not shown.

※N.S – statistically not significant

Table 10-6: Relationship between Socioeconomic Characteristics and Attitude on Globalization: "The effect on labor market caused by the migration of people, goods and capital between cities and countries."(Ordered Logit Model)

	China		Japan		Korea	
	N	Standard Error	N	Standard Error	N	Standard Error
Education	N.S		.061	(.021)**	.039	(.018)*
Income (34-67%)	N.S		N.S		N.S	
Income (top 33%)	N.S		.337	(.143)*	N.S	
Clerical work, Sales, etc. (ISCO 3, 4, 5)	N.S		.249	(.123)*	N.S	
Executive, Professionals, etc. (ISCO 1, 2)	-.351	(.132)**	N.S		N.S	
Unemployed	N.S		N.S		N.S	
Subjective SES	N.S		.084	(.028)**	N.S	

Source: EASS (2008)

※1: very negative on globalization, 7: very positive on globalization

※Control variables age, sex, marital status, family size, size of residence are not shown.

※N.S – statistically not significant

tude toward immigration and labor market. Most foreigners working in Japan are unskilled or low-skilled laborers. Therefore, most Japanese who hold higher-paying jobs are likely to assess foreign workers as non-threatening to the labor market. To add, since most high SES people are well knowledgeable about the economic structure and industry trends, they would most likely to have judged that most Japanese would not be threatened by the migrant laborers concentrated at the lowest tier of the labor market. For Korea, only the educational level has relevance to the attitude toward immigration and labor market. Higher educational level was associated with lower likelihood of connecting migrant laborers to negative effect on labor market.

In general, socioeconomic characteristics were found to be associated at statistically significant levels to attitudes on globalization and immigration in all three countries. Education levels positively influenced globalization attitudes in Japan and Korea while showing no statistical relevance in China. Income levels positively shifted both globalization and immigration attitudes in all three countries. Korea showed the highest influence of occupational status on attitude toward immigration and globalization. One interesting finding is the positive association between higher job positions and nationalistic attitude in Japan. In China, people with higher occupational status were found to hold an attitude that foreign workers will compete with domestic laborers in the labor market.

5. GLOBALIZATION AND IMMIGRATION IN THREE CITIES: A BLESSING OR A BURDEN?

Shanghai, Tokyo and Seoul are widely recognized as global cities. However, moving away from Sassen's contention, these three cities share both similarities and differences in immigrant characteristics and relationship formed between immigrants and native-borns. In regards to one of Sassen's core propositions that global cities will assimilate to share similar functions and structures, the three cities do indeed show similarities in their functions as part of the world economic system. However, in regards to immigration—commonly regarded as a product of globalization—the three cities show some differences. Foreign population in Shanghai is mostly comprised of international students and workers in international companies, finance and professional fields. However, foreign population in Seoul and Tokyo are comprised of: ethnic groups left behind after Japanese colonialism including Koreans in Tokyo and Korean Chinese in Seoul; and migrant laborers from China and Southeast Asia that have filled labor needs created by the neoliberal order. The foreigners in three cities are from different backgrounds, have dissimilar reasons for migrating and hold different socioeconomic statuses. Simply put, since the foreigners in three cities hold different socioeconomic positions, it is natural for the native-born from each city to have contrasting attitudes regarding foreigners and form dissimilar relationships with them. For those residing in Shanghai, foreigners are overseas workers who have come to China to help boost the economy. For Tokyo and Seoul residents, frequency of contact with the foreigners have increased but there is still a feeling of reservation toward accepting migrants as part of the society.

The three cities are in the process of undergoing quantitative and qualitative transitions to continue to develop as global cities. Immigration is at the core of these transitions. Shanghai is advancing efforts to transform the city into an environment where foreigners would want to settle permanently. Seoul and Tokyo are strengthening aspects of diversity within city areas settled by foreigners. Further, both cities are promoting urban renewal programs to attract high-skilled and professional workers from abroad. All three cities have embraced the importance of immigration in the age of globalization and forming strategies to effectively manage the inflow of people to the city's advantage.

The analysis of EASS data reveals that anxiety coexists with hope in regards to immigration in all three cities. In China, attitude towards immigration and globalization seems hopeful as more citizens hold positive views toward them and believe economic prosperity can come from them. However, a nationalistic sentiment is still very strong for the Chinese. The Chinese stance on immigration more closely resemble acceptance based on national interest rather than embrace of foreign culture through globalization and immigration. Therefore, whether the positive attitude will continue to remain in the future with foreign population increase and frequent contact between foreigners and native residents remain to be questioned. Would the Chinese be able to let down their guard and view foreigners as their equals when migrants start penetrating their daily lives with encounters of awkwardness and inconvenience? The nationalistic attitude shown in China is prevalent in Tokyo as well. Japan was the first Asian country to have experienced labor migration during the capitalistic development. However, their immigration policy is extremely exclusive and the state tends to view migrant laborers as "human resources" rather than "persons." Stemming from the distinct work culture and Japan-centric values, most Japanese view migrant laborers as people who "do the dirty work." In this context, we may wonder how effective multicultural social integration or urban development projects will be in the future.

Similar scenes unfold for Seoul. As shown by the global city indexes, Seoul shows weakness in procuring human capital even as a developed city. In other words, most foreigners in Seoul are low-skilled and from a low SES background. Even the biggest immigrant group *joseon-jok* face financial hardships in Korea working in low-paying jobs including childcare, restaurant and construction work. Koreans are well aware that migrant laborers are supplying the work necessary for Korean economy and that *joseon-jok* have acquired Chinese nationality while fighting against Japanese colonial rule. Koreans have maintained a positive attitude toward them until the late-1990s and early 2000s. However, Koreans are now at the crossroads of deciding between taking immigrant groups as their own or rejecting their presence now that immigrant population is becoming larger. The combination of increased permanent residents, illegal overstay of laborers and naturalization of *joseon-jok* have increased the chances of personal encounters between immigrants and the native population. The immigrant groups they have acknowledged as abstract possibilities have now become their neighbors. Whether Koreans can fully accept their presence under the same rights and social structures is a question left to be answered. Similar to Japan, the Korean state is making effort to attract high-skilled workers to the country but it remains to be known whether these workers can find a reason to permanently settle in a land where other immigrant groups have failed to integrate successfully. The groups that have failed to fully integrate include the migrant laborers who have continued to support the Korean economy and the immigrants of Korean descent who have once fought for the liberation of Korea.

REFERENCES

AT Kearney. (2016). *The AT Kearney Global Cities Index.* Available at: https://www.atkearney.com/research-studies/global-cities-index

Beaverstock, Jonathan V. (2012). Transnational elites in global cities: British expatriates in Singapore's financial district. *Geoforum*, 33, 525-538.

Burnley, I. H. (2016). Developments and Complementarities in International Migration Paradigms. *Journal of International Migration and Integration*, 17, 77-94.

Castles, Stephen and Miller, Mark J. (1993). *The Age of Migration: International population movements in the modern world.* New York: The Guilford Press. Translated in Korean by Korean International Migration Studies, 2013. Seoul: Ilchokak.

Choi, Jaehoon. (2013). A Disaggregated Mediator. *Korean Journal of Sociology*, 47(2), 319-348.

Country Digest. (2016). *Shanghai population 2017.* Available at: http://countrydigest.org/shanghai-population/#Foreign_population_in_Shanghai

East Asia Forum. (2016). *Japan and its Immigration Policies are Growing Old.* Available at: http://www.eastasiaforum.org/2016/06/07/japan-and-its-immigration-policies-are-growing-old/

East Asian Social Survey. (2008). *East Asian Social Survey 2008.* Available at: http://www.eassda.org/modules/doc/index.php?doc=intro

Immigration Bureau of Japan. (2016). *Immigration Control Report.* Available at: http://www.immi-moj.go.jp/english/seisaku/index.html#sec_02

Gries, Peter Hays. (2004). *China's New Nationalism: Pride, Politics, and Diplomacy.* Berkeley, CA: University of California Press.

Kim, Seokho. (2015). Social Distance toward Immigrant among Koreans. *Journal of Contemporary Korean Studies*, 2(2), 45-67.

Kim, Seokho, Noh, Minha and Yang, Jonghoe. (2015). What Made the Civic Type of National Identity More Important among Koreans? A Comparison between 2003 and 2010. *Development and Society*, 44(3), 535-563.

Kim, Seokho and Park, Eun-Sun. (2016). Is National Identity an Obstacle to the Acceptance of Foreign Immigrants as Kookmin (Korean Citizen)? *Korea Journal of Population Studies*, 39(4), 29-59.

Kim, Seokho., Shin, In Chol., Ha, Shang E. and Chung, Kiseon. (2013). Measuring Social Distance Using Knowledge Space Theory: The Case of South Korea. *Korea Journal of Population Studies*, 36(1), 1-20.

Kim, Yongshin, Kim, Doo Hwan and Kim, Seokho. (2016). *Who is Nationalist Now in China? Some Findings from the 2008 East Asian Social Survey.* Available at: https://muse.jhu.edu/article/640274

Kodama, Takashi. (2016). *Japan's Immigration Problem- Looking at Immigration through the Experiences of Other Countries.* Available at: http://www.dir.co.jp/english/research/report/others/20150529_009776.pdf

Lee, Myon Woo. (2015). Nationalist Turn of Japanese Politics and its Influence on Japan's Multicultural Policy. *The Journal of Multicultural Society*, 8(1).

Massey, Douglas S., Arango, J., Hugo, G., Kouaouci, A., Pellegrino, A., and Taylor, J. Edward. (1993). Theories of International Migration: A Review and Appraisal. *Population and Development Review*, 19(3), 431-466.

Sassen, Saskia. (2001). *The Global City: New York, London, Tokyo. Princeton.* NJ: Princeton University Press.

Seoul City. (2017). *Seoul Statistics.* Available at: http://stat.seoul.go.kr/jsp3/index.jsp

Shanghai Municipal People's Government. (2016). *2015 Statistical Communique of Shanghai on the National Economic and Social Development.* Available at: http://www.shanghai.gov.cn/nw2/nw2314/nw2318/nw26434/u21aw1109178.html

Shanghai Social Science Research Center, Shanghai University. (2014). *Survey on the living conditions of foreigners in Shanghai.*

The Japan Times. (2016). *Japan sees record high number of foreign residents: Justice Ministry.* Available at: http://www.japantimes.co.jp/news/2016/03/11/national/japan-sees-record-high-number-foreign-residents-justice-ministry/#.WGn-9m2weUk

Tokyo Metropolitan Government. (2016). *Tokyo's History, Geography, and Population.* Available at: http://www.metro.tokyo.jp/ENGLISH/ABOUT/HISTORY/history03.htm

Tsuda, Takeyuki. (2008). Local Citizenship and Foreign Workers in Japan. *The Asia-Pacific Journal*, 6(5).

Wickramasekera, Piyasiri. (2002). *Asian Labour Migration: Issues and Challenges in an Era of Globalization.* International Labour Office(Geneva).

Yoon, In-Jin. (2016). Characteristics and Changes of Koreans' Perceptions of Multicultural Minorities. *Journal of Diaspora Studies*, 10(1). 125-154.

Zhang, Jie. (2015). Specific Xenophobia?-Japanese Acceptance Attitudes toward Chinese Immigrants. *Journal of the Graduate School of Asia-Pacific Studies*, No. 30.

Zolberg Aristide. (1999). Matters of State: Theorizing Immigration Policy. In Hirsehman, C., Kasinitz, P. and DeWind, J. (Eds.), *Handbook of International Migration. New York: Russell Sage Foundation*, 71-93.

Conclusion

Daishiro Nomiya, Dukjin Chang,
Haidong Zhang

As outlined in the introduction, we started this book project with two big questions in mind. Our first question relates to similarity and differences across Seoul, Tokyo, and Shanghai. How similar or different are the social settings of these three mega cities? Our second question concerns developmental trajectories of three cities. Do these three cities follow the same developmental patterns, allowing for the differences in historical time when these cities enter certain stages of development? Using the metaphor of a long running train, with Seoul, Tokyo, and Shanghai as passengers riding in different cars in it, we have laid out a bold speculation that the developmental processes of three cities may be similar, as these cities eventually view the same scenery. However, the scenery may look different because the three cities view the scenery at different time points.

In our effort to answer these questions, we have examined the nature and characteristics of three cities from different angles and perspectives. These angles include family and household, social mobility, job structure, working mothers, dining practice, general trust, attitude toward global change, and community change and policies. To conclude our project, we attempt to answer our initial questions, using as our point of reference empirical findings the preceding chapters have provided us with.

In this concluding chapter, we first return to each chapter, summarizing its findings and arguments. Based on the observations in all chapters, we proceed our attempt onto drawing a big picture of the developmental trajectories in three mega cities in East Asia.

In chapter 3, Zhang, Kim, Sato, and Yao try to examine social mobility in Seoul, Shanghai, and Tokyo. Data limitations for the city of Tokyo would not let the authors do straightforward analyses of three cities with their cautious use of the Japanese data, however, they have managed to draw a big picture that could depict trends in social mobility in three cities in a comparative manner.

The authors see similar mobilization patterns in Seoul, Shanghai and Japan (not Tokyo), arguing that high and active mobilization had existed before the mobility started to stabilize gradually. This pattern, the authors contend, is due to industrialization and coming of information society that create an array of new job categories. The observation in this chapter also echoes with the one expounded in the previous chapter, viewing that the above pattern is seen in different times across three countries, with Japan first, then Korea, followed by China. Social mobility across both jobs and generations has been weakened after the mid-1990s bubble burst in Japan and the 1997/8 Asian Financial Crisis in Korea respectively, while it is still on the constant rise in China.

In chapter 4, Koo, Hayashi, Weng, and Bi discuss job structure and its change in three cities, focusing on similarities and differences across them over the years. In their discussion, they are careful in their treatment of the data, trying to pick up some nuanced details in their observation of the differences, as when they examine workers composition of service industry of three cities in 2014 and compare their observations with those of 2007, or when they point out the difference between Seoul and Tokyo in their labor force participation rates. Overall, however, their examination of the data leads them to find substantial similarities between Tokyo and Seoul, leaving Shanghai as showing a different picture in its job structure. This difference, the authors argue, is due to the different positioning of Tokyo and Seoul, on the one hand, and Shanghai on the other, in the process of industrialization and de-industrialization development. Here, they find mega social change working behind the change in the job structure in three-cities. As industrialization progressed, the three cities all witnessed more supply of decent jobs. However, Tokyo, with its high level of de-industrialization, could not avoid polarization due to a decrease of middle-income jobs and the increase of low-paying ones. In Seoul newly created jobs tend to be concentrated in upper classes; at the same time, the city begins to witness the increase of low-paying jobs because of welfare expansion and aging which bring in the growth of medical and social service. Shanghai predominantly enjoys an increase of good jobs.

In chapter 5, Kwon, Nishimura, and Meng discuss difficulties today's working mothers face in three cities. Their focus is on the tension working mothers experience between regular full employment and child rearing. As expectations become high for a child to attain high academic achievement, mothers feel an increased responsibility to be "educational coaches". This feeling, coupled with the lack of a reliable child-care system, takes mothers to a point where they are "torn apart" in between job and child-rearing. Ways to deal with this difficulty vary; in Tokyo, mothers choose part-time employment so that they can set their work time as they wish; in China, often grandparents cut in and take the role of child-care while mothers work full time; in Korea, mothers choose either work full time or "stay-at-home". The authors show a high sensitivity to their subject of investigation. In fact, they are cautious enough not to leave out possible country-specific sources as factors explaining the differences among mothers in three countries in general and three mega cities in particular. These factors include national policies on daycare facilities, parental leave regulations, and national cultural traditions. While differences exist in the nature and causes of this modern mothers' difficulty across three cities, the authors also argue that there are certainly undeniable similarities. These similarities become apparent especially in the comparison between Tokyo and Seoul. Furthermore, the authors never fail to see a possible convergence in the change process of mothers' roles in three cities - increased importance in child's educational achievement itself is a prime example- and in so doing they view macro trends as forces working in the backstage of this phenomenon, such as capitalistic development, women's participation in the job market as work force, and educational expansion, in conjunction with traditional family values.

In chapter 6, Kim, Ishii-Kuntz, and Huang point out that starting in the latter part of the 20th century, three-person or four-person household became a central, or "normal," household category in three cities. This trend, however, has gradually been overtaken by an increase in single-person-household (SPH). While differences in data categorization do not allow them a complete comparison of demographic characteristics, this trend seems to be today's mainstream in three mega cities. What is more, the occupational categories of SPHs in three cities appear to be concentrated in high paying professionals, clerical workers, and low-paying professionals in sales and service work. Citing Beck's argument, the authors interpret this increase in SPHs as manifestation of individualization, which features weakening ties in traditional relationship and resultant increase in "burden" on the side of the individuals to make decisions by themselves and at the same time "liberate" them from traditional webs of human relationship. All these trends and characteristics appear to fit in modern life in three cities, which in turn suggests that, at least, part of city life is governed by some mega-trends, such as economic activities and a general pattern of life course. Additionally, a finding that cannot be neglected in this chapter is the differential time of change in the dominant household category in three cities. Tokyo came first, followed by Seoul, and Shanghai the last. This time differentials fits well to our original conjecture that the developmental trajectory of

Japan, Korea, and China is similar but come in different time.

It is interesting to note that in chapters 3 and 6 their observations converge. While observing phenomena in different socioeconomic fields, both chapters find that three cities (or three countries) experience a similar pattern of change, and this pattern of change is experienced in different times. The similarity in the experiences in three cities may be attributed to larger macro-trends, such as industrialization and de-industrialization, information society, urbanization, and concomitant economic development and demographic change. At the same time a closer look into the lives of people living in three cities such as SPHs suggest that the different timing of arrival of the same trend may result in different composition of the seemingly same phenomenon. In Tokyo where industrialization and de-industrialization had arrived first, it is the elderly generation SPHs that is most vulnerable while the younger generation SPHs seem ready to face a new type of society as witnessed in their high economic participation rate and home-ownership percentage. In Seoul where these macro trends arrived perhaps twenty years later, it is the younger generation SPHs that needs more policy attention. Unlike their Japanese counterpart, they have to find stable jobs while at the same time trying not to be driven out of their current living spaces. In Shanghai where SPHs arrived with globalization, most people living alone are foreigners.

Cheong, Mizukami, and Hao revisits the theme discussed in chapter 6, that is, individualization. In chapter 7, they do so, however, by focusing on different aspects of modern life in three cities. While chapter 6 observes individualization from types and size of household, chapter 7 views it as emanating in individual attitudes and their social life. The authors argue that change in human relationship in modern city life manifests itself in such phenomena as "dying alone," "me-generation", and "eating alone." While the authors never fail to find similarities across people in our three cities, they also are keen in detecting differences in social life in these cities. A prime example is their analysis of eating alone. While eating alone becomes more of a trend in all three countries today, the authors contend, factors working behind the practice of eating alone are complex and different across three countries. In Korea, a norm still exist that people should eat together, while in Japan, there is no such a norm. Apart from these two countries, eating together is still considered as the cultural centerpiece in China. These various factors give different looks to the act of eating alone practiced in each country.

In chapter 8, Byun, Nomiya, and Zhang look at change in human relationship in urban areas as well as policies to address the problems associated with the change. They observe that mounting problems exist in today's East Asian mega cities. Some localities in urban cities, for instance, suffer heavily from malfunctioning of safeguard mechanisms, such as protection from crimes and mutual aid in times of natural disasters, which traditional communities were able to provide decades ago. The authors argue that in the heart of these problems lie separation and inequality among city dwellers. In a way, residents in mega cities live a difficult life characterized by solitude and segregation among themselves. What are the ways to cope with these problems? While details differ, Tokyo and Seoul share the fundamental ideas and goals for their community rebuilding projects; policies are being laid out to regenerate urban life, including economic and cultural revitalization through gentrification in Seoul and social innovations in Tokyo. Throughout chapter 8, similarity is a distinctive character between Tokyo and Seoul. Urban policies in these mega cities are essentially the same in their basic ideas and goals. This testifies to the thesis that these two cities have experienced similar macro transformational forces; macro trends have pushed the two cities in the same direction. Shanghai appears somewhat different from Tokyo and Seoul in its community life, as demonstrated by the fact that close-knit communal life is still alive in the neighborhoods in Shanghai. In this regard, as shown in the previous chapters, the city of Shanghai may be experiencing a different mixture of forces that transforms the city in a direction different from that of Tokyo and Seoul. Yet one needs to notice that, as seen in the emergence of gated communities, today's Shanghai is increasingly exposed to segregation and separation across social classes, a characteristic Shanghai has begun to share with Tokyo and Seoul. Thus, it is safe to say that at least some part of community life in Shanghai resembles that in the other two mega cities in East Asia.

Sasaki's interest lies in interpersonal relationship. Especially in chapter 9 he focuses on the structure of trust among mega city dwellers. A mega city may provide social settings that are different from other localities, which in turn leads to new patterns of trust among residents. In mega cities, for example, we might see reduced importance of particularized (personal) trust as compared to general trust in association with rapid pace of in- and out-flow of population. He examines general trust among people in Tokyo, Seoul, and Shanghai by looking at other associates as represented by optimism, individual attributes (such as age, gender, education, and well-being), personal network, and success. Some of Sasaki's findings are interesting as they show stark differences from the mainstream findings of the literature in this field, such as women more trusting than men in three cities, and less educated people being trustors as compared with educated people. Albeit these different findings between his research results and previous literature, Sasaki's overall finding in his within-three-city comparison points to one direction: similar trust structure among dwellers in our three cities. This finding itself is intriguing as it comes regardless of their different national traits and different timing of arrival of macro trends. One explanation is the effects of being a megacity may supersede those coming from being different countries. Another explanation may be the persistence of common traditional values (Inglehart and Baker 2000).

In chapter 10, Kim, Zhang, and Takenoshita keep a keen eye on peoples' attitudes in times of globalization. As is increasingly becoming evident, globalization is bringing up changes in various fields of our life, such as an increase in foreign migrants and inflow of foreign commodities and cultures. To this change people respond: some accept, and others resist to it. The authors attempt to identify similarities and differences in the way people respond to the effect of globalization in three countries in general, and in three cities in particular. During their investigation, the authors stay careful not to exclude both the impact of globalization and characteristics uniquely present in respective countries as possible determinants of peoples' attitudes. Their finding is that, in many instances, Chinese people's attitudes seem to be different from residents in Korea and Japan. This is not to say that attitudes of the Japanese and the Koreans are the same; rather, these two countries are closer as compared with the distance they have with the Chinese people. One distinctive difference that people in Shanghai show is the degree with which they want to protect the national interest in the face of globalization; 80% of Shanghai residents respond in favor of the protection of national interest, whereas 59.8% and 41.1% of residents do the same in Seoul and Tokyo respectively. The authors infer this Chinese inclination for national interest as an outcome of a newly constructed value system in China in recent years. In sum, while the authors see some macro social forces, such as the inclusion into the world economic system and globalization, as contributing to the creation of similarities among the residents of three mega cities, governmental policies, together with national traditions and characteristics, do work to form different attitudes toward globalization. In a sense, people's attitude may be a product of joint work of big overarching macro societal forces and state's initiatives. Particularly in China, there is another issue we may want to pay attention to: institutional inconsistency that may exist between socialist China and its penetration into the mostly capitalist globalization. Globalization is largely known to have a converging effect among capitalist countries. However, globalization from the perspective of

China may mean penetration into the global market on the one hand and the persistence of the rule of the party on the other, posing a *fundamental paradox* (Liu Kang. 2003)

Throughout this book, we compare city dwellers in Seoul, Tokyo, and Shanghai from various perspectives, trying to detect similarities and differences in their attitudes, perceptions, and social structures that condition their ways of life. Our first and instantaneous finding from this comparison is that both similarities and differences exist in these mega cities. For example, in chapter 6, we find receding three-person and four-person households in all three cities; instead rising are single-person households (SPHs). At the same time, differences exist as to who constitutes single-person household. In Tokyo, men account for more SPHs than women, whereas in Seoul, women are dominant. As compared with Tokyo and Seoul, Shanghai carries low rates of SPHs in the total household structure. In chapter 3, we find that in all three mega cities, service sectors are developing, often showing relatively high shares in the job structure. However, within the service sectors in three cities, compositions are different, with Tokyo and Seoul witnessing a growth in high value-added sectors, while Shanghai still a mixture of manufacturing and value-added sectors. Still in chapter 6, the authors see differences among three cities in the way mothers cope with the decision to choose between job and child-rearing; at the same time, they do not fail to discern a possibility that some of these differences may converge in the future.

It is not that we find similarities and differences evenly across all results of our work. Rather, our finding is that similarities are detected more in between Seoul and Tokyo, while differences more in between Shanghai and the other two cities. Thus, in chapter 8, we see similar city governments' responses to the erosion of traditional community life in some areas of Seoul and Tokyo. Likewise, the authors of chapter 7 find that "eating alone" is a commonly accepted practice in Seoul and Tokyo, while in Shanghai it is not.

Where do these similarities and differences come from? In this book, we do not have data nor tools to answer this question in a convincing manner. Yet it is intellectually stimulating to conjecture possible answers to this question, using our authors' arguments as a steppingstone. As for the difference, it is safe to say that differences, at least in part, come from national traits, national traditions and culture, and governmental policies of the nation. Policies that control the number of children in a family certainly affect the conception of the "normal family" in respective countries; working age population would differ as country's tradition and culture dictate who should be in and out of the labor force.

Illustrative examples of this commonsensical understanding can be found in many chapters in this book. In chapter 6, a high concentration of SPHs in the age group 25 to 39 in Seoul is attributed to city's unique history of spacial formation, and a small number of SPHs in Shanghai must be attributed to the hukou system, a traditional family register system unique to China. Also, as found in chapter 3, this hukou system contributes to the continuation of dual labor market system in China. In these cases, Seoul's spatial formation and China's hukou system are the consequences of unique historical development and governmental policy in respective country. Findings in chapter 10 echo the conclusions in chapter 3 and 6. In chapter 10, the authors argue that recent Chinese state policies may actually be creating attitudes and responses toward globalization in its residents.

In addition to country-level traits and policies, we can also think of two larger variables that may explain the differences among our three cities. One is the different timing of the arrival of mega trends. When neoliberal stronghold and de-industrialization hit these three cities simultaneously in the latter part of the 20th century, people of Tokyo might have been relatively better prepared because they had already been in the bubble burst for more than a decade. Those in Seoul seems to have been a much less prepared for an unexpected attack because the growth rate was still high and the job market was easier to enter. Shanghai was protected from this impact because it still enjoyed burgeoning manufacturing sector. The other is the ever-present possibility of inconsistency between global mega trend and national institutions, as witnessed by China's unique type of globalization. Global trends do not necessarily bring about convergence. They mix up with national institutions and end up something unexpected.

What is it that is creating these similarities, then? Again, our commonsense tells us that we may think of a big social force encompassing all three mega cities, and that social force may contribute to an increase in shared traits. Such a force, it is considered, would set the conditions with which all three cities develop and transform themselves, and thus mold their compositions and shapes more or less in the same direction. Many authors in this book apply the same line of logic in their effort to understand the sources of similarities: there are macro trends and forces that push each country and city to move toward the same direction. True to this presumptive understanding, we find an abundance of similarities across our cities, as shown in many chapters in this book. In chapter 5, for instance, the authors argue that an increase in SPHs in three megacities can be traced back to the dramatic shift in modern society, namely, individualization and concomitant decrease in collective bonding. The authors in chapter 3 also find industrialization and information society as macro forces strongly associated with the change in the mobility patterns in our three mega cities. It is not only modernization and other forces associated with modern societal formation that work as an engine in the creation of similarities across three cities. In chapter 5, in their finding of today's mothers being pressed to choose in between job and child-rearing, they often refer to traditional patriarchy system and value system placed on family as conditions for the emergence of this difficult decision. As in chapter 7, when the authors' concern centers around big social forces, such as urbanization and individualization, they do not fail to see similarities across three mega cities.

Note that we do not know that these similarities are the characteristics shared only by our three cities. It might as well be the case that these shared traits go beyond our three cities and cover more mega cities in the world. While we need to leave the answer to this question to yet another research endeavor, it is certainly safe to say that some societal forces send our three cities to a certain direction.

Throughout this book, these encompassing forces are often referred to as industrialization, de-industrialization, urbanization, modernization, and globalization. Now, does the strong presence of similarities mean that these mega-trends are working to cancel out the effects of other forces that create differences in three countries and cities? Here discussions from our authors vary. The study of trust in chapter 9 might seem to put us to side with the strong presence of modern macro-trends. Whereas in chapter 10, in which similarities and differences in peoples' attitudes toward globalization are discussed, the authors tend not to draw a strong conclusion that favors either encompassing macro societal forces or national distinctiveness.

Here, comparison of Seoul and Tokyo might provide a valuable perspective with which we proceed with this discussion. Despite differences, similarities certainly stand out between these two mega cities. In fact, almost all chapters in this book take notice of substantial presence of similarities. There is a certain time differential between Tokyo and Seoul, as Tokyo and entire Japan entered first in the industrialization phase and modern economic development. However, if seen from the viewpoint of developmental process, both of these cities seem to have followed essentially the same path to the present stage of socio-economic development. This is evidenced in many aspects of city life, such as decline in multiple-person household and concomitant increase in single-person household, structure of general trust, and attitude toward change associated with globalization. In between Seoul and Tokyo, one can find some shared macro-level traits. Both cities lead capitalistic economic development in respective countries, with relatively minor interferences from their national governments. They are heavily involved in the transnational flow of people and materials in the global economy. These observations lead us to think that various forces associated with modern societal and economic development exert strong influences over peoples' ways of life, often diluting national characters that would otherwise work to augment the differences. While it is tempting to think this way, we still do not know the definite answer to this question.

What about time differentials between our three cities? In the outset of this book, we conjectured that these three cities may be riding on the same mega waves of social transformation, using an analogy of three passengers riding in different cars in the same train. Behind this analogy lies one big sweeping transformational power, be it composed of one force or multiple forces, that nullifies national differences. Now, we have already answered to the question of the existence of such a sweeping power. At this moment, we cannot say such a powerful trend is present in our three East Asian mega cities; what we can say is there are certainly some social forces that substantially change the life of residents in these three cities in a similar direction. We do not know yet that such social forces can be powerful enough to supersede the national differences. Thus, going back to our analogy again, we do not know if we are riding on the same train; we may as well be riding on different trains. The definite answer to this question lies ahead of us.

REFERENCE

Inglehart, Ronald and Wayne Baker. 2000. "Modernization, Cultural Change, and the Persistence of Traditional Values." *American Sociological Review* 65(1): 19-51.

Liu Kang. 2003. *Globalization and Cultural Trends in China.* University of Hawaii Press.)

List of Contributors

Introduction
Dukjin Chang: Professor, Seoul National University
Daishiro Nomiya: Professor, Chuo University
Haidong Zhang: Professor, Shanghai University

Ch.2
Wonho Jang: Professor, University of Seoul
Tatsuto Asakawa: Professor, Waseda University
Xiaocong Lu: Professor, Shanghai University

Ch.3
Haidong Zhang: Professor, Shanghai University
JiYoung Kim: Assistant Professor, University of Seoul
Yoshimichi Sato: Professor, Tohoku University and Kyoto University of
    Advanced Science
Yelin Yao: Lecturer, Shanghai University of Engineering Science

Ch.4
Hearan Koo: Research Fellow, Seoul National University
Yusuke Hayashi: Professor, Musashi University
Dingjun Weng: Professor, Shanghai University
Jingqian Bi: Lecturer, Ludong University

Ch.5
Hyunji Kwon: Professor, Seoul National University
Junko Nishimura: Associate Professor, Ochanomizu University
Meng Chen: Assistant Professor, Shanghai University

Ch.6
JiYoung Kim: Assistant Professor, University of Seoul
Masako Ishii-Kuntz: Professor Emeritus, Ochanomizu University

Suping Huang: Associate Professor, Shanghai University

Ch.7
Byeong-Eun Cheong: Associate Researcher, Seoul National University
Hao Yuan: Associate Professor, Shanghai University
Tetsuo Mizukami: Professor, Rikkyo University

Ch.8
Miree Byun: Senior Research Fellow, Seoul Institute
Daishiro Nomiya: Professor, Chuo University
Dunfu Zhang: Professor, Shanghai University

Ch.9
Masamichi Sasaki: Professor Emeritus, Chuo University and Hyogo University of Teacher Education

Ch.10
Seokho Kim: Professor, Seoul National University
Haidong Zhang: Professor, Shanghai University
Hirohisa Takenoshita: Professor, Keio University

Conclusion:
Daishiro Nomiya: Professor, Chuo University
Dukjin Chang: Professor, Seoul National University
Haidong Zhang: Professor, Shanghai University